The Artificial Southerner

The Artificial Southerner

Equivocations and Love Songs

Philip Martin

The University of Arkansas Press
Fayetteville
2001

05 04 03 02 01   5 4 3 2 1

Designer: John Coghlan

⊗ The paper used in this publication meets the minimum requirements of the
American National Standard for Permanence of Paper for Printed Library
Materials Z39.48-1984.

Library of Congress Cataloging-in-Publication Data

Martin, Philip, 1958–
     The artificial Southerner : equivocations and love songs / Philip Martin.
          p. cm.
A collection of essays, most of which were originally published in the Arkansas
democrat-gazette.
     ISBN 1-55728-716-3 (pbk. : alk. paper)
   1. Southern States—Civilization—20th century. 2. Southern States—Intellectual
life—20th century. 3. Popular culture—Southern States—History—20th century.
4. Southern States—Biography. 5. Group identity—Southern States. I. Title.
     F216.2 .M37 2001
     975'.043—dc21

                                                          2001003853

For Miller and Jordan and, as always, Karen

Acknowledgments

I owe much to my faithful sounding boards: Bill Jones, Rufus Griscom, Jim Nosari, and my southpaw lawyer, Paul Bowen. Griffin Smith, Jack Schnedler, Werner Trieschmann, Ellis Widner, and Paul Greenberg have been kind and patient with me. I want to thank Larry Malley, Brian King, Archie Schaffer IV, Karen Johnson, and everyone at the University of Arkansas Press as well as my colleagues at the *Arkansas Democrat-Gazette.* Karen Martin is the best friend and editor a fella ever had. Bork, Coal and Sherpa are good dogs. (Hi, Mom.)

✧ ✧ ✧

P.S. Most of these pieces were first imagined as newspaper articles; most of them were published in some form in the *Arkansas Democrat-Gazette.* "The Apotheosis of Elvis Presley" can be considered original for this collection, but I feel compelled to point out that parts of the essay have appeared in my various newspaper columns about the King. "The President Next Door" was prepared especially for this collection, but it also borrows some from an earlier piece, "Notes on a Boy President," that serves as the introduction to David Gallen's 1994 book, *Bill Clinton: As They Know Him.* The collection's penultimate piece, "Riding with the Sun King," appeared in *Spectrum Weekly,* a Little Rock alternative newspaper.

I think it is important the reader understand that some topical references remain while others have been edited and revised to reflect current situations and heighten whatever resonances may exist between the essays. I have tried to achieve at least the simulacrum of literary cohesion here, though these pieces were all occasional and I never gave any thought to the possibility that they might one day hang together in anything as formal and intimidating (to this author) as an actual book.

I'd like to acknowledge an antecedent—my friend and colleague Gene Lyon's autobiographical essay, "The Artificial Jewboy," that appeared in *Moment: The New Magazine for America's Jews* way back in 1975. I discovered Gene's essay in his 1988 collection of essays, *The Higher Illiteracy.* I probably never would have imagined collecting my own pieces were it not for his example.

From time to time a headnote will attempt to explain what a particular piece is doing in this particular collection—sometimes these may seem like rationalizations. I will confess right now that I approached the sequencing of these essays the way a record producer (I know, it's all CDs now) might approach the sequencing of a LP; I tried different lineups and this is the way they felt best. Some of these pieces might seem like odd choices for a collection about the South, but give them time—perhaps there is something about the pacing or the language or the sensibilities delimited or evoked? Perhaps I am pleading for a break here. In the words of Southerner Michael Stipe, "I've said too much. I haven't said enough."

✧ ✧ ✧

> *It is not from criticism but from this world that stories come in the beginning; their origins are living reference plain to the writer's eye, even though to his eye alone. The writer's mind and heart, where all this exterior is continually* becoming *something—the moral, the passionate, the poetic, hence the shaping* idea—*can't be mapped and plotted.*
> —*Eudora Welty*, The Eye of the Story

As this book was being prepared for publication, we received word Eudora Welty had died. She was ninety-two years old, so when the word came on a hot July morning, I could hardly pretend to be surprised—though to tell the truth I was genuinely shocked. Somehow I had figured Miss Welty was one of those folks who would outlive us all, a stubborn miracle who might quietly achieve Methuselahian longevity. She would persist because we needed her hopeful example.

As I write this, I realize those inchoate thoughts were silly; flesh and blood is flesh and blood, and there is a limit to how long the animating spirit can hole up in a faltering ruin. People die and the rest of us survive their dying. Anyway, there are things about Eudora Welty I've only learned since her death, since the flood of obituaries and appreciations have hit the newspapers. For instance, I have learned that the inventor of the e-mail program Eudora, a man named Steve Dorn, named his program after her because he was impressed by her famous story "Why I Live at the P.O."

I have it on rather good authority that Miss Welty never messed around too much with smart machines; she probably never went on-line to cruise the Internet. She got her mail the old fashioned way—she didn't need silicon sandwiches and silicon blips to draw the whole world to her door. Still, I think it was a nice gesture on Mr. Dorn's part

About the Cover

The author would like to extend his heartfelt appreciation to Frederick James Brown, the artist whose painting, *Hero,* appears on the cover of this book.

As a writer, I'm not generally overly concerned with the visual impact of a book's cover—or for that matter, any of the practical aspects of book making. I generally trust that others know better than I, and I try to let the people who know better do their jobs. It's difficult enough to get the words close to right.

However, from the first moment I glimpsed *Hero,* I was convinced it conveyed some of the same sense of the transient, impermanent and assimilated nature of the of the Southern character and experience that I wanted to express. It seemed to me to depict a kind of self-manufactured being, a Southerner, a bluesman, part black, part white, partly self-willed, partly an accident of nature and circumstance. It was a striking, haunting image, and I was gratified when others agreed it might make an appropriate cover image.

Though I didn't realize it at the time, I was familiar with some of Mr. Brown's other work, specifically a series of portraits of blues artists he created in the 1980s. After talking to him, I realized we shared many of the same concerns and experiences. Both Mr. Brown and myself were born in Georgia, both of us have spent considerable time on Chicago's South Side. We've both lived in Arizona. And we share a deep love for the folk music called "the blues."

Hero resides in the permanent collection of the Arkansas Arts Center in Little Rock. Mr. Brown resides in Arizona. But he says he may come for a visit. I'd like that.

Contents

Encounters and Equivocations

Bill Clinton Time

Introduction: The Artificial Southerner

I don't hate the South. I don't hate it. I don't. I don't.
—Quentin Compson

I clicked on the little envelope icon and the message popped open. It was from an appreciative reader who said he always looked forward to reading my columns in the newspaper. My correspondent meant no offense, and for that matter none was taken. I suspect he meant the remark to be neutral—for if he meant it as a compliment he surely understood that it might be taken as insulting. I don't really know how to respond; I must admit I find his message—or at least his opening statement—a little baffling.

What he wrote was this: "You don't sound Southern."

I suppose I should point out that my correspondent—known to me only by an e-mail signifier—was referring not to my speaking voice but to my writing style. As far as I know, my electronic friend has never heard me speak, and if he had he might or might not hold the same opinion. I have one of those accents that tends to wax and wane—I am never more Southern-sounding than when I am in New York, Chicago, or Los Angeles.

On the other hand, I've always thought—perhaps flattered myself is the better characterization—that my writing did sound Southern. After all, I am a Southerner, Savannah-born to Southern parents, and the fact that I've lived elsewhere shouldn't void my nativity. Even though I live in Arkansas, which is at least as much apart from the South as part of the South, I think my sensibility is Southern. I still say "sir" and "ma'am" a lot. I like grits.

I should not be surprised if people thought I did sound Southern—I would be eager to confess to being unduly influenced by Walker Percy or Hank Williams or Flannery O'Connor. I have a fondness for acoustic Delta blues and greased-up rockabilly, and more than once I have been to Graceland and experienced something more profound than the silly giggles of imagined superiority.

But does that mean I am Southern? Or that Southernness means anything any longer in a cyber-gridded America pimpled with shopping malls and Stepford suburbs? When MTV and *South Park* and Matt Damon are as available to the youth of Birmingham and McComb and Texarkana as they are to the citizens of the great coastal metropolises is there any reason to believe that the empires of Hollywood and Madison Avenue and Disney won't soon subsume—if they haven't already—what is odd and wonderful and distinct about this place?

I know some people think the Southern sensibility isn't such a good thing to claim to have, but these are unsubtle people, with what we might call vulgar minds. They don't know the South, just the unflattering propaganda.

And perhaps my correspondent's statement might be read another way—the extent to which I do not sound distinctly Southern might have as much to do with the pervasive nature of the Southern voice. I think Scott Fitzgerald sounds Southern, and Hemingway too, in his best moments.

That is, of course, my prejudice, a belief that springs from my desire to believe it. It is very Southern of me to nevertheless honor that prejudice.

✧ ✧ ✧

In the main, I am a newspaper writer. I work for the *Arkansas Democrat-Gazette,* a statewide newspaper. I live in Little Rock, near a Rockefeller and the mother-in-law of Bill Clinton. My neighbors are schoolteachers and doctors and tire salesmen. I am married and keep three dogs.

Regardless of how I might sound, I consider myself a Southerner. My mother's family comes from a farm near Savannah; some of them still live on Seedtick Road. My father came from Asheville, North Carolina; there is a family legend—easily disproved if I had the inclination—that my grandmother may have befriended Scott Fitzgerald during those months Zelda languished in a local asylum.

There is white trash in my blood, no doubt some of my ancestors were bigots. Surely there were horse thieves and bad debtors and bust-head imbibers. Some of them were ignorant and mean and hard; were I of their time, I might have turned out to be just like them.

I was not the first in my family to go to college, though I was the first to go directly there and stay until they gave me a degree. I have played in blues bands; I have picked tobacco. I have taken offense when I've heard people say ignorant things about the people who live where I live.

I have been gainfully employed in the journalism trade for more than twenty years and have been a columnist at the *Arkansas Democrat-Gazette* since 1993. The ascension of Bill Clinton raised all boats around here; I maintain a kind of low-grade cable-network level of renown. I sometimes appear on television, usually as a representative of the Southern—or more particularly, Arkansan—point of view. The producers seem to think I do sound Southern, or at least Southern enough for their purposes.

Still I am not an unreconstructed Southerner; I am not preoccupied by the old grievances. I do not brandish a rebel flag. Lincoln might not have been fully compliant with the Constitution but he was right. I am the first to concede that there is something willed about my Southernness, that it is, to one degree or another, something decided upon.

✧ ✧ ✧

Indulge me a moment; maybe I can better explain what I mean. As I am writing this essay, meant to be something like an introduction to a collection of diverse but not dissimilar essays, there is a blip in the news about the governor of Arkansas moving his family into a fancy trailer while the mansion is being renovated.

I suppose I winced when First Lady Janet Huckabee insisted that it wasn't really a trailer they were moving into but a manufactured home—a two-thousand-square-foot triple-wide, to be precise. To be honest, I generally admire the Huckabees for their lack of pretense, but Sugar Button's insistence on the politically correct nomenclature reminded me of things about myself I'd rather not think too much about—such as the reason I think it's vulgar to use a real estate agent's word like "home" when what you mean is "house." I think it is a class indicator because I've read that it is a class indicator, that only people of a certain outlook and education, people who are perpetually striving to sound posh, misuse "home" in that fashion. I mean, someone wrote it, so I believe it. I also believe it's much more brave and honest—and therefore "classier," another word that classy people don't use—to say you live in a trailer than to coo about your manufactured home.

I have all kinds of basically arbitrary rules like this, rules I more or less believe in even though I understand how silly they would seem if—like now—I ever tried to explain them to anyone. I don't believe there is any such thing as a short-sleeved dress shirt, for instance. And while I know that there are those who think my soft-collar button-downs are déclassé, I choose to wear them because I think they bespeak a certain Southernness.

Don't get the wrong idea; not everything I believe is as calculated as that. I wear my button-downs because they're in my closet and they're clean; but I own them because I think of myself as the kind of person who wears soft-collar button-downs. I have a seersucker suit for the same reason. I understand there are people who believe, for perfectly good reasons of their own, that seersucker suits are ridiculous. And for the most part, I would agree with these people. But some people—people like me—can wear them.

I would be ridiculous if I wore a bottle-green velvet suit. Yet I have a friend who wears one, and I have to admit that it serves him well. But my friend can wear that suit because he lives in New York, went to an Ivy League college, and works in a creative industry. I went to a land grant university and drink bourbon.

In other words, my friend can wear his ratty—did I mention that it's ratty?—velvet suit because he is who he is, an authentic member of the upper class, a kind of American aristocrat. I, on the other hand, have to be careful not to let people know that once upon a time I lived in a trailer.

It was a long time ago, when my parents were young, but I remember the trailer park, a loop of gravel around a balding common, with the trailers extending out like spokes from a hub. It was minutes from the air base where my father worked. We lived there while he was waiting to secure base housing.

Some of my relatives still live in trailers—though I believe they, like the Huckabees, have recently upgraded to triple-wides.

In high school, I had a friend who lived in a trailer—several friends, actually, but one who was a better friend than the rest. He used to joke about it and I used to feel bad for him.

✧ ✧ ✧

One of the prerogatives of Americans is that we can invent ourselves. We can go to college—if we have the requisite talent and ambition, we can even go to the best colleges—and we can make money and have our neighbors think well of and envy us. A Bill Clinton can emerge from the jungles of Arkansas and grow up to be president. It happens all the time.

It is painful for me to remember all the things I trained myself to do and not do. In fifth grade, I trained myself to cross my sevens in the European style. Now when I write a check or fill out a form, I look down and notice my hand has learned well. Perhaps someone once picked up on this trait and assumed perhaps I went to school on the continent. Probably not—most of the teenagers who take a class trip to Paris come back crossing their sevens; at least that's what I think when I see those precious slashes.

I taught myself to dress, to resist synthetic fabrics and ventless Italian jackets, to prefer red wine to canned beer. I worked to eradicate my accent—and then to put just a touch of it back when I felt I needed it. I spent a lot of time thinking about who I wanted to be and how I could get to be like that.

At some point I decided to be a Southerner, though I could just as easily have decided to be a New Yorker or a Californian, since I lived in those places during my formative years. I can even say that I made this decision in part because I thought that it would be easier for me to assume a quieter, less aggressive approach than that of some of the people I knew, that I might be able to somehow exploit this assumed Southernness. I decided to tame my language, to be softer and less demonstrative. I worked on becoming the kind of bemused snob I think I often am. I decided it was a costume I could wear comfortably, a persona I could inhabit without drawing undue and unwelcome attention.

Later I decided I would travel; I would be passionate about movies and books and music and baseball. I decided I would play the guitar; I would write songs; I would sing—no matter that I had little talent. I would play golf; I would wear deck shoes without socks; I would keep dogs and drink my coffee strong and black rather than fool around with milk and sugar.

I don't know if we all do this or not, whether some people are genuinely more natural than I sometimes feel I am, or whether we are all basically the product of whatever forces have been exerted on us. I do know that while we can affect all kinds of outward modification, while we can change our hair, our face, our dress code, and even our body type, there are inner hollows and eddies removed from our training and experience. There is a primal skittering, a dark twitch that we might read as a fear of being exposed as utterly, sadly human.

I do know that I overthink sometimes, that equivocation is what I do best. I wince at Janet Huckabee's statement, then almost immediately feel a kind of solidarity with her. She can call it what she wants—there is power in the naming of things.

This artificial Southerner wears khakis and a red tie to work, he moves through his day like an actor in a movie, unperturbed and easy in his skin. He makes his calls; he thinks his thoughts and sets about sorting them into his column. It is not a bad life for him, he thinks, though he realizes he has imagined—or constructed—it all.

❖ ❖ ❖

I am thinking of an episode that took place in 1997 and might have been the catalyst for this book. I am in Los Angeles to interview the actor Nicolas Cage. It will be a friendly, routine (at least for Cage) exchange; he is working to promote his new movie, a big summer action affair called *Con Air*, I am a card-carrying member of the American media, the great engine of hype. I am here to record what Cage says about the film, to serve as Cage's linkage to Arkansas moviegoers, his most remote public.

Without trying to, I find myself liking Cage; he is an intelligent, alert man who seems gentler and more deliberative than any of the characters he plays. He is genial, seemingly anxious to please. He smiles at me. We both understand this is acting—in the course of our interview Cage will say to me the same things he's said to dozens of entertainment reporters in the past few days.

Neither of us has any illusions about the transaction we are to conduct. Cage is here to charm, to get me to say good and noncontroversial things about his movie. Presumably, I am here to land an interview with a big movie star. Cage can't know that I really don't much care about the interview, that it's only happening because a studio publicist insisted I talk to Cage as a condition of seeing the movie in advance of its release date, that I'm not at all sure any of Cage's words will end up in the newspaper for which I write.

He can't know that I am not particularly fond of talking to celebrities, that I always seem to have trouble asking them questions that are answerable and interesting. Cage's job is simply to stay on point, to steer the conversation to promotional ends. He can't know that I consider this business unpromising, that I am perhaps just as reluctant as he is to deconstruct this summer blockbuster.

Yet there comes a moment when I ask Cage about his portrayal of Cameron Poe—the heroic convict who saves the day. Cage plays this Poe with a rather broad Southern accent, a character point that seems not entirely necessary to the role. There is no real reason for Poe's Southernness, he might just as well have been a Californian or a Midwesterner.

I ask Cage about this—and as I do I feel my voice soften and slur, just a intimation of Savannah creeps in.

He understands immediately. He knows I represent an Arkansas newspaper. He rushes to reassure. Nicolas Cage does not hate the South. He doesn't. He says that he not only admires Poe, but likes "that type of guy," the type of guy who works on his Chevy in his front yard (not "lawn"), who drinks regular beer and enjoys monster truck races.

"I like that guy," the actor emphasizes. "What some people call 'white trash' is, to me, a way of looking at the world, a kind of aesthetic."

Cage's famously limpid eyes plead not to be misunderstood. He knows this is dangerous ground and some people might take offense. But why? His character is, after all, the hero of the piece, a decent but quick-tempered man wrongly sentenced to prison who risks his life to protect the innocent on board a prison transport plane taken over by some of the most dangerous criminals in the federal prison system. (It doesn't make sense; it's a summer action movie.)

In fact, the move's writer, Scott Rosenberg, says Cage decided to make Poe a Southerner precisely because the actor wanted to draw on the South's chivalric tradition. Rosenberg said he wrote the character as a generic working-class roughneck; Cage thought his selflessness and heroism would be more credible if he spoke with a soft Alabama accent.

On the other hand, maybe it is understandable that Cage, a thoughtful and sincere actor, might be made uncomfortable by the line of questioning. In his mind he's being interviewed by a seemingly legitimate Southerner about his portrayal of a Southern character. While perhaps not as daunting as being quizzed by, say, an Asian journalist on his portrayal of an Asian character, there is a palpable edge to the situation. Cage wants something like an assurance that he did all right.

He doesn't hate the South.

❖ ❖ ❖

Cage's reaction is interesting. It raises some prickly questions. Is there any such thing as a legitimate Southerner anymore? In a country overrun with homogeneous shopping malls and fast-food joints, when the World Wide Web buzzes in every fourteen-year-old's bedroom, does it make any sense to try and define a set of attributes that are distinctly Southern?

What, if anything, makes the South Southern anymore? For Nicolas Cage, it is more than an accent and a sort of deferential bearing, it is a kind of code. His Cameron Poe is a knight-errant who puts the defense of the weakened above his imminent return to his family, to the daughter he so poignantly has never seen. (He wouldn't even allow her to visit him in prison, he didn't want her to see her father in such a condition.)

But *Con Air* is just a movie, and a big blow-'em-up cartoon of a movie at that, loaded with all kinds of stereotypes, from Ving Rhames's opportunistic black nationalist to John Malkovich's evil genius. Movies necessarily develop a kind of shorthand to telegraph the attributes of their characters; while we might agree that some stereotypes are offensive, they are an essential starting point for any character development. The fact that a character is a Southerner tells us something about that character—it's kind of like Mr. Potato Head's potato. And even if real Southerners aren't in fact much different than real Midwesterners, for the sake of the movies they must be.

❖ ❖ ❖

Yet, in fact, we are different. At least that is what I have come to believe.

While there are no doubt people who are born in the South and dwell in the South but have no sense of any innate Southern quality, there are still Southerners here as well. The character Cage played in *Con Air* is a Southerner, not just someone who was born and reared in the South, so is the perverse, power-mongering character that Gary Oldman played in *The Fifth Element*—a Hitlerian figure with a soft Southern drawl that he says he based on Ross Perot. (Oldman said he adopted a Southern accent for the role because his greatest fear is that the South will not only rise again but take over the universe.) Southerners are not necessarily heroes; perhaps they are more often portrayed in movies as villains, ineffectual or dissipated romantics, or inbred know-nothings.

It is probably true that the Southern character is more quickly moved to violence and more afflicted by grievance than any other kind of American; in many ways we do tend to be provincial. The flip side of our famous hospitality is a certain suspiciousness and distrust of outsiders. And while—like the rest of the country—we look to the urban Northeast for validation, we also maintain a tendency to dismiss homegrown excellence as merely local news.

Even in an age that is rushing toward post-literacy at cyberspeed, Southerners retain long memories. We know our histories, both public and personal. While sophisticated people may find the persistent Southern obsession with the War between the States quaint, the emotional attachment of the Southerner is genuine and not bound up with any queasy feelings of racial superiority. We understand slavery was a vile and hateful practice that needed to be abolished, but we also understand the Stars and Bars is not a symbol of racial hostility or a suggestion that the hegemony of the white masters over black people was anything less than an abominable sin.

(This said, the Southerner must also allow that certain emblems of the Confederacy have been adopted by a number of bigoted hate groups who would—if they could—install it as a banner of oppression. In fact, the best argument for not incorporating Confederate imagery in any state flag or flying it from any public standard is simple propriety. It might be rude to do so. Then again, the question of whether we ought to allow jerks and idiots to confiscate our history is a legitimate one.)

Southerners know the fact that the South lost the war does not mean that the South's constitutional interpretation was insupportable. They know this, whether or not they imagine things might be better had Lee's armies been better supplied and had a new nation been brought forth.

While the Southerner still exists, the Yankee has by and large been assimilated into a greater America. Few people from Ohio remember the Army of the Potomac the way that some of us remember the Army of Northern Virginia, in that Southerners have the advantage of being a conquered people. The South may be indivisible with America—Washington, Jefferson, and Madison were Southerners—but the South is a part of America that has heard the bootfalls of an occupying army.

For the descendants of Yankees, the Civil War is as remote as the reign of Caesar; here in Arkansas—one of the least Southern of the states of the old Confederacy—we commemorate the execution of the teenaged Confederate spy David O. Dodd.

While I consider Lincoln a hero, I don't necessarily think there's anything wrong with that.

✧ ✧ ✧

It is probably true that Southerners are less polite—more American—than they used to be, though this is probably more of a consequence of rubbing up against the rude than of any genuine failing of instinct. Only a fool insists upon being taken advantage of time and time again; sooner or later patience fails. Our society is becoming less civil because there are fewer people who feel constrained by the conventions of manners. The impulse to mock the Southerner's exquisite and intricate sense of social rights and obligations as phony, patronizing or archaic is simply a by-product of coarsening times—a reaction to the otherness of mannered discourse.

An infectious informality has all but obliterated the need to show respect for people with whom we are not altogether familiar; similarly, the addictive habit of confession has become a staple of our popular culture. The Southerner's inherent reluctance to participate in these touchy-feely festivals of revelation draws immediate suspicion. What is he hiding behind that gentle drawl and those old-fashioned table manners?

It is also probably true that Southerners are less well-educated than they might be, but the same must be said for the rest of America. While the South is famous for illiteracy, it is also famous for William Faulkner and Eudora Welty. In the South, the people who can read do.

The Southerner is acquainted with what is tragic and what is true. While the South has not always been kind to truth-tellers—Erskine Caldwell was hounded out of Georgia after writing *Tobacco Road* and *God's Little Acre,* and W. J. Cash hanged himself in a Mexico City hotel room six months after the publication of his terribly true *The Mind of the South*—the Southern character has borne up and persisted despite all attempts to rehabilitate it. Part of what makes the South the South is its inability to forget ("Forget Hell!" the novelty plates still read) and its acquaintance with guilt.

Beginning in 1928, a group of writers—including Robert Penn Warren, John Crow Ransom, Allen Tate, and John Gould Fletcher—held a series of discussions at Nashville's Vanderbilt University; these discussions evolved into a seminal collection of essays urging the South not to abandon its "moral, social, and economic autonomy" for the industrial model of the North.

I'll Take My Stand: The South and the Agrarian Tradition has been dismissed by some critics as an antiprogressive manifesto, but there is an undercurrent of spiritual defiance that runs through many of the essays. According to Ellen Glasgow, "To defend a civilization would seem to us as impertinent as to defend time. Certainly the South needs defenders as little as it needs apologists. . . . We are, I think, less interested in any social order past or present than we are in that unknown quality which we once called the soul."

Elsewhere in America it might be possible to believe in our own innocence, in Manifest Destiny or Mickey Mouse; the pragmatic South has always known and understood guilt. Where elsewhere there was plenty, this land knew privation. The South is more real than the rest of the country; at least it has lived through more.

$$\diamond \ \diamond \ \diamond$$

Perhaps that is what Nicolas Cage was trying to get at by alluding to a white trash aesthetic. His Cameron Poe—little more than a cardboard Southerner, a caricature of a Southerner really—wasn't some desperate bottom feeder, no white trash redneck cracker, but a poor but honorable man attached to some inviolable code. He was a man resigned to the facts of existence—he understood that sometimes Daddies die before they see their little girls, that sometimes bad people prevail, that there is a kind of insurmountable unfairness to a man's life—but he was determined to do his best nonetheless.

Cage was afraid that the genuine Southerner might mistake his intent and think his accent a burlesque, that his performance might have somehow given offense.

But the South has always endured parody, as we have, perhaps just as often, invited it. Billy Bob Thornton's *Sling Blade* is no less a film because it presents Southerners the way it does; there *are* Snopeses and Jeeter Lesters about. Cage was right to make his hero a Southerner, the tweaking adds some ballast to the character and makes a willfully slight film just a tad more textured.

The South is still around, for there are still Southerners, though most of us have decided upon our Southernness. And while in the age of glass office towers and jet travel and the cyberhalls of the Internet the South may exist more as memory than as fact, so long as it is remembered—or misremembered as myth—it will persist.

Every American has a South within, a conquered territory, a old wound settled into a scar. Forget, hell—the thing is to remember and to imagine.

In these essays I hope to explore some of the implications raised by the still extant South and the Southerners who have both fled and embraced it. I want to describe some encounters with Southerners and non-Southerners—with Barry Goldwater and Ralph Ellison—and express some equivocations—about rock 'n' roll and literature, about life and love—which, at least by this artificial Southerner's lights, proceed from that inner, self-created South.

March 15, 2001

Southerners: Actual, Imagined, and Absentee

The Apotheosis of Elvis Presley

I was born too late for Elvis, at least for the real Elvis.

I was eighteen years old when he died, a bloated glutton, in an upstairs bathroom of a vulgar lower-upper-middle-class house in Memphis. When I heard the news I was working at Lorant's Sporting Goods in Shreveport. In a moment of entrepreneurial inspiration I went into the back room and got a dozen boxes of cheap black T-shirts—irregular stock we'd normally sell for $2.99 apiece—out of inventory and began pressing Elvis's iron-on image onto them. I arranged two-inch felt letters and numerals tombstone style:

Elvis Aron Presley
1935–1977

I stuck one in the window with a $10 tag on it and sold them to the suckers.

The ones that didn't sell I took back with me to school, where I sold or gave them away. Some of the frat boys wore them without irony—ironed-on T-shirts were somewhat fashionable in 1977—but the punks ripped my shirts with razors, splattered them with paint and, in one case, alleged pig's blood. Some of them scrawled hateful slogans on their Elvis shirts; after Johnny Rotten it was punk convention to scribble "I hate" over the logo or image of a popular band or performer. I didn't much care what people did with the shirts I sold.

I made a few dollars ripping off the King after he died.

I'm sorry about that now. I'm sorry I missed Elvis when he was still around. I had plenty of chances to see him perform; he made the rounds of the South's fairground coliseums and civic auditoriums, but I never was much interested in the unhip fat man sweating in his jumpsuit. I wasn't interested in the greasy youngster either; back then I was snob enough to think that Elvis didn't matter to me and that he never could, that he was a kind of cultural pirate, a white hope hip-shaker who had provided an alternative to the messy implications of Ike Turner and Chuck Berry. In my ignorance, Elvis seemed the safe option, a competent Pat Boone. He didn't mean anything to me, for I had heard Huddie Ledbetter sing his blues and Bob Dylan snarl his poetry and I thought that whatever Elvis might have meant to the blue-haired and the duck-assed, he could never mean to me. I thought he was an ignorant, probably bigoted, cracker boy who rode the main chance as far as he could before retreating into his pharmaceuticals and his ridiculous Cadillac trash style of living.

I didn't care that he died before I came to know him. I didn't think the redneck King could teach me anything.

✧ ✧ ✧

I know better now.

What Elvis did, at first unconsciously and later with terrible self-consciousness, was nothing less than establish the vocabulary of gestures that we now recognize as rock 'n' roll. That's not all he did, but it's a reasonable start. He was a pop singer but that's not why he is important. Pop singers dissolve with the passing of their moment; Elvis has become an American icon as recognizable as Mickey Mouse or Coca Cola.

Indeed, the further away we get from the historic Elvis, the boy from Tupelo who cut some sides for Sam Phillips at Sun Studios, who fell asleep at night listening to Sister Rosetta Tharpe on Dewey Phillips's radio show, the longer his shadow grows.

We all have our own Elvis, our own hot glow of what he means. He growls; he curls his lip and grinds his hips, parodying his own Elvishood. He speaks to us all, yet maybe he's not saying the same thing.

✧ ✧ ✧

In those few months in the mid-1950s when he was only a regional star on the Louisiana Hayride, he stayed in Bossier City at the David Motel ("For Nicer People" the sign still reads) and hung around the Southern Maid Donut Shop near the state fairgrounds. In those days, he was just a shy kid who wanted to be Bing Crosby or Dean Martin and wasn't quite sure how it all was going to turn out.

"We had nothing before, nothing but a hard way to go," he once said about his childhood. His daddy, Vernon, once told him he ought to make up his mind and be either an electrician or a guitar player. Vernon added he'd "never seen a guitar player worth a damn."

And as a guitar player Elvis wasn't worth a damn, not really. He used the instrument as something to beat, to keep time with—he was better on bass and piano. But he was some kind of electrician, turning on the world.

Now he's just another pop touchstone, another hero in amber, trapped in his movies. He died young but ignobly. He will always be remembered, but not necessarily as a Promethean artist or even as a skillful pop singer.

◇ ◇ ◇

Or perhaps he won't be remembered as anything. That's the argument implicit in this copy of *Newsweek*, dated January 1, 2000. A chart in the magazine short-lists a number of items that the editors believe will or will not survive the next hundred years. Among the things that make it to the year 2100 are Halloween, whipped cream, and the Beatles. Among the things they predict will not make it are psychoanalysis, corrective eyeglasses, and—disturbingly enough—Elvis Presley.

Now we probably ought not make too much of this; the plain fact is that *Newsweek* was simply making up this chart as it went along. The writers wanted something to balance their prediction that the Beatles would still be around a hundred years from now, and Elvis happened to be their sacrificial icon. They needed a figure of sufficient cultural weight, and no matter what the SoundScan figures tell us, Garth Brooks just isn't in the millennial league. Elvis was the only righteous yin for the *Newsweek* Beatle yang.

It's certainly not anything to get too upset or defensive about—though it's obvious that Elvis, and more particularly, Elvis fans, are safe targets. It's silly to pretend anything so ephemeral as popular music will be remembered by anyone other than academics and specialists a hundred years hence. While improved technologies have ensured that a lot of twentieth-century popular music will "survive" the next hundred or even thousand years, it's unlikely that any of it will be familiar to the general public in Y3K. Elvis will probably be as obscure as Ozymandias a thousand years from now; in future popular histories, our times might be compressed to a single paragraph or line.

On the other hand, it's only right that we acknowledge the implicit slight. *Newsweek* regards Elvis as less important than the Beatles, probably for some of the same reasons I was so cavalier about his passing. Elvis was a poor white Southerner who died ridiculously, on the toilet, after a tabloid life characterized by child brides and white Vegas jumpsuits. Elvis has not been treated well by biographers (Albert Goldman told such authoritative lies about him that they have acquired the pure knell of truth), by his record company (RCA squeezed his catalog for every drop of short-term profit), and most of all by a certain kind of fan who insists on treating Elvis as a kind of quasi-religious figure. Every August, during the Elvis Week which commemorates his death, Memphis is flooded with "Elvis people" who come to light candles and wear black and debate the slender possibility that the King, having faked his death to get away from the pressures of stardom, still walks with us.

Of course the Ivy League editors of *Newsweek* are liable to snicker at such a figure—the Church of Elvis is an institution as preposterous as it is ongoing. While many of the most devout of the Elvis people are concurrently devout Christians—and there are those who think that referring to Elvis as "the King" is blasphemous—there is a strain of Elvis worship that veers close to necrolatry. Any hero held close by the blue-haired trailer trash is fair game for the editors of a publication as august and culturally alert as *Newsweek*.

Never mind the fact that Elvis Presley was as important as any American who lived in the 1900s and that the surviving Beatles would likely be among the first to acknowledge that without him they'd never have evolved beyond skiffle. Elvis Presley—with the help of Sam Phillips and Chuck Berry and Ike Turner and a handful of underappreciated ancestors—started a fire that spread over the world. It doesn't matter that he didn't write his own songs or that he wasn't a proficient musician or that his taste was absurd. Elvis Presley might have been a wondrous accident: it's for sure he didn't know the consequences of what he was doing; he just wanted to be another show biz kid, make some records then move into movies like Dean Martin; it's for sure he didn't seek to be transformed into a kind of alternative Jesus who, instead of offering the promise of forgiveness of sin, instead allows license to violate social norms.

Elvis was ridiculous when he died, a caricature of cape-whirling decadence. But he isn't ridiculous now, not in the long run, no matter how druggy and empty the end was. I think Elvis seemed ridiculous because he wasn't wrenched from us violently, like James Dean or Sam Cooke or Buddy Holly or Jimi Hendrix or Janis Joplin or Jim Morrison or JFK or Kurt Cobain. He just died, like somebody's loser uncle, on the toilet.

Elvis died young, but he didn't leave us the necessary beautiful corpse. What Elvis left behind was ugly and stinking—he was years past mattering in anything but a crass commercial sense, past caring about anything beyond hit records and the creature comforts those hit records provided. There was plenty of reason to resent the smug, fatted Elvis at the end, plenty of reason to want to storm his walls and break his glass and drag his leopard-skinned sofa out into the street and set it afire.

At the end Elvis was emptied of meaning: a swollen man in a tight white jumpsuit, goofing on his own songs, peeling silk scarves off his neck to hand them to frumpy female fans. There was no menace left, nothing left for the world to fear.

✧ ✧ ✧

That was the first Elvis that I knew, but it wasn't the real Elvis. The real Elvis was still in there somewhere, trapped and horrified at the spectacle he had become. I imagine he felt helpless.

There's no doubt the quasi-religious fervor of Elvis fans and the still-emerging details of the singer's apparently bizarre personality combined with the myth-manufacturing capability of the media to obscure the real face of Elvis, to reduce America's greatest pop singer to a white trash icon, a snide, sad joke.

As with Jesus, Mohammed, and Buddha, Elvis Presley's death was not an end but a transformative event. They died so they might live again. Though the tabloid sightings have decreased in frequency, Elvis lives—the apotheosis of the hillbilly cat is complete.

During Elvis Week the faithful gather in Memphis, wearing black and carrying flowers. There are tears and candles and somewhere someone will claim to have been visited by the King.

While Americans tend to convert dead celebrities into durable cultural phenomena—remember Jim Morrison on the cover of *Rolling Stone* in 1977, "He's Hot, He's Sexy, and He's Dead"?—there is something unique about the elevation of Elvis from pop singer to quasi-religious figure; in his particular case there is a genuine blurring of the lines between the spiritual and the aesthetic.

This transformation is possible only because Elvis is dead.

Had he lived, we would not see the multitude of Elvis imitators we see now, some specializing in the young Elvis, some in the decadent Vegas Elvis. Had Elvis lived there would be but one Elvis, the actual Elvis, and he would be retired or recording, in the midst of a revival or restricted to the periphery of the public consciousness. It seems certain that a living, breathing Elvis would, in 2000, be less vital than the Elvis industry that has thrived since his death in 1977. An elderly Elvis might be irrelevant; while it is a cliché to say that death is sometimes a good career move, it is a cliché that has proven true.

✧ ✧ ✧

In 1995, at the inaugural International Conference on Elvis Presley held in Oxford, Mississippi, Mark Gottdiener, a professor of sociology at the State University of New York in Buffalo, delivered a paper titled "Dead Elvis as Other Jesus."

"The fact that Elvis is so popular dead, and so widely imitated after death," Gottdiener said, "suggests to me that the presence of Elvis is very comforting to people, and, in fact, that deep down people love him in the true sense of the word. People have to love Elvis to want to see or be his imitators frequently. Consequently, above all else, the Dead Elvis phenomenon is about obsessive love for Elvis as the Other Jesus."

Gottdiener argues that Elvis, instead of offering the promise of forgiveness of sin, instead allows license to violate social norms. Through death Elvis has been converted from a darkly sinister figure—a man enamored of handguns and pharmaceuticals—into a kind of cuddly mascot, a social convention that permits the loosening of inhibitions. Elvis dead is Elvis expunged of complications, Elvis arrested at whatever point in his career the individual particularly fancies.

There are all sorts of campy artifacts—Elvis as bourbon decanter, Elvis as ashtray. In the gift shop at Graceland you can buy Elvis deodorant and Elvis air freshener and plastic sunglasses that resemble those the old fat Elvis wore on stage in Las Vegas.

Dead Elvis—the title of a excellent 1991 book by cultural critic Greil Marcus—is more about wearing stupid trashy junk than setting the world on fire. Yet Elvis was the point at which the black aesthetic laid siege to the majority culture; Elvis was the Trojan horse who smuggled in the jungle rhythms and hell-bent jive. Those White Citizen's Council members in the 1950s knew what they were talking about—Elvis was about miscegenation, genetic riots, and a world arock.

Elvis was a threat. In 1956, a Des Moines preacher declared, "The spirit of Presleyism has taken down all morals." And it wasn't just the preachers who were wailing—the old pop stars and songwriters understood what the ascension of Elvis meant. Bing Crosby always hated him, for Elvis was not only competition but competition that completely changed the rules and rendered the crooner if not obsolete at least old-fashioned. Elvis—with help from World War II—created what we call "the youth market."

"Elvis never did a damn thing for music, " Crosby said in 1975, and in an odd way he was right. Elvis did more for nonmusicians than for musicians, though Crosby couldn't read music any better than Elvis—neither of them were really competent with any instrument, though Elvis could bang on a guitar. The rock 'n' roll that Elvis exemplified was by and large a medium for impassioned amateurs. It didn't demand virtuosity or even technical proficiency but instead put a premium on the authenticity of the emotion.

At his best, Elvis was indivisible from what he was singing—whether it was a rockabilly one-off or "Amazing Grace." His best, his most important work is absolutely without irony, whether his eyes are squeezed tight in religious rapture or his lip is curled into that famous, remarkable (and ever marketable) sneer. Elvis betrayed himself when he became an entertainer, capable of—as one of his record albums had it—"fooling around on stage." When Elvis became aware of his own Elvishood—and you can hear this as early as 1956—he began the long slide down.

Elvis was saved by death, in the sense that it kept him from becoming obsolete. We can always make use of a good tragedy, of a rich man dying young. Elvis's story can be admonitory, cautionary, a tragedy or a romance, depending on who is telling and what motivates the telling. Elvis is a ghost, but as dead as he surely is—and despite the tabloids he must be dead, mustn't he?—he haunts the world, appearing in all sorts of unlikely places.

❖ ❖ ❖

It is important that we understand there is a meaningful difference between the symbolic Elvis who is with us now and the historic Elvis who died in 1977, though that Elvis is at risk of being occluded by the legend. A whole generation has grown up since August 18, 1977; there are adults born after Elvis's death.

This doesn't mean they can't know Elvis. They can know Elvis as well as most of us ever knew Elvis; technology has made singers and movie actors immortal. We can still listen to Elvis singing "Blue Moon of Kentucky" in 1954 (for that was when he sang it) or watch him, starved to perfection and resplendent in black leather, in his 1968 comeback special. The real Elvis still exists, but he is a minor part of the Elvis industry, and so, if one regards the Elvis industry as silly or unseemly, it is possible to dismiss Elvis's performance of "Mystery Train" or that sublime moment when he charges through "Trying to Get to You" on that television special.

It is possible because you don't have to hear or see Elvis to be aware of him and because the Elvis one is likely to see or hear by accident is likely to be inferior Elvis, singles like "Heartbreak Hotel" or "Hound Dog," or clips from television appearances designed to demonstrate his Elvisness, clips that invariably emphasize the jokey, playful, boyish side of Elvis Presley: Lil' Abner with a microphone.

While these clips—like the one from the Steve Allen show where he sings to an actual hound dog—may make Elvis seem like a nice guy, a good sport, a kid eager to please his audience, the effect they have on people who have no real reference point, no real understanding of what Elvis was, is disarming. They make Elvis seem lightweight, a showbiz type, a kind of Southern mush-mouth Ricky Ricardo.

Even those who grant Elvis his Elvishood, his unique and towering place in American culture, are likely to understand him as a freak, a gifted hillbilly of limited intellectual gifts. Elvis's genius is but an outsized talent, a facility for song, the genetic roulette of bone structure and lush hair like "hot buttered yak wool." No one allows that Elvis might have imagined himself—he's always portrayed as the Frankenstein creation of Sam Phillips, as the white boy who could sound black, when in reality Elvis absorbed black culture on his own and bought his clothes at Lansky Brothers, the Beale Street department store that catered to an ethnic clientele. Charlie Feathers, the rockabilly eccentric, has even suggested that Elvis might have had a black grandfather.

The further away we get from the historic Elvis, the boy from Tupelo who cut some sides for Sam Phillips at Sun Studios, the longer his shadow grows.

Elvis dead is Elvis immortal—at least until his followers have died out (which, according to *Newsweek,* surely won't take another hundred years).

Are you lonesome tonight? There is an Elvis for you, a Latin Elvis, a black Elvis, a hip-hop Elvis, an Elvis to serenade your sweetheart as you propose marriage, an Elvis for any purpose one can imagine. Death has exploded Elvis and the resultant pink flecks have all grown into unsubtle variations on the theme—hydra-headed Elvis, cut off one meaning and two or eight or a dozen grow in its place. Elvis is everywhere, Mojo Nixon sang, and it is true. Elvis is ubiquitous, spread thin, one part per billion in the air we breathe.

Dead Elvis can be made to stand for everything and so means nothing; he occludes the real and devastating meaning of that boy from Tupelo, the "Hillbilly Cat," the "Memphis Flash." He was the one, the founder of a secular religion. And as it is with the founders of other religions, it is often those who profess the greatest devotion who do his legacy the most harm.

I'm sorry I was ever cruel to Elvis. I'm sorry that it took me so long to wise up.

2000

Richard Ford: The Reluctant Southerner

He looks less like a writer than an actor playing a writer: pale, intelligent eyes, high forehead, slim shoulders and hips, health's translucent glow in his face. He looks younger than the part in which he has been cast, but never mind that—there is a delicate precision to his features, a certain annoying prettiness to be left unmentioned or shrugged off with an athlete's shamble. In his gray greatcoat, scarf, and black shirt Richard Ford looks posh and urban—like Jonathan Pryce in those Lexus commercials—but there is still a trace of Mississippi in his mouth.

"I'm not as nice as my characters," he warns. But he is smiling as he says it.

He is taller than expected, maybe six foot two or three, with a hint of the West in his silver-buckled belt, a belt familiar from his jacket photos. He is gracious and gentle and confident behind the wheel of his dark blue 1994 Lincoln Continental with Montana plates. A few weeks before, he drove the car east across a couple of states to teach a class in magazine writing at the Medill School of Journalism of Northwestern University. A couple of weeks from now he will drive the car down the center of the country to New Orleans, where his wife of thirty-one years is the executive director of the city's planning commission and a key member of Mayor Mark Morial's kitchen cabinet.

Then he will go to Paris for a while—maybe the Fords will buy an apartment there as well. Maybe not. "If it feels right." He is getting to an age when maybe buying a place in Paris is something that could be done. But that is later; tonight there is work.

Tonight he is reading one of his short stories—a piece called "Optimists," from his *Rock Springs* collection—in a gallery at Northwestern University. The university president shows up, asks how his squash game is going. An ex-student introduces him. He reads a story about the night a family came apart, and then answers questions for students.

The penultimate question comes from one of those touchingly serious young men one often sees waiting outside the office doors of certain superstar professors. Through his anarchist's beard the young man asks, in light of the critic Leslie Fielder's distaste for post modernity and the lamentable tendency of writers working in the late twentieth century to do little more than record the moment-by-moment arc of consciousness, if there isn't any more serious work that the novelist ought to be doing. Or something like that.

"As if there were more important things to write about than people," comes the sotto voce hiss from a woman across the aisle from the earnest student. But Ford seems unshaken by this young man's implication that he has failed to become a Balzac or Trollope for our times. He answers the question, offering the gentle opinion that Fielder had focused his attention so finely that he missed the larger truth, which is that writers have always written about things other than the internal monologue. Ford himself tells stories. He is interested in the ways people make accommodations with the world, the ways we court affection.

◇ ◇ ◇

Ford, the Pulitzer prize and PEN/Faulkner Award–winning novelist, was born in Jackson, Mississippi, but it is only that accident of birth that prevents him from thinking of himself as an Arkansan. And insofar as Arkansas is at least as much of the West as it is of the South, it is fitting that Ford—a writer who has actively resisted the delimiting constraints of "Southern" writing—should feel a great affinity for this city. He has many friends in Arkansas; he returns occasionally to sign copies of his books.

His mother, Edna Akin Shelley, was born in Benton County in 1910, very near the Oklahoma border. In 1928 in Morrilton, she married Parker Ford, who worked as a produce stocker in a Little Rock grocery store.

In 1932, Parker lost his job in the grocery and went to work as a traveling salesman for the Faultless Starch Company of Kansas City, a company for which Huey Long had also worked. For fifteen years the couple lived an itinerant existence. They spent the Great Depression in hotels and restaurants, driving in a company car from Shreveport to Texarkana, from Fort Smith to Memphis, while Parker called on groceries and prisons and conducted clinics to teach newlywed women how to use his product.

When they had days off, they repaired to Little Rock, but mostly they traveled, until Edna became—unexpectedly, after so much time—pregnant. With a baby on the way they moved to Jackson, near the geographical center of Parker's territory. At first they rented, but later bought, a brick duplex at 736 North Congress Street, next door to a school and across from the house where Eudora Welty had lived as a girl.

After Parker suffered a heart attack when their son Richard was eight years old, the child was shuttled back and forth between Jackson and Little Rock, where he stayed in the old Marion Hotel, managed by his grandfather

Ben Shelley. Then, on a Saturday morning in 1960, Parker woke up gasping for breath. As his sixteen-year-old son fought to revive him, as his wife looked on helplessly—"pushing her knuckles into her temples, becoming hysterical," Ford remembered in *Harper's* years later—he died.

Mother and son then took up more or less permanent residence in the Marion, eating huge room-service meals in their upstairs apartment or in the kitchen or in the dining room—the Green Room. The family car was washed every day. They had maid service. Their laundry was done for them.

And Little Rock, Ford says, somehow seemed more like a place people came from than Jackson. It wasn't Deep South, with a complex set of social obligations and expectations. It was rawer and less settled, a place of possibility.

He visited his high school friend Frank Newell's home and marveled at the books that spilled over their shelves and onto the floor and imagined that he might someday want to live that way. His grandfather arranged for young Richard to caddy for a hotel porter when he went to play golf at Fort Roots, the only local course where blacks could play.

Chester, the porter, dressed in plus fours and a Ben Hogan cap, and the sight of a young white boy carrying the clubs of a middle-aged black gentleman was certainly unusual, but not so unusual, perhaps, as to draw rude comments. At least Ford doesn't remember any.

He remembers it as a gentle time. Ben Shelley's name was dropped in the *Arkansas Gazette,* the editorial writers goofing on his habit of running his bird dogs—Brittany spaniels from France—along the river where La Harpe Avenue would eventually be built. It was a good way to grow up, among the itinerants, the salesmen, and the celebrities who passed through the Marion, drinking in the Gar Room and loitering on the long green leather couches in the lobby.

He remembers Win Rockefeller, a friend of his grandfather's, before he was governor—"a great big old guy who had on dusty cowboy boots and some old khaki pants and a white shirt"—churning dirt on Petit Jean Mountain in a big maroon Cadillac.

"He'd say, 'This is kind of my run-around-the-farm Jeep,'" Ford says. "I thought, that's a nice Jeep.

"He was the first really rich guy I ever met. He was really a decent guy; he had such a good heart as far as Arkansas was concerned."

✧ ✧ ✧

Time went by. Ford grew up a little, learned to box, got in a little trouble, nothing too terrible but enough to worry his mother. He was dyslexic, and "enough of a delicate flower" to wince at his middle name—Carrell—and want to get shed of it as quickly as he could.

He had no real plans for the future, just an idea, planted by his grandfather, that maybe he wanted to get into hotel management. Michigan State University had a good program in hotel management. Otherwise the impulse for education was largely self-generated.

"I think if I hadn't wanted to go to college my . . . mother and my grandfather would have been OK about it," he says. "Neither of them had gone to college. . . . I think they wanted me to go to college; they didn't care where I went—all of those decisions got made by me and me alone."

At Michigan State he joined the ROTC program, effectively enlisting in the marines. But he contracted hepatitis soon after and was promptly given a medical discharge.

"I began to think, when I was a sophomore in college, that I had just frittered away a lot of time," he says. "And I thought that if I didn't catch hold *right then* I was going to fritter away a lot more time."

So he went to the counseling center at Michigan State and signed up for a battery of aptitude tests. As Ford tells it, it was a purely pragmatic move to discover a direction for his life.

"And they told me that what I really liked to do was read," he says. "They said, 'You probably should be a better writer than you are but you probably would like to write.' I guess I showed some evidence of liking language. And I just kind of let that guide me to taking a degree in literature."

It might have seemed a strange choice, given that Ford still struggles with a mild form of dyslexia.

"So I had to work hard to read books," he says. "That sense of what I had to do to read, to get it into my brain, became my ethic when it came round to trying to write. I just saw everything as a kind of challenge and sometimes a hardship, so I work at everything real hard because I learned those habits when I was real young."

✧ ✧ ✧

He graduated in 1966 and applied for a series of jobs. He took a test to become a reporter with the *Arkansas Gazette*—they put him in a room with some files and told him to write a story from the clippings within.

"I did pretty badly," he says. "They never called me."

He applied for a job with the Arkansas State Police but didn't get it, possibly because an applicant with an English degree from an out-of-state college seemed a little fishy to the sergeant who interviewed him. He taught junior high school and coached baseball in Flint, Michigan. He moved to New York and for a time worked as an assistant science editor with a trade magazine called *American Druggist*. He was offered a position with the CIA, but he didn't take it. He enrolled in law school at Washington University in St. Louis, but realized his mistake after a single semester.

By then he was married to Kristina, the daughter of an Air Force test pilot; he'd met her while an undergraduate at Michigan State. Finally, he thought he might like to write fiction, so he applied to graduate school, settling on the University of California at Irvine because they were the first to admit him. He says that he knew nothing of the program, that he was unaware that E. L. Doctorow and Oakley Hall were then teaching at Irvine.

He took his master of fine arts degree in 1970, but it was 1976 before his first novel—*A Piece of My Heart*—found a publisher. And though it was well-received by critics and nominated for the Earnest Hemingway Award for Best First Novel, it didn't sell very well and Ford was slightly irritated to find himself routinely described as a "Southern writer."

"Once I wrote *A Piece of My Heart* I couldn't really write about the South anymore because I didn't know anything else," Ford says. "It's everything I knew. And I tried in that book to make a case for landscape being important, for place being important. The book didn't fail, but I think in some ways it proves that landscape isn't very important. I don't think it is."

At least one Arkansas writer is glad that Ford consciously decided not to set any more novels in the South.

"I have the highest regard and envy for Richard Ford," Donald Harington, the Fayetteville-based author of eight novels, almost all of which are set primarily in Arkansas, says. "And also a bit of gratitude: if he had chosen to do more Arkansas subjects in his fiction, he'd have left me lost in his wake or his dust. I rushed out to buy *A Piece of My Heart* as soon as it came out . . . and I've followed his career with amazement ever since."

But the response to Ford's second book—*The Ultimate Good Luck,* set in Mexico and published in 1981—was discouraging. With Kristina teaching at New York University in Manhattan, Ford decided to quit writing fiction and took a job with *Inside Sports* magazine, a glossy publication designed to challenge *Sports Illustrated.*

Had the magazine not folded a year later, Ford might still be writing sports.

"I would have kept that job and never written another book if I could have," he says. "It was a wonderful job for me, particularly since I felt that I'd sort of dogged out as a novelist. To have then the chance to run around the world on an expense account and write about athletes and go to ball games, hang out with Mordecai Richler and people who were sort of heroes of mine, it was a died-and-gone-to-heaven kind of job."

After he lost it, he was more than a little lost. But losing the perfect job compelled Ford to write fiction again.

"I started writing *The Sportswriter* in 1982; it was shortly after my mother died, and it was shortly after the time I decided to myself that I should really probably try to find other work," he says. "And I had found other work and it had all fallen away from me. *Sports Illustrated* wouldn't give me a job; they kept saying I was a novelist and I kept saying, 'I'm not a novelist; I *was* a novelist; I kind of failed at being a novelist; let me have a job.' And they said, 'Oh, no, no. You're a novelist and you wouldn't work out here.' So I was tossed back on my own resources and the only resource I had was to be a novelist."

✧ ✧ ✧

The Sportswriter follows a divorced Everyman named Frank Bascombe over the course of a few days surrounding Easter 1983. Frank works for a magazine much like the one Ford worked for, is divorced and still fond of his ex-wife. As the story opens he is meeting her for a private ceremony commemorating what would have been the thirteenth birthday of a son who had died four years earlier.

Published as a paperback original by Vintage Contemporaries in 1986, *The Sportswriter* was named one of the year's five best books by *Time* magazine and was a finalist for the PEN/Faulkner Award. It sold sixty thousand copies in its first year (since then sales have more than tripled) and a hardcover edition was published by Knopf last year. It was a last-second shot to beat the buzzer—had *The Sportswriter* not found an audience, Ford likely would have given up writing fiction again.

"In fact, in 1984 while I was working on *The Sportswriter,* my agent said, '. . . Ford, this better be a good book—because it's your last shot.' And I thought to myself, 'Well I'm sorry to hear that news coming from you, but you're right.'"

A collection of short stories, *Rock Springs,* followed in 1987. When *Independence Day* was published in 1995, it was greeted as a major literary event. It won the Pulitzer prize and the PEN/Faulkner Award and suddenly Richard Ford was not only one of America's most important writers but one of its most famous as well.

But literary fame is not debilitating. He is able to go out, to eat in restaurants, to travel. Kristina grew weary of his pathological restlessness a few years ago and mostly stays in New Orleans while Ford moves between Montana and Paris and this small sunny corner apartment not far from Northwestern University.

The day before he had sent away his puppy Scooter to be trained as a hunting dog in Tennessee; a few weekends ago Kristina was here for Valentine's Day. Her birthday is coming up—Ford has bought her a photo by WeeGee, a picture of the movie chimp Cheetah being led by the hand across a littered lot by a young woman dressed in a bareback rider's costume. The circus is breaking camp.

"I look at that photo and think that must be what it's been like for her to live with me all these years," Ford says.

He is a man at ease with himself, a patient and gracious man. He likes his little apartment here; he likes the fact that he can spread his clipboards out, read his Chekhov, watch sports on television. Soon he'll be back in New Orleans, in the big house on Bourbon Street where Kristina is remodeling the slave quarters to accommodate his clutter—then on to Paris, where some of his most recent writing has been set. Maybe they will buy that apartment.

And sooner or later he will be back in Arkansas, to a reunion of his father's family in Atkins or Russellville, to sign at Wordsworth Books or at his friend Rod Lorenzen's bookstore, to visit Frank Newell. Something will call him back. His mother is buried here.

He is finished. He has an appointment—he's speaking at a high school in Oak Park, a school Hemingway once attended.

"I've lived a rather sort of typical kind of middle-class writing life in America," he says finally. "I didn't go to Vietnam, though I joined the Marines. That would have changed my life, if I hadn't got sick. . . . I haven't been a foreign correspondent. I mostly haven't taught. I've been married to the same person; I'm not an alcoholic; I've never done anything but write books and try to stick to my word.

"Truthfully, I don't know if my life is the fodder for very interesting stories. That's OK with me, because I like my life, A; and B, I think it makes more difference to me if my books are good books—not that my life is an interesting life."

1998

Educating Jimmy Carter

There is something about Jimmy Carter that still resists easy characterization. At seventy-six years old, the thirty-ninth president of the United States, a man renowned for his quiet intelligence and preternatural compassion, seems to retain a remnant of boyish pride and pique—perhaps even a flash of humanizing vanity or a need for approbation.

He seems to have something yet to prove, even at this late date, when he seems above politics, when even those Reagan-worshipping radio talk boys concede Carter's integrity. Is it faint praise to be considered, almost by acclamation, the greatest ex-president of the twentieth century, a man whose very name has become a kind of synonym for decency?

Sure, it might rankle. But what can one do? There will be revisions to history, little touch-ups, but the twentieth century is over. Carter, the peanut farmer from Plains, Georgia—that's what they called him, though he was a scientist and a navy man and businessman and a politician as well—who became an unlikely president in the Watergate-rattled post-sixties, told us the somber truth about our "malaise"—a word some of his critics had to look up—and served one crimped and tortured tour of duty plagued by oil crises and hostage takings.

We rejected his somber, clerical fact-facing for the cheery, magical pragmatism of Ronald Reagan. The voodoo spell worked; the eighties boomed and Jimmy Carter went on to supervise elections and build houses for poor folks and almost—but not quite—win a Nobel Peace prize.

"Maybe people think I won one," he muses, in what might be half a joke.

But if it's a joke, it's a joke that contains just a hint of plausibly deniable hurt. It's enough, perhaps, to supply some evidence of Carter's longing. He would like to have the prize, sure, though it doesn't mean that much to him, not really. It's not an accomplishment he'd list on his tombstone. He says as much. And he didn't even raise the subject.

Yet Carter is on the phone. And he's on the phone because he's willing to suffer the questions of opinion journalists and arts and entertainment reporters in an effort to sell his latest book, his fifteenth and arguably his finest. It's not former president Jimmy Carter on the line, it's Jimmy Carter, author. And even though he's got a cold, even though he's still rehabbing a shoulder he injured last November (ever the self-improver, Carter hurt the shoulder when he fell during an early morning jog on a San Diego beach), Carter is willing to do the things authors do when they want their books to sell.

He's obviously proud that his memoir, *An Hour before Daylight: Memories of a Rural Boyhood,* has spent a few weeks atop the New York Times Bestseller List. He is even prouder of the almost uniformly excellent reviews the book has received. He is willing to do rounds of phone interviews from his home in Plains to push it.

He ought to be proud of the book. It is keenly observed—remembered, actually—and written in a sometimes terse yet evocative and above all confident literary style. Carter's prose is remarkable for its clarity and lack of pretense, yet it has hollows and wells and ringing echoes. Carter cites James Agee as an influence, but one hears Willie Morris, Will Campbell, and Rick Bragg as well as some of Arkansas poet Miller Williams's plainsinging lyricism.

It's something at which Carter says he's worked. Though he's one of the few public personages who writes "every word" of his books, he was not too proud to seek help. For the past decade or so, Williams has been perhaps his prime literary tutor.

"I have always had a kind of frustration about not having had an adequate liberal arts education," Carter says. "So, I've tried to make up for it by studying and writing myself. Maybe ten years ago I had written a few poems, not even good enough for me to want to show them to anybody in my family. And Miller Williams came down to Plains; I got to know him and I told him that I would really love to learn more about poetry. In effect he took me under his wing as a student and was a very tough taskmaster in assigning me the same kind of literary textbooks he used in college courses. I began to struggle with poetry then."

Carter spent thousands of hours over an eight-year period writing what became his first book of poems, *Always a Reckoning.*

"The wonderful thing that I had with Miller was that he could tell me that a line or a word was inferior, but I never let him give me a word instead," Carter says. "That was the deal we had and I stuck with it. So he would say, 'This line has an artificial rhyme and you're straining to say something. You should be more natural.' He would recognize it, and I would try to correct it."

✧ ✧ ✧

So he has made himself into a real writer. The *New Yorker* has called his memoir "an American classic." He will even admit to working on a novel, set in the South during the Revolution, a book still inchoate, whose early pages are yet unread by anyone, not even by his wife, Rosalynn, whom he calls his sternest editor.

"It's very strange to me to write fiction because the characters have taken on a life of their own, which is a surprise to me. And, you know, when you don't have to worry about the facts and you can just kind of dream . . . it's really delightful in a way. I don't have any judgment about the quality of the novel, yet."

But that is the future, and what's now is Carter's past, specifically, his boyhood, his formative years in the Georgia backwoods on the same farm he lives on today. It is a memoir of pranks and punishment, of a rural, sentimental education.

"My most persistent impression as a farm boy was of the earth," he writes. "There was a closeness, almost an immersion, in the sand, loam, and red clay, that seemed natural, and constant. The soil caressed my bare feet, and the dust was always boiling up from the dirt road that passed fifty feet from our front door."

An Hour before Daylight takes its title from young Jimmy's routine—each morning he was awakened at five A.M. by an iron bell rung by a neighbor, a black sharecropper named Jack Clark.

Carter credits Clark's wife, Rachel, as a large influence on him; he writes that his "childhood world was really shaped by black women" who cared for him while his father worked on the farm and his mother practiced nursing.

"Much more than my parents, she [Rachel] talked to me about the religious and moral values that shaped a person's life, and I listened to her with acute attention."

Carter writes that until he was about fourteen, he had closer ties to his black neighbors than to the white community. Then, he noticed his black playmates began treating him with a little more "deference."

"We still competed equally while on the baseball field, fishing, or working in the field," Carter writes, "but I was not reluctant to take advantage by assuming, on occasion, the authority of my father. I guess all of us assumed this was one more step toward maturity, and there we were settling into our adult roles in an unquestioned segregated society."

Looking back, he says he's amazed at how closely black and white neighbors could live in an age of legal segregation. Maybe it was simply economic necessity.

"It's almost impossible for Americans to realize how poverty stricken everybody was," he says. "There was just not any money. And, for instance, Mother was a nurse, twenty-four hours, and her pay was six dollars, but mostly people who she nursed didn't have any money. So, they would agree to bring Mama a dozen eggs a week for a year or something like that. That was the way we lived.

"We were drawn together, the black and white people. I didn't have any white neighbors; we were probably drawn together closer because we shared that common poverty. I never was hungry and most of the people on a farm weren't, either. We had a garden and we had firewood, all that we could burn, and we had wild animals that we could harvest and that sort of thing."

And, perhaps, Carter muses, it was different in rural areas.

"I think the intimacy was really limited to two things," he says. "In the towns like Plains, mostly south of the railroad is where the black people lived and north of the railroad was where the white people lived. There was some overlap, but on the farm there was no separation. You know, all of the immediate neighbors of mine that lived within fifty yards of our house, all of them were black. That was the first thing, is that we were in a rural area.

"The second thing was that we had that closeness when I was growing up, from the time when I was four until I was fourteen, which is a long time. I slept at my neighbor's house; I ate dinner and supper with them. You know, we played cards together, we played checkers with each other, we went fishing in the same stream, we fought each other, we wrestled with each other, we made toys together, and that's all I knew. I mean, I never realized it was a different kind of life."

Carter says he understood the ways things were, but it never occurred to him—or anyone else—to question the status quo.

"We weren't separate and we weren't equal because I knew that when we went to the picture show in Americus that we sat in separate parts of the theater. We rode on separate buses and trains marked colored and white, but it didn't really affect me."

Carter left the family farm some fifteen years before the Civil Rights movement had gathered any momentum, and when he returned after a career in the navy, he supported the rights of local black tenant farmers to vote in the face of white opposition. Carter doesn't go into any of this in detail in his book—he says he took pains not to "insinuate" into the narrative the idea that the author might grow up to be an important person—but he refused to join a local White Citizens Council and as a result his business, the peanut business, was hit with a boycott.

Yet despite his unassailable civil rights record, Carter is more than a little ambivalent about the effects of desegregation. In the book he writes, "In the dramatic changes we have witnessed, something has been lost as well as gained. My own life was shaped by a degree of personal intimacy between black and white people that is now almost completely unknown and largely forgotten."

And he doesn't think that kind of intimacy can easily be recaptured.

"I think now, with equal legal rights, people have decided voluntarily to segregate themselves geographically in housing areas, and also culturally there are some natural differences," he says. "For instance, we go to church and I start Sunday school at 10:00 A.M. I get through at 10:45 and the preacher starts preaching at 11:00, and if he's still preaching at 12:03 the whole audience is restless.

"But when we go to the predominantly black churches in Plains, you know, it's completely unstructured and much more full of vitality and life and exuberance, and if the preacher is still going at 2:30 in the afternoon, then so be it. So, it's kind of a different culture. And so we voluntarily have segregated ourselves.

"And so that's not mandatory, it's not legal segregation, but it's just as segregated as it was when I was growing up."

Yet Carter still sees some of the black friends he made growing up—he was with a couple of them just the other night, he says. They still laugh together; they still share.

If he is the slightest bit sad, it is sadness for the world, not for himself. He still gets up at 5:00 A.M., an hour before daylight, and works at his word processor, sometimes just clacking out words and parts of words in a stream-of-consciousness spew. It sounds like the kind of thing a young aspiring writer might do. There is something touching in his ambition, something vulnerable. It is strange to think of an ex-president this way: Down in Plains, where his heart has always been, Jimmy Carter fills up line after line in his electronic dream book, the characters tumble, to be later mined for sense, and even wisdom.

—2001

Back Home with Willie Morris

I miss Willie Morris. We became friendly after I wrote this piece, exchanging a few letters. He invited me to come visit him in Jackson sometime but we were never quite able to connect. I regret that deeply.

> *Yet, finally, when a writer knows home in his heart, his heart must remain subtly apart from it. He must always be a stranger to the place that he loves, and its people. His claim to home is deep, but there are too many ghosts. He must absorb without being absorbed. When he understands, as few others do, something of his home in America—Mississippi—that is funny, or sad, or tragic, or cruel, or beautiful, or true, he knows he must do so as a stranger.*
> *—Willie Morris, "Coming on Back"*

Every Southerner eventually comes home, Truman Capote said, even if it's in a box. Willie Morris came home fifteen years ago, when he was still a relatively young man, to become a legend-in-residence at the University of Mississippi at Oxford.

Even today, as he sits in a dingy, nearly deserted classroom at the University of Arkansas at Monticello, with his body a sack of potatoes and the pale, watery gaze of a sage, there is something of the wunderkind in Morris. At sixty, he is still the brightest boy in the classroom, still shot through with promise. His manner is courtly, his stately Southern storyteller's cadences flow like bourbon through silk. He retains an unruly shock of hair and a subversive eye twinkle he uses for punctuation.

There is no doubt he has lived, often well and often hard. Morris seems easy, in the Southern way, with decay. Nothing about him suggests that he might like to live forever; there is no suggestion of California tone or a special longevity regime. He drinks, he smokes, and when the man who has become president of the United States comes to visit him, they are likely to drive over to Doe's in Greenville and eat about two steaks apiece.

Morris might be one of the quiet men one sees eating breakfasts of pork chops and fried eggs and grits in the little diners that still exist in the little

Delta towns too small to attract the attention of McDonald's. His sports jacket is a little frayed; he asks permission before lighting his first Viceroy. Even though the Memorial Classroom Building is officially a no-smoking zone, permission is granted. He taps his ashes into an institutional green tin trash can with a plastic liner.

He is from Yazoo City, Mississippi, a place name that sounds ridiculous—a Dr. Seuss name—to those of us who did not grow up there. But it does not sound ridiculous in Morris's mouth.

"The Yazoo River is the eternal river of death," he says. "Did you know that? That's what it means, 'river of death.'"

❖ ❖ ❖

To be Southern is to live among the dead, to acknowledge them. Southernness commands remembrance of the days of occupation, of ancestors' bones in the buried caskets. In the jacket photo of *New York Days,* Morris leans against a tree in a graveyard, his eyes cast up, headstones picketing in the background.

To be Southern is to understand the stubborn persistence of the South, to apprehend the claim the dead have on the living. Morris has come home to find the little girls he once knew are now grandmothers, and the grandchildren wear the faces of their ancestors.

"I confuse the generations," he says. "In Mississippi, everyone looks alike anyhow. And they're all talking. . . . My wife and I went to a Christmas party in Yazoo City, at a friend of mine's parents' house. It was the hundredth anniversary of that house. He invited all of what they call 'Old Yazoo'—people that I hadn't seen in forty years. It was like something out of Fellini's movie *8 ½*—remember that march of life around Fellini's past? It was bizarre to see all these old people—they were the same; they had just shrunk. I recognized everybody, everybody recognized everybody else, and they all took for granted the terrible passage of time; they kind of made fun of it. There's something very satisfying about that. They'd just stayed there forever—like the trees."

Morris once thought of running for governor of Mississippi, an idea that does not seem so far-fetched once you give it a little thought. Where else might a writer be king but in Mississippi, Faulkner's land, where firemen and state legislators turn into novelists, where the banal pain of living poor is converted into something as beautiful as the blues?

Yazoo. The river of death. Words are important to Southerners. Morris likes the roll of them, the way they knock together and make sparks, their capacity to delight and vex.

❖ ❖ ❖

Born in 1934, Morris graduated from the University of Texas and went to Oxford as a Rhodes Scholar. He came back to Austin to edit the *Texas Observer*—a liberal alternative newspaper that was at the peak of its influence in the late '50s and early '60s. In 1962 he received a letter from John Fischer, the editor-in-chief of *Harper's* magazine. Fischer matter-of-factly informed the twenty-eight-year-old editor that he was looking for a successor and that he believed Morris might be the man. Morris directly embarked on a high-level apprenticeship, and then, at the age of thirty-three, became editor-in-chief himself.

Just before he assumed the editorship, Morris published, with the help of a Houghton Mifflin Literary Fellowship, an extraordinary *Bildungsroman* that carried our hero from his youth in Mississippi, through his days at Oxford, and into the Harper's offices in Manhattan. *North toward Home* has become an essential part of the Southern literary landscape, a kind of touchstone for every young person straining to escape the emotional gravity of the small-time South.

❖ ❖ ❖

When Morris took over *Harper's,* it was a staid, fading magazine labeled "Squaresville" by *Esquire* in the 1963 edition of that magazine's annual map of the literary universe. Under Morris that all changed; he sought pieces from Southern soul mates like Marshall Frady and Bill Moyers. His *Harper's* published George Plimpton, Joan Didion, and David Halberstam, Seymour Hersh on the My Lai massacre, Joe McGinniss on the selling of a president, Irving Howe on the New York intellectuals.

"I am the editor of one of the most respected magazines in the history of America, and the most long-lasting," Morris wrote in *New York Days,* the 1993 sequel to *North toward Home.* "The best writers will write for us, and not for the money. *Harper's* is what this town calls 'hot.'"

"One of the things that distinguished our *Harper's* back then was the whole mood of the '60s themselves," Morris says. "We were very much an expression of the '60s. There was such great excitement about the magazine business back then. We had some fun. It was hard work, but we had some great people.

"I knew Larry L. King when he was worth about twenty-five cents. Now he's probably made $25 million off of *Best Little Whorehouse in Texas* alone. The rest of those boys haven't done badly either."

Ironically, Morris's pursuit of talent probably hastened his departure from *Harper's*. In *New York Days,* he spends a chapter recounting his courtship of Norman Mailer, who wound up writing several landmark pieces for the magazine.

The testosterone-soaked bull genius wrote about the 1968 political conventions in Chicago and Miami Beach; twice Morris dedicated entire issues to Mailer's pieces: "The Armies of the Night," a story detailing Mailer's role in an antiwar demonstration at the Pentagon, ran close to ninety thousand words; the second story, "The Prisoner of Sex," a rumination on feminism, was even longer.

It was also the last issue of *Harper's* Morris edited. In 1971, Morris was summoned to a meeting in Minnesota with publisher William Blair and John Cowles Jr., president of the media group that owned the magazine. After a three-and-a-half-hour meeting, Morris caught a plane back to New York, where he abruptly resigned.

"It came down to the money men and the literary men," Morris wrote in a news release announcing his resignation. "And, as always, the money men won."

✧ ✧ ✧

When *New York Days* was published, it met curiously polarized reviews. Though the book had only one real villain—the short-sighted Cowles (who eventually wound up deposed, dancing naked with his wife in bizarre theatrical productions)—most of the players were still around to take issue or concur with Morris's version.

Morris shrugs. It was his book, his memories. He allows that it is subjective and "terribly, terribly difficult" to re-create the time after a quarter century has passed. It was not an easy book for him to write; he sat for hours a day in a basement room—"my dungeon"—that his second wife, JoAnne, set up for him in their home in Jackson, and wore out 180 felt-tip pens, scribbling it all out longhand.

"One of the gratifying things about it was going back to the bound volumes of *Harper's* from the '60s up into the early '70s," he says. "Those bound volumes were like a diary to me, a story or an article would bring back in a rush to me all the memories. I started getting back in touch with old friends and colleagues, and a few enemies, and I sent portions of manuscripts out to various people I was dealing with."

He sent Mailer the section that dealt with him. Mailer sent it back, with his comments penciled in the margins.

"The first time I saw Mailer I was at a cocktail party in Greenwich Village, about 1963," Morris says. "It was a hot night and the air conditioning wasn't working in this apartment; he was talking away to somebody in a crowded room. Next thing I knew he was lying on the floor with a bloodied lip.

"He writes in the margins of my draft, 'Absolutely nonsense, Morris! I've only been knocked down once, and that was in Mexico. I think I told you that story but you're confusing it with me getting knocked down in Mexico.'

"So I changed the sentence to say, 'So I looked over the next time and saw him standing there with a bloodied lip.'"

Comes the twinkle. Willie's version.

✧ ✧ ✧

After leaving *Harper's,* Morris retreated to Long Island, where he lived for nine years. It was an admittedly difficult time for the still-young writer.

"I missed the perquisites and attentions of high station," he says. "All of a sudden, the phone was not ringing. It was wintertime and it was snowing and there was a great silence out there. I talked to Bill Moyers and he said, 'Well, you're only thirty-seven and you've still got a typewriter.'"

So Morris sat down and wrote a children's book. He wrote an account of his friendship with his Long Island neighbor, *From Here to Eternity* author James Jones. He settled into the routine of the professional writer; another expatriate Southerner in a Yankee culture thick with expatriate Southerners.

In 1980 he was offered the opportunity to become the writer-in-residence at Ole Miss. He jumped at the chance and settled into a bungalow on faculty row, where he was visited by the likes of sixteen-year-old Donna Tartt.

"When Donna came here, she lived . . . just up the street," he says. "She'd come down to my house and she showed me some of her early stuff—it was really amazing, powerful stuff for a kid of sixteen, seventeen. For various reasons, she didn't want to stay in Mississippi, so I encouraged her to apply at Bennington [College] to study writing under Bernard Malamud. I wrote a letter for her. She went there, and though Malamud had pretty much retired, she found a pretty good writing teacher. Her campus in *The Secret History* looks a lot like Bennington.

"Donna's real; she could be one of the great ones. She's from Grenada, Mississippi, just a little bitty girl."

Morris also had a hand in finding a young writer named John Grisham a literary agent; and the president of the United States has cited Morris as his favorite author.

"I met Bill Clinton when he was twenty-one years old," Morris says. "A

longhaired, baby-faced kid, he was on his way to Oxford on his Rhodes scholarship, and he stopped off in New York for a few days. I remember one night
we went to Elaine's, and he was talking to these writers about watermelon.

"Jules Feiffer asked Bill about watermelon: 'Bill, what's so great about
watermelon? Isn't it a parasite?' And Bill told him, 'No, it's not a parasite.
First of all, it's good to eat. And second, Arkansas is a poor state and it's good
for the economy.'"

Morris remains fond of Clinton, whom he has kept in touch with over
the years. Mississippi went for George Bush, he remembers. Another
twinkle.

$\diamond \ \diamond \ \diamond$

Even in an age of cable television, franchised fast food, and shopping
malls, the South persists.

"I think the Southern sensibility is still with us," Morris says. "Despite
the whole relentless urge to national sameness, when you get off the main
thoroughfares in Mississippi, the South is still there in all its color and complexity. All the traditional Southern literary themes, you have them there. So
much of what the South is about is remembrance anyway."

Morris talks about a University of Arkansas at Monticello faculty member, whom he'd met the night before at a reception.

"She was from California," he says. "She came up to me and whispered,
'This place is a lot crazier than California.' And I smiled, and I said I'd consider myself lucky to be here, then."

Morris sees technology as a great leveler of experience and, more
depressingly, a silencer of conversation. Today's kids tend to be more impres-
sionistic and less verbal, more solipsistic and less connected to the world at
large. Reconstruction couldn't dissolve the South, but the cyber age might.
This worries Willie a little.

"A couple of months ago, I went over to talk to Eudora Welty—she lives
up the street from us in the house where she was a girl," Morris says.

"I asked her, 'Eudora, are you going to take any trips soon on the information superhighway?' She said, 'What's that?' And I didn't know much
about it myself, but I'd got my son to fill me in on the general idea. So I told
her. And she said, 'That's scary.'

"I asked her if she had a fax machine. She didn't know what a fax
machine was . . . so I tried to explain to her. She said, 'Oh, faxes. They're
going to be like fairies.'"

1995

A Thing Worth Staying With: Larry Brown

With practice, a man can teach himself just about anything. He can teach himself to tear down an engine and put it back together with no parts left over, to build a house or maybe to strum a few chords on the guitar. It starts with something like will, with the wanting to and the unutterable belief that maybe it will all work out.

You look at Larry Brown and you don't see much that seems extraordinary; a wiry little guy with receding chestnut hair and sad-dog eyes patting his pockets for that pack of Marlboros. You get close and see his face is tanned and creased like a farmer's, and when he speaks the words back out slow and careful, like eighteen-wheelers creeping to the loading dock behind the Wal-Mart. He sounds deep Mississippi—which he is—kudzu cadences and soft solemn vowels.

He sure doesn't look like a genius and likely he is not, at least not in the way that word is usually overused. He looks like a good carpenter and a steady guy, someone you might rely on to watch your house and feed your dogs when you're out of town—what up in New York folks might call a real mensch.

He doesn't look exactly comfortable now, but not quite uncomfortable either, as he looks up from his typed notes and comes level with the eyes of some of the twenty or so people who've come to hear him talk this afternoon. He's done tougher things.

Brown enlisted in the marines right out of high school, before they could draft him. For sixteen years he worked as a firefighter in Oxford, Mississippi, eventually rising through the ranks to become a captain. He has helped extricate dying people from cars and pulled out the charred bodies of babies in the aftermath of house fires.

Now he's here, at Lyon College in Batesville, Arkansas, in this spanky-nice little auditorium, to talk about what creative writing professors call "process," the way that humans begin to put down their ideas on paper, the way they make up stories and save them.

This is something Larry Brown has become quite good at, something he does.

At forty-four, he is your genuine Southern writer, literature division, which is kind of ironic if you understand that he got into the writing trade for mercenary reasons. He figured he might be able to make some money at it, maybe get on the best-seller lists like Stephen King or Harold Robbins, figured that writing for a living had to be easier than cutting pulpwood or installing chain-link fences for Sears or cleaning carpets or painting houses or farming or working in a convenience store or any of the other odd jobs he took when he wasn't knocking down fires as a member of the Oxford Fire Department.

"I had been wondering how people went into a room and, just out of their imaginations, created a book," Brown says. "I figured these were regular people, but I wanted to know how they did it. Did they go to college and take a course? Did they take a correspondence course? Did they just go into a room and start doing it?"

So, in 1980, when he was twenty-nine years old, Brown drove over to his sister's house and retrieved his wife's portable Smith-Corona typewriter. He went into a room and started typing. When he emerged seven months later, he had written a novel of sorts. He had 327 single-spaced pages about a bear running amok in Yellowstone National Park.

"I didn't have the advantage of ever having been to Yellowstone National Park," he says. "But that didn't concern me."

He packed it up in an envelope and sent it off to a New York publisher, "fully expecting to get back a check for a million dollars." But the manuscript came back. So he packed it up again and sent it off again. Again it came back, and again, and again.

"I sent it out enough times to know it was never going to be taken," Brown says. "But all I did was sit down and start writing another novel. I went through that process five times."

None of the early novels met with any success at all. But Brown had always enjoyed short stories, so in 1982 the motorcycle magazine *Easyriders* accepted one of Brown's first attempts at writing a short story for publication.

"At that time I was just trying to write anything I could to get published," he says. "I remember the day that that story got accepted; it was a horrible day. It was February; it was raining; it was muddy and cold. Let's see: my wife was pregnant and my oldest son was sick and we were on our way to the doctor's office. We didn't have money to buy gas to heat the house and probably didn't have enough money to pay the doctor either. I thought I'd go down to the mailbox and check the mail before we left, and in there was this acceptance letter from Malibu. They were going to buy the story; they were going to pay me $375 for it. It became the greatest day of my life—I thought I was going to publish everything I'd write after that."

It would be another two years before Brown had another story accepted for publication—anywhere.

Always a ferocious reader, Brown had—quite by accident—stumbled into the works of Mark Twain and Oxford's own William Faulkner as a boy. But he was well into his twenties before he realized there was any difference between a Harold Robbins paperback and Flannery O'Connor's work.

"I used to read Greek mythology—just for the stories," he says. "The Bible had some good stories in it, too. And I grew up hearing stories told—but I think everybody grows up hearing stories told."

Brown's mother encouraged his habit, but his sharecropper father, who died in 1968, had no use for books. Neither did Brown's fire chief.

"I had to go read in back," he muses. "He thought guys playing poker, with money right out on the table, that that was all right, but that it looked bad to have me sitting there reading a book."

Brown shakes his head at this, not angry, more amused, as though it all seems a long time ago. It's been five years since he retired from the fire department. Does he miss the work?

"There's times when I miss it; any time I see a fire truck go by I miss it. I miss the boys I work with; it's like a family in a way. You live with each other for twenty-four hours at a time; you eat meals together; you sleep together. . . . The only thing I don't miss is the boredom, the hours when nothing is happening, when, just from my own point of view, I wished I was home writing."

Things started happening in 1987, when Shannon Ravenel, an editor for Algonquin Books in Chapel Hill, North Carolina, noticed one of Brown's stories in *Mississippi Review.* The next year Algonquin published *Facing the Music,* a collection of Brown's short stories about the poor and nearly desperate people of rural northern Mississippi. Over the next five years, he cemented a burgeoning literary reputation with another short story collection, *Big Bad Love,* and two novels, *Dirty Work,* the story of two battered Vietnam vets trading histories over the course of a long night in a VA hospital, and *Joe,* a white trash coming-of-age story.

In November 1993, Brown published *On Fire,* a pellucid memoir of his days as a firefighter. Now he's finishing another novel, with the working title *Father and Son,* a book about difficult homecomings.

And somewhere in there he figured out he needn't be the next Stephen King or John Grisham. His choice of reading material improved; he began to meet other writers—fellow Mississippian Barry Hannah was the first—and he discovered the work of Raymond Carver, Cormac McCarthy, and Flaubert. He decided that what he wanted to do was write good books, quality fiction.

"I was really obsessed with it, and even though I didn't have much success at first I began to feel it was a thing worth staying with," he says. "My family couldn't understand it; it was taking up an incredible amount of time, but I had this unshakable belief—there was no way to prove it—that if I kept writing that eventually I'd learn how."

So he has.

Larry Brown stacks plain word after plain word until he's got a solid book. He can stare into the thrilling pain at the center of most human relationships and not turn away. With a few quick strokes, he can gut a character, dumping his innards out on the floor like he's field-dressing a deer. There's an almost mathematical elegance in the way he uses language; like an Eskimo whaler, he wastes nothing.

Take, for instance, this passage from *On Fire,* in which Brown describes the odd mingling of cynicism and fear that infects firefighters and police officers and soldiers—those who know they may be called upon to die in the line of duty:

> *Sometimes there was a weird callousness about the work we did. We couldn't let it get too close to us because we didn't want to be touched by it. We didn't talk much about the bad ones. When they happened, we dealt with them.*
>
> *Then we went back and ate or watched a movie or went on another call, or washed the trucks and polished the chrome. We got through our shifts and then we went home and went fishing or hunting or made love to our wives or played with our children. We hoped the bad things we saw would never claim us. We hoped we wouldn't die in smoke and flames or torn steel like the people we couldn't save.*

There are no big words in that passage, no writer's tricks. Only "torn steel" seems poetic. But there is rhythm and a sense of aptness to the passage—something that is not so easily deconstructed. There is something honest in the words.

"What's hard about writing is that it comes from some secret place down inside us," Brown says. "And the hardest thing for a writer is to let someone else peek into that secret place, to just get it down and be completely honest about what you're feeling—and to never back off."

Larry Brown is a writer now, not a fireman who writes. He doesn't do as well as Mr. Grisham, but he does well enough; he still lives in the house he built with his own hands a few years ago with his wife, Mary Annie. His oldest boy is nineteen, wondering what he's going to do with his life. Brown tells him he's got plenty of time to decide.

1995

Rednecks: The Army That Fights for Dignity

We got no-necked oilmen from Texas
Good ol' boys from Tennessee
College men from LSU
Went in dumb, come out dumb too
Hustlin' 'round Atlanta in their alligator shoes
Getting drunk every weekend at the barbecues . . .
      —*Randy Newman, "Rednecks"*

You might be a redneck if your good deed for the month was hiding out your brother for a few days.
      —*Jeff Foxworthy*

It wasn't so long ago "redneck" was considered a pejorative term. Some people might still consider it a mild slur or hold it in some gray area, like "Arkie" or the self-descriptive Cajun "coonass." At the very least, "redneck" carries some strong connotations. Most people have an idea of what rednecks are and how they behave. The redneck is prone to violence. It was rednecks who shotgunned Peter Fonda and Dennis Hopper to death at the end of *Easy Rider*. The redneck is ill-educated and disaffected. The redneck is white trash, Strother Martin in mirrored shades in *Cool Hand Luke* drawling about a "failure to communicate." The redneck drives the pickup with the Confederate flag screen on the back window, obscuring the view of his gun rack. The redneck has no manners.

The redneck is a safe target in this politically correct world. You can't make fun of most folks who can claim membership in some underprivileged class or other. The overweight and the left-handed have their lobbies, psychiatry has banished evil by turning ogres into victims, and you can't say anyone is stupid unless it's obvious to everyone that he isn't. But you still can make fun of rednecks; you can get your own television situation comedy and houses on both coasts and one of them big speedboats.

It's safe to make fun of rednecks because most rednecks generally don't mind. You might be a redneck if you think comedian Jeff Foxworthy is funny. Which isn't to say that every redneck does. The Reverend Will Campbell, civil rights activist, Baptist preacher, and author of *Brother to a Dragonfly*, doesn't think that redneck jokes are funny at all. He thinks agrarian Americans are the most discriminated-against folks in America.

"Jeff Foxworthy says you might be a redneck if you eat squirrel for breakfast," Campbell says. "Well, Mr. Foxworthy, I've had squirrel for breakfast, out of necessity, because we couldn't afford to buy meat so we had to eat what we could shoot."

All right, there's one in every crowd. But rednecks are generally amiable about being called rednecks. Most of them seem fairly content to be what they are, and no matter what kind of success they achieve—and there are plenty of overachieving rednecks—they never "get above their raising."

This leads us to the putative First Redneck, Bill Clinton, who actually isn't a redneck at all. He may be "Bubba" to some; he might be a cousin to Bill Faulkner's hardscrabble Snopes and a brother to Roger Clinton—who certainly is a redneck—but he's not one himself.

In itself, this isn't a good thing or bad thing, just the truth.

✧ ✧ ✧

So exactly what is a redneck? We all have our ideas. A colleague says rednecks are simply members of "ball-cap-wearing America." By his lights, white trash is a redneck subgenre—to wit, "a redneck who won't work."

For Will Campbell, rednecks are poor rural white Southerners. To Randy Newman, whose 1973 album *Good Ol' Boys* can be read as a defense of rednecks, they are "white Christians who like to do and hate the same things. For instance they hate guys who wear silk underwear and tweed jackets. They like country music, pickup trucks, Harleys, sex, God and Mama. They may look tough, but their hearts are tender."

Newman is quoted in *Redneck Heaven: Portrait of a Vanishing Culture*, the new book by Bethany Bultman, a New Orleans–based documentary filmmaker. The book is a handy compendium of redneck cultural signifiers—she includes lists of "redneck bumper stickers" and recipes for "Coca Cola cuisine"—and a celebration of the lifestyle.

Bultman says she spent five years researching her book and found rednecks indigenous to all parts of the country, from Maine to California. She finds much to admire in rednecks, whom she considers regular working people, without pretensions, who favor acting on instinct over intellect—heart over head, emotion over reason.

Although she doesn't mention W. J. Cash's seminal work on the

American caste system, *The Mind of the South*, there are some congruencies. Cash found the spirit of the South in "the savage ideal" and said the dominant trait of the Southern mind was "an intense individualism—in its way, perhaps the most intense individualism since the Italian Renaissance and its men of 'terrible fury.'"

In her book, Bultman visits gonzo journalist Hunter S. Thompson and finds him disinclined to talk about "ethno-culturalism" until she offers the opinion that rednecks are basically a species of Anglo-Saxon.

Thompson corrects her, in a way that echoes Cash's description of the typical Southern "savage" as a Scotch-Irishman freed from civilizing obligation by the vastness of the American frontier.

"Bikers and biker gangs are rednecks too," Thompson says. "I rode with the Hell's Angels for two years. It didn't take more than a few hours with 'em to get a sense of déjà vu for Scots-Irish clans. There's that same sulking hostility toward outsiders, that honor code and those long bodies that never look right unless they're leaning on something."

Yet being a redneck has nothing to do with genetics.

Being a redneck is an act of volition. You have to want to be one to be one. So Bill Clinton is not a redneck because he aspires to be a part of an American aristocracy. Even from the presidency, he courts celebrities and indulges in social climbing.

Real rednecks don't have the kind of pretensions our president has affected. They might be star-struck in the presence of Dolly Parton or David Allan Coe, but they'd never imagine themselves the star or publicly consider their own place in history—their legacy.

So just because your mama or your daddy was a redneck doesn't necessarily mean that you will be one, too. And just because you're born a redneck doesn't mean you'll stay one. You can overcome your redneckedness, just as it is possible to achieve redneckedness. Country singer Jerry Jeff Walker, who started life as a Jewish fella from upstate New York, is perhaps the best example of a self-made redneck.

And while it's possible to occasionally adopt redneck ways (as our president sometimes seems to do), a real redneck doesn't go back and forth.

✧ ✧ ✧

There are several theories about the origins of the term "redneck." According to the Oxford English Dictionary, "red-neck," as a term of derision for religious dissenters, was in use as early as the seventeenth century. Bultman places the first American use of the word in 1830 or 1831, to describe the "Presbyterian proletariat" of North Carolina's backcountry.

Many people assume "redneck" is a simple descriptive term: A farmer who toils in the fields all day invariably ends up with a red neck. Bultman favors a story she says a miner named Sam told her.

According to Sam, when coal miners began to complain about conditions in the late nineteenth century, the bosses imported workers from Greece and Italy to do their jobs.

Bultman quotes Sam: "But they were uncooperative, too. So the company brought in black railroad workers to do the mining. But the thing the company didn't bargain on was that the miners would put aside their distrust of one another to fight for a better life, together. . . .

"When all the trouble blew up in 1921 on Blair Mountain, West Virginia, near the Kentucky border, it quickly turned into a civil war involving tens of thousands of miners and their families. The rebels didn't have uniforms, just their work coveralls or their World War I service uniforms. They tied red kerchiefs around their necks and called themselves the Rednecks—the army that fights for dignity."

1996

Don't Call Me That: White Trash a Go-Go

Americans instinctively understand that class matters, despite what we were told in high school civics. As uneasy as we are about the subject, most of us are to some degree insecure about our place in the world—and we may even long for clean, bright lines of division.

While Americans do have a kind of fiscal mobility and are perhaps as likely as anyone else to equate worth with wealth, there still are certain inescapable facts of life. However egalitarian we imagine our society, through the real world snake countless lines of social demarcation—hidden trip wires for the nearly and the not-quite.

There are social classes in America; and our place in society is determined not only by how much money we make but by our parents, where we went to school, what we do for a living, where we live, how we behave, even where we were born. As the radio commercial for a company called Hooked on Phonics announces, "People *do* judge you by the words you use."

They certainly do. And there are hundreds of other variables that figure in to where we fit in. Although we Americans have been trained not to think in terms of class, we are constantly (and often unconsciously) making distinctions and ranking people, places, items, and even ideas.

What you are backing into, ever so gingerly, dear reader, is a story about a style of low-class living and people called white trash; what W. J. Cash, author of *The Mind of the South,* described as "the people to whom the term 'cracker' (is) properly applied—the 'white trash' and 'po' buckra.'"

No, dear reader, I don't mean you. I'm speaking of a style that has become ever more prominent as our society abandons traditional notions of shame and regret, as the idea becomes commonplace that repression is inherently a bad thing (a popular misreading of Freud).

Welcome to the white trash decade, here and across America. If the 1980s belonged to the smug yuppie, the '90s belong to the tasteless, the shameless, and the crude, then white trash—in all its manifest forms, from the relatively benign Branson, Missouri, boom to the gut-grinding horror of the Susan Smith murder case—is upon us. White trash is riding high via junk television, obscene gestures, rude celebrities, and sleaze of all sorts. White trash is what happens when civility leaves the room, when guilt evaporates, when certitude and stridency are sufficient to carry the national debate.

Now, we all know that "white trash" is an inflammatory term. Even in this guiltless age, it is a term that still has power to sting. It carries overtones of not only class, but also race—America's other forbidden thought. For generations, it has been used as what the French critic Michael Foucault would call an "exterminating gesture"—an epithet designed not only to disparage but also to crush.

Yet lately the term has become somewhat denatured. A couple of years ago, a Little Rock theater group anticipated the trend with a revue called *White Trash a Go-Go.* At mid-decade, *New York* magazine ran a lengthy cover piece titled "White Hot Trash!" Movie magazine *Film Threat* proclaimed the advent of "White Trash Chic." James Carville, one of the minds that engineered the election of Bill Clinton, doesn't hesitate to claim membership in Club White Trash.

So let's establish right off that there is no shame to come from white trash. My mother's people were Georgia tobacco farmers, barely one generation removed from sharecroppers. My father's family story is more complicated; they were fallen Carolina aristocracy—shabby genteel to us, perhaps, but not to their creditors. I have relatives who've been in drunk tanks, who've done things decent people would consider irresponsible and immoral.

At a stylish dinner party the other night, a friend revealed that he has kinfolk who enjoy the occasional cockfight. We'd never suspected that, but it shows that a white trash skin can be shed; a generation or two with money can give anyone the sheen of gentry, just as a week without money can starve a king.

The concept of white trash may have originated with whites themselves, as a way of explaining how individual members of their "superior" race could behave so badly. It is a term usually associated with the South, which more than other parts of the country has always accommodated the idea of a hierarchical social order that allows for and accepts human inequality (not necessarily tied to race). In the South, where there was never any illusion of classlessness, "white trash" was the term for shiftless white folk, the petty criminals and the dissolute.

It was codified by an Atlanta newspaper reporter named Erskine Caldwell in his novels *Tobacco Road,* in 1932, and *God's Little Acre,* a year later. Jeeter Lester and his brood were shockingly raw, nearly feral people.

In the book an older woman persuades a sixteen-year-old named Dude to marry her in exchange for a car. Dude promptly drives the car without oil, ruining it. It goes up on blocks in the yard.

Caldwell, the truth-teller, was summarily run out of the South. Jerry Lee Lewis, who once married his thirteen-year-old cousin, was so trashy he was nearly driven out of the United States. The indignant mob ran him right off the pop charts and into what was then called hillbilly music.

White trash was what you became when you fell out of the working class and into disrepute. It always bespoke an attitude that respects nothing and no one, that believes nothing matters and so what if it did. White trash lives fast, dies young, and leaves a frightening wreck of a corpse.

It used to be that "white trash" was a term of opprobrium. Now, in the nonjudgmental '90s, it has become a nearly neutral term. White trash today knows no regional or racial parameters. White trash is an attitude, a way of thinking (or, perhaps more correctly, not thinking) about things.

The best country music is unabashedly white trash, as is some of the best rock 'n' roll. Rupert Murdoch's Fox network provides essentially white trash television; it also produces arguably the most audacious and original programming of the big four commercial networks.

Melrose Place is white trash. Reality-based shows like *Cops* and *America's Most Wanted* are white trash. So is Matt Groening's *The Simpsons*—especially paterfamilias Homer. And, of course, Al and Peg Bundy of *Married . . . with Children* are perhaps the most uncouth white trash couple on TV.

Roseanne—formerly Roseanne Arnold, formerly Roseanne Barr—is perhaps more white trash off screen than on. There was the incident when she and then-husband Tom Arnold jointly "married" Tom's assistant, a woman named Kim Silva. In her petition for divorce from Arnold (not Silva), she claimed she had been "a classic battered and abused wife." During the course of that marriage, Arnold had sold stories about his wife to the *National Enquirer* and had been arrested for public urination. Roseanne, meanwhile, claims she used to turn tricks in the parking lot between stand-up comedy gigs. Both she and Arnold assert they were sexually abused as children. Roseanne has said that her father—who once sold 3-D portraits of Jesus door-to-door—regularly involved her in scatological sex play.

Even if true, all this would seem to belong in the "I would'na tole that" file. Yet the unredeemably trashy Roseanne remains one of America's biggest stars; last year, NBC and Fox broadcast docudramas based on her life and legend.

Beavis and Butt-head—MTV's latchkey fourteen-year-olds—are white trash. They have single moms, live in ratty houses, love heavy-metal music, and spend every penny they can lay their hands on for concert tickets and porno mags. In fact, all of MTV is white trash, from the politically conservative V. J. Kennedy (who is prone to brag about her supposed sexual exploits with Rush Limbaugh) to the misogyny of *Yo! MTV Raps.* Black people can be white trash, too—think of rapper and heavy-metal thrasher Ice-T and Elvis son-in-law Michael Jackson.

The movies are full of white trash heroes, such as Thelma and Louise. The most ferocious scene in Jonathan Demme's *Silence of the Lambs* had Anthony Hopkins as Hannibal Lecter telling Jodie Foster's earnest young FBI cadet,

> "You're a well-scrubbed, hustling rube with a little taste . . . desper-
> ate not to be like your mother. . . . But you're not more than one genera-
> tion out of poor white trash, Officer Starling. Is it the West Virginia
> Starlings or the Okie Starlings, Officer?"

In 1993, Foster portrayed another sympathetic white trash character—the wild child in *Nell.* Forrest Gump, with his unwed mama, was endearing—and white trash. The serial-murdering antiheroes of Oliver Stone's *Natural Born Killers* were white trash of the nasty breed. Other white trash variations included the swanky denizens of Quentin Tarantino's imagined underworlds as well as the serial killers and Elvis-mongers of dozens of other recent films. Think of Kevin Costner in *A Perfect World,* Brad Pitt, Johnny Depp, Drew Barrymore, and Juliette Lewis in anything.

White trash is hot; it's all the rage.

❖ ❖ ❖

Even our president, while not white trash himself, especially if you accept lassitude as an essential component of white trashiness, is a white trash icon. The late dear Virginia Kelley loved the ponies, was married four times, and had a soft spot for Elvis. Clinton has described his car-salesman stepfather, Roger—known, like the character in *Tobacco Road,* as "Dude"—as an abusive alcoholic. And the president's half brother, also named Roger, has outdone himself.

Young Roger, who in the 1980s went to prison for cocaine trafficking, fancies himself an entertainer; when last heard from, he was working the lounge circuit in Seoul, South Korea. He has parlayed his genetic proximity to the president into an acting role in the movie *Pumpkinhead 2: Blood Wings.* He's also done commercials for a cable comedy channel, seated behind a desk in a fake Oval Office.

The president has been known to slip; talking about one's underpants on MTV is not exactly suave. Ditto his remarks about laying AstroTurf in the back of his pickup. The mere fact that he has admitted knowing Gennifer Flowers—much less that he may have carried on an affair with her—seems tacky enough.

And if he behaved the way Paula Corbin Jones claims he behaved toward her in the Excelsior Hotel, then that's certainly white trash. As for Jones, her own family has suggested that she's white trash, and those pictures in *Penthouse* don't exactly help her case. (If that weren't enough, her husband, Steve Jones, had a brief part as Elvis in the Jim Jarmusch film *Mystery Train*.)

And if Clinton is at least partly of the white trash breed, what about the new speaker of the House, Newt Gingrich? As the *New York Times*'s Frank Rich has pointed out, some of the biographical similarities between Clinton and Gingrich are eerie. The president and the speaker were favored eldest children—mama's boys—brought up by tough, doting mothers in less than affluent circumstances.

Their moms were physically abused by their husbands—who had problems with the bottle. Neither Clinton nor Gingrich ever knew his biological father; both had strained relationships with their adoptive fathers. And some of the anecdotes about Gingrich, the husband—how he served his hospital-bound first wife with divorce papers, for instance—raise as many questions about his character as the tales of womanizing raise about the president's. Meanwhile, the speaker's mom, Kathleen Gingrich, seems poised to take over for the president's late mother as the nation's bawdy old broad of choice.

Some have suggested that what she was really doing when she leaned forward and told Connie Chung she couldn't tell her what "Newty" said about the first lady was just asking permission to say the "B-word" on television. And what kind of boy talks like that around his mama, anyway?

✧ ✧ ✧

So you may as well revel in this golden age of white trash. America has become an uncivil landscape, where "abuse" excuses and psychobabble relieves all guilt, where afternoon chat shows have become a kind of public confessional, with high priests such as Oprah, Phil, Montel, and Jenny Jones offering absolution through revelation. The white trash ethos seeps into every area of our culture. Ranging beyond entertainment and politics, there are at least a couple of white trash icons for every aspect of American life.

What about literature? Bret Easton Ellis, James Ellroy, Pete Dexter, and Carolyn Chute. Religion? Easy. How about Tony Alamo, Jim Bakker, and Jimmy Swaggart, for starters. Sports? The Philadelphia Phillies, John Daly, and, of course, Tonya Harding. Harding is so trashy that even No Excuses jeans company—which has stooped to hire such luminaries as Donna Rice,

Fawn Hall, and Jessica Hahn for its commercials—wouldn't touch her. The truck-driving, pool-hustling figure skater with the rabbit fur coat and the bad perm was forced into the national consciousness after the botched attack on her rival, Nancy Kerrigan. Harding skated to ZZ Top and once worked at a fast-food place called Spud City. For a bodyguard, she chose Shawn Eckardt, who drove a 1974 Mercury with missing hubcaps. Her on-again off-again ex-husband, Jeff Gillooly, taped their wedding night and sold it as an X-rated video. (We may see it one day on pay-per-view.)

But I'll tell you a secret. I'm kind of fond of Tonya Harding. A lot of us are. In a perverse way, knowing the white trash tendencies that may lurk in some deep recess of even the most toffee-nosed Americans, we admire the overtly white trashy among us and their blithe capacity for tackiness.

Some people, the old song goes, can do what they want. And some people do: Harding, the Menendez brothers, Joey Buttafuoco and Amy Fisher, Anna Nicole Smith and her octogenarian husband—the white trash parade winds on and on, with no end in sight. Who's next? Stay tuned.

Maybe part of what we find fascinating here is simple Schadenfreude— the pleasure derived from another's misfortune. A lot of our inquiring minds' curiosity could simply stem from a smug belief that we are surely a better sort of person ourselves. But there is also envy in our fascination; part of us wants to be so brash, so free of conscience, so bereft of shame as these savants of gratification.

1994

Johnny Cash: The Damned Saint

Like an American Rasputin, Johnny Cash oscillates between iniquity and redemption, between the dark urges of the flesh and the thrill of intimacy with the divine. He understands that without sin there can be no forgiveness, so that every transgression can bring the penitent closer to God.

Maybe he understands that this convulsive path to heaven has its risks, that there are pits vast and dark, and that no man knoweth the hour or the day, but he surely knows that being good all the time is just no damn fun at all.

We are talking about a fictional Johnny Cash here, a construct that the real Cash is complicit with but separate from. The real Johnny Cash has never been in prison but to sing. The real Johnny Cash is sick and dying (as we all are, in the long run). The real Johnny Cash is someone we—unless we can count ourselves among his friends and kin, and maybe not even then—can't know.

No, the Johnny Cash we are talking about, the only Cash accessible to us, is in all likelihood the more interesting Cash, who exists only in photographs and memories, in digital code on magnetic tape, as bumps and hollows on silver discs. The Cash we can talk about, the Cash we can hear, wears a preacher's coat and a long black duster and a heavy .44. He's Stagger Lee, another one, a crazy white boy with an ancient face and a gothic, bone-deep voice. Remember that wonderful, perfect photo of him flipping his middle finger at the camera way back in his younger days?

He shot a man in Reno, just to watch him die. He's the reason Delia's gone. And while he may be remorseful about it, he doesn't see any way things could have turned out different. The only thing to do now is turn to Jesus, sweet Jesus.

"Johnny Cash doesn't sing to the damned, he sings with the damned," U2 singer Bono writes in the liner notes of the latest Johnny Cash compilation, "and sometimes you feel he might prefer their company."

Maybe you know Johnny Cash's story. Maybe it's a little bit like your story—or your granddaddy's story. Born near Kingsland in 1932, the son of an Arkansas dirt farmer, John R. Cash's family moved to Dyess Colony, a New Deal socialist experiment, set up by the Roosevelt administration, that started new farming communities on uncleared land near the Mississippi River.

Cash hauled water for a road gang when he was six years old, chopped cotton when he was twelve, the same year he saw his older brother Jack killed in a chain-saw accident.

He was singing on the radio while he was still in high school in Blytheville, Arkansas, but he didn't learn to play the guitar until he enlisted in the army in 1950. He was stationed in West Germany, where he typed coded radio messages and learned how to drink whisky and chase frauleins.

When he returned from his four-year hitch he settled in Memphis, marrying Vivian Liberto, a girl who had written him while he was away. He sold appliances and went to broadcasting school on the GI bill. In Memphis he met guitarist Luther Perkins and bass player Marshall Grant. They played together, then went to Sam Phillips, the Sun Records owner who discovered—and possibly created—Elvis.

Phillips thought they sounded too country, so they went back and worked some rockabilly into their act. In 1955, their second audition with Sun led to a contract. Soon they were appearing—just like Elvis—on the Louisiana Hayride in Shreveport. Cash had a couple of hits in the couple of years he was with Sun, but, again like Elvis, he was destined for bigger things. He signed with Columbia in 1959 and moved to California. He bought Johnny Carson's old house in Encino.

By then, he had four daughters, a wrecked marriage, and was addicted to barbiturates and amphetamines. He crashed cars and sank boats and was almost killed when he jumped from a truck just before it dove over a six-hundred-foot cliff. He accidentally set fire to a national forest and was one of the first citizens sued for the cost of putting out the fire. (He eventually paid $82,000 in restitution.) His daughters were taunted as "Cash trash" at school.

Finally, in 1966, Vivian filed for divorce. Two years later, in London, Ontario, Cash impulsively proposed to his longtime friend and duet partner, June Carter, on stage during a concert. She tried to laugh it off, but Cash—and the audience—insisted. She said yes.

The next year Johnny Cash sold more records than anyone in the world. He got his own TV series—he had Bob Dylan and Kris Kristofferson on as guests.

While the legend holds that June saved Johnny, and while in actuality that may have been exactly what happened, Cash still had trouble with drugs and alcohol right up until 1992. There have been a couple of interventions that the general public knows about. Now, with a progressive nerve disease that prevents him from performing—when he appeared at the Wildwood

Festival near Little Rock in 1996 he had trouble playing his guitar—Cash has essentially retired to his compound near Montego Bay in Jamaica.

A cynic might consider the latest Cash project an exercise in Elvisian repackaging for profit-taking—there is no revelatory material on the new three-CD retrospective *Love, God, Murder,* and most of the tracks are available elsewhere. (Each of these three discs is also available separately.) The concept here is to divide Cash's career into a convenient trinity, with the singer himself selecting his favorite tracks that fall under these rather broad categories.

The first disc contains sixteen of Cash's love songs, including "I Walk the Line," "Ring of Fire," and the haunting (despite its country-politan arrangement and straining lyrics) "Flesh and Blood." The second—the one for which Bono wrote liner notes—covers his gospel career. The third and most interesting disc is filled with songs about bad men and victims.

A cynic might complain that it's not a comprehensive box set (six years ago Columbia released *Johnny Cash: The Essential Recording*), and casual fans might be disappointed to discover the new release doesn't include a lot of the great man's greatest hits (there's no "A Boy Named Sue" or "Hey, Porter" or "Ballad of a Teenage Queen"), and you could make the argument that quality is compromised for the sake of thematic consistency. For example, Cash is a sturdy, effective gospel singer because his battered voice resists sentimentality, but do we really need an entire disc devoted to this part of his career?

Well, maybe—the point is that Cash, presumably the real Cash and not the icon, wanted that disc. And so the inclusion of it adds another level to the myth. Cash realizes the contradictory nature of his image, and he wants us to know that he recognizes it. With Elvis, you got the feeling that he sang gospel music because he'd always sung gospel music, because it was a part of him, because he loved the music. Elvis was an innocent.

Cash is anything but innocent; there's always a dark, controlling intelligence, a self-awareness, present in his performances, in his songwriting and choices of songs. Elvis was always natural grace; Cash's talent, his rumbling eloquence, always seems hard-won and provisional. No question the angels loved Elvis; he seemed one of them when he joined the choir. Cash is a more difficult case. Cash's gospel singing seems like an act of contrition rather than joyful noisiness. He's got a grudge in his voice, a little broken, human edge. The *God* disc sometimes sounds like an offering, a pagan's stab at appeasing an erratic and vengeful parent. These aren't Cash's best songs, but they are important to anyone who wants to understand the artist. And they're obviously important to the artist—Cash uses them as a talisman, a smear of lamb's blood on his door. Evil spirits, don't bother 'round here.

So the best way to look at the new compilation is as an act of thoughtfulness, a gift from a reformed crank seeking both to explain himself and ask for absolution. At sixty-eight, Cash might finally be done (though the post-'60s albums he made with Rick Rubin, *American Recordings,* and *Unchained* hold up with his best work), and all that's left is his summation. Cash's final answer? Murder.

"These songs are just for listening and singing," Cash warns in his remarks that accompany the album. "Don't go out and do it."

(Johnny Cash—the real one—never did anything like what men, and it is always men, do in his songs. He was usually jailed for being drunk.)

Murder is reminiscent of Nick Cave's 1996 album *Murder Ballads,* but it's entirely possible that Cash has never heard of the Australian singer, and Cave certainly would never have recorded his album without the influence of Johnny Cash. In his liner notes for Cash's *Murder,* filmmaker Quentin Tarantino makes a rather strained equation of Cash's lyrics with the novels of Jim Thompson and the narratives of gangsta rap—an insight that isn't original with Tarantino, who seems to be using the occasion to argue for a tradition of aesthetic violence. (That such a tradition exists doesn't make Tarantino's essay any less self-serving.)

Tarantino almost gets it right when he argues that what separates Cash's tales of blood and bad men from the nihilism of the thug life is that Cash's antiheroes invariably express regret. That's almost it. What it really is is the empathy Cash's killers have for their victims, even if they believe their victims need killing. After all, it was a man who got shot in Reno—and that man deserved better than what he got.

"I know I had it coming / I know I can't be free," Cash sings at the end of "Folsom Prison Blues." But knowing the consequences are deserved and living with them are two different things. Unlike the gangsta rappers, who insist that a thug is a thug and there's no reason to expect a man can change, none of Cash's killers are unsalvageable. They regret so that they might be redeemed. As hard-boiled as it might at first seem, Cash's murder ballads are almost always tempered with hope.

Rap is conservative and postmodern—criminals can't change and you're a fool if you think otherwise. Cash is old-fashioned and deeply humane—if dangerous. Think of him as Robert Mitchum, in *Night of the Hunter,* a psychopathic, hymn-singing preacher with "LOVE" tattooed across the knuckles of one hand and "HATE" tattooed across the other.

That may not be the way he really is—the real J. C. is probably a sweetheart—but that's the way he wants to be and will be remembered. A walkin' contradiction, partly truth and partly fiction, his buddy Kristofferson called him. That'll do.

2000

That Bad Man: Cruel, Cruel Stagger Lee

At the core of the American story is the outsider rebel, the misunderstood underdog, the mumbling antihero. Yet a young country, born of revolution, America gave the world the myth of the gunfighter (black-hatted Gregory Peck), Al Capone, Jay Gatsby, and Doc Holliday, shambling in from Georgia. We love our big criminals, our men above the law.

America is best understood as an idea, a construct of the individual personality. Hollywood conquered the world through the images it crafted: James Dean in his red windbreaker, Marlon Brando in his torn T-shirt, Elvis Presley curling his lip at the understanding little girls. America made martyrs of murderers like Jesse James and Cole Younger and Billy the Kid and John Dillinger and Clyde Barrow. "Murder is the case," Snoop Dog reminds us, as the ghosts of Tupac and Biggie and a million wanna-bes swirl like incense around the unblinking MTV. We have cultivated a near-religious reverence for our weapons; we insist on the right to own and hold instruments designed solely to spit out death.

No wonder the world—as barbarous and cruel as it can be—thinks there's something dangerous about us, something sticky and cold at our core. We baaad. We're a nation of Stagger Lees. Popular taste has a strange way of transforming bad men into glamour figures; and though almost everyone who's spent any time around them can tell you that thugs and killers are mostly sad and dull and ugly, there is in most of us a vestigial nerve that is excited by the possibility of sudden violence. We feel the potential deep inside—buried, sublimated, under however many insulating levels of civilization—for acting out. We bracket the objects of our rage in our sights— the impudent teenager, the thoughtless driver. We have always had our bad men, and they have always had a claim on our rough and rowdy hearts.

Just look at Latrell Sprewell. In his Italian suit, with his cornrows and fine gold frames, the New York Knicks' soft-spoken shooting guard can look thoughtful, nearly genteel. He shows up at camp a few days late, without bothering to let his employer know he'd be tardy—so what? Without Sprewell, the Knicks wouldn't have made the NBA finals last year. He had a good year after they picked him up last January; he didn't try to choke his coach one time.

That's right—you knew he sounded familiar. Sprewell was the Golden State Warrior who took offense to something his coach said—perhaps something offensive, though it's been reported that Sprewell became upset when his coach told him to "put a little mustard" on his passes during a shooting drill—and attempted to strangle the man. He locked his long, powerful fingers around the coach's throat and tried to act out Miles Davis's fantasy of slowly strangling the white man to death.

Sprewell didn't manage to strangle P. J. Carelismo to death, of course; there were too many witnesses around for that. Instead, he was physically separated from the coach by his teammates. He stalked out and was suspended by the league for a year.

He didn't go to jail, like another person might have, but he did lose millions of dollars in salary. But, after the Knicks picked him up and he contributed mightily to their unlikely run through the playoffs, Sprewell signed an endorsement deal with an obscure athletic shoe company called And 1.

In one spot he looked into the camera as, in the background, Jimi Hendrix's electric guitar version of "The Star-Spangled Banner" played, and said, "People say I'm what's wrong with sports. I say I'm a three-time NBA all-star. People say I'm America's worst nightmare. I say I'm the American dream."

He was right.

Billy Preston's question notwithstanding, the evidence is clear that the bad guy does win a substantial portion of the time. In some versions the sheriff arrests ol' Stagger Lee, but in most of them, no human being can touch him.

◇ ◇ ◇

Stagger Lee—or Stack O' Lee or Stack-o-lee or Stacker Lee or Skeeg O' Lee or whatever—is one of the defining legends of America. He is a character that appears again and again in our mythology, a kind of murderous trickster, Loki with a .44. He is part of us, the flip side to Roy Rogers and Tom Mix, the Dionysian Bruce Wayne answer to Apollonian Clark Kent. He is Fonzie to Richie Cunningham, Latrell Sprewell to the impeccably behaved good citizen Tim Duncan.

He is the American answer to Milton's Dark Angel. He gets most of the good lines.

There are at least sixty-three—and probably many more—documented recordings of songs that mention this character. While the lyrics vary from version to version, the story line and the essential thrust of the story remain the same: Stagger Lee was a bad man who shot poor Billy Lyons (or Billy De

Lyons or Billy the Lion, etc.) during a game of chance (usually dice) in which the doomed Billy won Stag's cherished Stetson hat.

In most versions of the song, Billy is not only killed but humiliated; he begs Stag to spare him because he has children and a "sickly" (or is it "shapely"?) wife to support. But Stag doesn't care, he pops a cap in Billy and picks up his hat and leaves.

Almost a quarter-century ago in *Mystery Train*, which may still be the best book ever written about rock 'n' roll, Greil Marcus began a monumental essay about the meaning of Sly Stone with a recitation of the Stagger Lee myth. Marcus pointed out the importance of the cruelty of Stag's actions—he noted that he shot Billy, "in the words of a Johnny Cash song, just to watch him die."

This murder is the very seed of the nihilism that runs through rock 'n' roll, though Stagger Lee existed long before Sam Phillips coaxed Elvis into singing his natural way, before Ike Turner and Jackie Brenston dreamed up "Rocket 88." A list of the artists who recorded the songs sounds like a who's who of blues history—Furry Lewis, Memphis Slim, Jesse Fuller, Ma Rainey, and Mississippi John Hurt are among the artists who committed versions to vinyl.

And the song wasn't solely the property of black artists: David Miller, a blind white man from Ohio, recorded a ballad called "That Bad Man Stackolee" in the early 1920s. In 1929, a record called "Stack-O-Lee" was issued by a mysterious band called the Fruit Jar Guzzlers. Doc Watson and Merle Travis each recorded the song. Cab Calloway had a crack at it.

Lloyd Price had the hit in 1959. Bob Dylan recorded it in 1993; Nick Cave did a thoroughly rewritten version three years later. (The Grateful Dead recorded an answer song—also called "Stagger Lee"—about how Billy's wife, named Delia by Dead lyricist Robert Hunter, extracted her revenge on Stag.)

And while Marcus suggested the legend grew out of a real incident ("It happened in Memphis around the turn of the century, in New Orleans in the '20s, in St. Louis in the 1880s"), he made no real effort to substantiate the story. It is enough that the myth—and the records—exist.

Still, it seems likely there was a historical Stagger Lee. One version points to a Confederate officer named Stacker Lee, whose family operated several steamboats along the Mississippi. One of the family's steamboats was named the *Stacker Lee* in his honor. (In her novel *Show Boat*, Edna Ferber set the action aboard the *Stacker Lee.*)

However, there is no evidence that this former Confederate was anything but an honorable man. It's been suggested that perhaps the legendary bad man was his illegitimate son. Or maybe the name "Stacker Lee" is a red herring; maybe the real key to finding the historical roots of the Stagger Lee legend lies in the other particulars of the legend.

As it turns out, a man named William Lyons was shot to death in a St. Louis saloon on December 28, 1895, by a man named Lee Sheldon. According to the St. Louis *Globe Democrat,* the men were friends who began to argue politics. When Lyons took Sheldon's hat and refused to give it back, Sheldon shot him with his revolver. At the end of the story the *Globe Democrat* noted, "Sheldon is also known as 'Stag' Lee."

That might solve the mystery, except there is some evidence that the song "Stagger Lee" predates the murder of William Lyons. In Lawrence Levine's book *Black Culture and Black Consciousness,* there is a reference to a source who claimed to have heard the song sung as early as 1895. Technically, it might be possible that a songster immediately set the tune to music and that Levine's witness heard one of the very first performances of the ballad, but it seems easier to believe that Stag has been with us always, a sulfurous shadow at the shoulder of the murmuring drunk.

✧ ✧ ✧

Understand that a lot of people who think that Latrell Sprewell should be locked up or banned from basketball also think that Pete Rose—an admitted and convicted criminal—should be in the Baseball Hall of Fame. Rose was a dishonest person and a selfish player (who never would have achieved many of the records he set had he not exercised the prerogatives of the living legend and insisted on playing long after his value to the team had become marginal), but he has his fans. Rose seems like a populist icon, the little talent that could, while Sprewell looms dark and aloof, the representative hip-hop thug.

A lot of that is cultural interference; a lot of the people who dislike Sprewell on sight wear their hair in a Pete Rose crew cut. A lot of people simply dislike the Otherness of Sprewell. OK.

That might be fine with Spree, just as it was fine with Bobby Seale (who named his son after Stagger Lee). Yet just because some people dislike him for the wrong reasons doesn't mean you can't dislike him or his arrogance and lack of impulse control and disregard for the consequences of his actions. Bad men are bad. You don't cuddle up to Stagger Lee; you don't rehabilitate him.

If you go after him, if you catch him, you hang him immediately. (In the song at least. In real life, Lee Sheldon died in prison, shortly before the advent of World War I.) You don't mess around with Stag.

But there are professionally moral people who insist that America is crumbling, that Spree and Stag are symptoms of a moral decay. Maybe they are right; maybe gangsta rap and Latrell Sprewell are worse than the old weird Child ballads and Ty Cobb. They are probably right in asserting that the world has gotten cruder and harder for the gentle-souled to negotiate. But it's not just our music and our sports and our movies and our television that got rougher and rowdier; the coarsening of the culture extends to the smash-mouth style of political discourse and the exterminating gestures of the cult of irony.

Some of those who complain the loudest about societal rot, about the tendency to "define deviancy down," are also bullies.

We all be Stagger Lee; we all be bad. We are, after all, Americans.

1999

James Brown, James Brown

Depending on the source, James Brown is either sixty-five or seventy years old. He says sixty-five, but then he would, wouldn't he? Five years isn't a lot to grant a self-made legend—after all, we allowed Dylan to kill off Mr. and Mrs. Zimmerman and wander in like a Dust Bowl orphan. If James Brown wants to be sixty-five, not seventy, there's no real reason to make an issue out of it, no real reason to charge in and start debunking his various and sundry claims—no, James, you did not invent rhythm and blues and rock 'n' roll, though you did help invent America—because everybody understands that the "Hardest Workin' Man in Show Business" is prone to exaggeration, that he isn't exactly the most reliable source for information about himself.

Man's got show biz in his genetic code; he's all whang and bomp and dit-dit-dit-a-wow-dit. Uh-HUH. Star time. I can't stand myself.

Like Dizzy Dean, James Brown isn't married to any one version of reality. Things get confusing when you start checking out the Godfather, and how can you expect the man to keep up with little details like when and where he was born? After all, that was sixty-five (or seventy) years ago.

Let's stipulate sixty-five. After all, Polydor—the record company in possession of most of Brown's recorded work these days—is using the occasion of Brown's sixty-fifth birthday to release three anthologies of Brown's work, including a previously unreleased live recording of an August 26, 1968, concert at the Dallas Memorial Auditorium (now the Dallas Convention Center Arena).

Say It Live and Loud, the concert album released in early 1999, is remarkable principally because it captures what we might assume to be a typical Brown show during one of his more vital and dynamic periods. It features what was arguably Brown's best band—Orchestra, featuring sax players Maceo Parker and Pee Wee Ellis, trombonist Fred Wesley, guitarist Jimmy Nolen, and drummer Clyde Stubblefield. It also contains one of the first live performances of Brown's extraordinary anthem, "Say It Loud—I'm Black and I'm Proud."

More on that later. Now, here's the star of our show, ladies and gentlemen, James Brown.

✧ ✧ ✧

Though Brown was most likely born in the piney woods outside Barnwell, South Carolina, when the Georgia legislature passed a 1997 resolution honoring Brown for "his distinctive voice, his legendary dance moves and his message-centered lyrics" that "have had an undeniable effect on our entire culture for more than three decades," they insisted he was "born right here in Augusta."

It's just a matter of a few miles, a few years. The more or less accepted legend holds that Brown was raised by his father, Joe Garner Brown, who was black and American Indian, and that his mother, Susie Benning Brown, was black with Asian blood. Young James was delivered stillborn and resuscitated by his Aunt Minnie, who blew into his lungs until the baby started caterwauling.

The Browns were so poor they were almost feral, living in a rude shack without running water or electricity and subsisting on the sales of turpentine. His mother ran away when he was four years old, and a few months later James and his father moved across the Savannah River to live with James's aunt, Handsome "Honey" Washington, a brothel-keeper and moonshiner. A few weeks later Joe moved out, leaving his son in the madame's care.

Brown earned his keep by running errands for soldiers at nearby Camp Gordon, entertaining them with his patter and "buckdancing," and inviting them to visit his aunt's place of business. He swept out the floors of the Trinity Baptist Church, and by 1946—when he was either thirteen or eighteen years old—he was a seventh-grade dropout fronting his own gospel trio. In 1949 he went to jail for petty theft. In 1952, he was released and almost immediately joined the Gospel Starlighters, a quartet led by Bobby Byrd. (When the Starlighters played secular gigs, they called themselves the Avons.)

Brown soon emerged as the quartet's star; and in 1955, renamed the Flames, they signed with Little Richard's manager. Within a year they had a record deal with King Records of Cincinnati. Now they were James Brown and the Fabulous Flames. The first track they recorded, the plaintive "Please, Please, Please," reached the *Billboard* R&B Top Five.

Their next nine singles flopped. It was nearly three years later when "Try Me" hit number one on the R&B charts, allowing Brown to finally hire a steady backup band and begin establishing his reputation as a perfectionist martinet who had every bloodcurdling scream, flying split, and knee drop precisely timed.

When King Records balked at releasing a live album in 1962, Brown put up his own money to release the epic *Live at the Apollo* a year later. It went to number two on the *Billboard* R&B chart, an unprecedented feat for a live album.

Then Brown imagined funk, in 1965, by accenting the first and third (rather than the second and fourth) beats in "Papa's Got a Brand New Bag," a record that is arguably the most influential pop recording ever. It sounds like nothing that had come before it, and every dance record since owes it a debt. With "Papa's Got a Brand New Bag," Brown laid the foundation for disco, rap, house, techno, and every other rhythm-based pop movement of the last thirty years. It is the basis of Brown's often cited claim that he "invented" rap, disco, and all those other genres he claims to have invented.

Over the years Brown has also claimed to have invented rock 'n' roll, country and western, Elvis Presley, Michael Jackson, the Afro, and probably mustard-based potato salad. The fact that some of these claims are not quite credible—it might be argued that the young James Brown was more an assimilator than an innovator and that he liberally borrowed from singers like Roy Brown, Wynonie Harris, and the obscure Johnny Tanner as well as from showmen like Louis Jordan and Little Richard—shouldn't obscure his genuine contributions.

❖ ❖ ❖

But if "Papa's Got a Brand New Bag" was a signal event in the way we listen to pop music, its lyrics were standard, literal pop song lyrics. The "brand new bag" Brown was alluding to was simply his new rhythmic approach. Had it been his only contribution it would have been more than enough to establish Brown as one of the century's most important musicians, but it might be argued that "Papa" wasn't even Brown's most important single record.

Few pop songs approach the sociocultural significance of "Say It Loud—I'm Black and I'm Proud." It can be read as a declaration of militancy by a figure that some suspected had been co-opted by the government in the wake of the murder of Dr. Martin Luther King Jr. Though there is no reason to suspect that James Brown's politics were ever terribly sophisticated or extended beyond the advance of his own self-interest—he was a role model, an exemplar of Emersonian self-reliance, a singer, and an entrepreneur, not a spokesman for a people—in the summer of 1968 powerful and irrational forces made "Soul Brother Number One" a kind of statesman.

The night after King's assassination, Brown was scheduled to play the Boston Garden. City officials attempted to dissuade Brown from performing for fear the show might somehow exacerbate the sporadic rioting. Instead,

Brown suggested televising the concert—after the city agreed to guarantee the box office receipts—on the theory that people would stay home to watch, resulting in a virtual truce. During the concert Brown made a plea for peace, a plea that seemed to palliate the tension.

Brown was flown to Washington, D.C., to speak on the radio and urge brotherhood. Again, he seemed to have some influence; the streets went quiet. He attended a dinner at the White House at the invitation of President Lyndon Johnson on May 8. Johnson wanted to personally thank the singer for having helped "save America."

A month later he went to Vietnam for several weeks, performing for U.S. troops there. He released a song, "America Is My Home," that some took as Uncle Tomming. He appeared with Vice President Hubert Humphrey and endorsed his presidential campaign at a rally in Watts on July 29.

There were whispers in militant black circles that Brown was an agent of the establishment. It has even been rumored that some militant blacks had urged Brown to make some sort of statement.

The statement was forthcoming. Brown knew it had the potential to galvanize the black community—listening to it during playback, he reportedly told one of the engineers that it was "the one fifty million people have been waiting for." He rush released "Say It Loud" as a single just two weeks before the Dallas show was captured on the Polydor disc. There are actually two versions on the record: Brown performs it first in the opening minutes of the show, after running through a smooth version of the ballad "If I Ruled the World." Brown introduces the song almost tentatively, and incorporates a plea for understanding.

"You know, one way of solving a lot of problems that we've got in this country is letting a person feel that they're important, feel that they're somebody. And a man can't get himself together until he knows who he is and [can] be proud of what and who he is and where he comes from," Brown begins; then he goes on to invite the white members of the audience to sing along as well: "A little love won't hurt."

This version is, if not tentative, at least careful. After Brown finishes, a palpable sense of relief descends. The audience exhales—the show can proceed.

Brown returns to the song as the final encore. This time he gives it a ferocious, wicked reading, ripping through it, exultant and defiant. It is a performance without apologies. The lyrics singe: "We'd rather die on our feet than keep living on our knees."

James Brown is sixty-five or seventy, and these days he's more likely to show up on the police blotter—he was arrested again early this year for possessing drugs and guns, the third time in the past ten years—than on the radio. But thirty years ago, when he was thirty or forty, or whatever, he was something.

1998

Whither the Blues?

Never has a white man had the Blues—'cause nothing to worry about.

—Huddie Ledbetter

Can white people play the blues?

Some, maybe most, blues fans might think the question a needless provocation. After all, they argue, blues is a music that knows no national nor racial boundaries; it belongs to anyone and everyone who would play it.

It ought to be obvious that white people do play the blues, and some of them do it with credibility and even authority. While Eric Clapton humbly resists calling himself a "bluesman," no one plays guitar with any more economy and emotion—he wrings more hurt out of a single note than anyone this side of B. B. King. And while people mightn't think of Richard Thompson's Celtic soul when they think of the blues, his playing betrays some of the same passion—so does Van Morrison's.

Stevie Ray Vaughn loved the form; he thought what he was playing was the blues. Bonnie Raitt probably thinks she's playing the blues. The Fabulous Thunderbirds think that's what they're about; any blues section of any halfway decent record store gives up the names of dozens of white artists who presume to sing and play the blues: John Hammond, Delbert McClinton, Duke Robillard, Peter Green—there's no shortage of would-be bluesmen.

On the other hand, there are those who insist that the blues is a uniquely black American form and that all others who try to play the blues are at best imitators and hobbyists and at worst plagiarists and grave robbers. Some folks feel the blues is a little like the Hopi Ghost Dance—if it ain't Indians dancing, it's counterfeit.

These people have a point—kind of. The real answer may depend on whether or not you believe in ghosts.

❖ ❖ ❖

"What is blues?" seems a reasonable, even essential question. If we answer it one way—if we say the blues is a musical genre bounded by certain conventions and agreed-upon rules, it is obvious the blues is available to anyone who would play it. After all, a guitar string doesn't know the color of the finger that plucks it, and vibrating columns of air are indifferent to the social and historical forces that have conspired to set them vibrating.

But is the mimic who does a perfect Ray Charles as part of his nightclub act actually "soulful"? Does picking through a I-IV-V7 chord progression mean you're playing the blues? Could a robot be built, could a computer be programmed, to play the blues?

If we define the blues as an arrangement of sound and set certain parameters to conceptually constrain the ideal, we lose the emotive context which most blues fans find essential. If we define the blues as a profound musical expression of the anguish of American black people, a form forged in the brutal segregation of the late-nineteenth-century Mississippi Delta, if we say genuine blues must arise from some reservoir of injury, then aren't we raising the specter of cultural separatism?

Under the circumstances, wasn't it presumptuous for middle-class British white boys to affect the inflections of ancient black men from Mississippi? Aren't the Blues Brothers a bit of a sick joke?

Maybe the argument seems academic and specious, but it matters to some blues fans—just as the question of whether a new folk song can be written or whether the songs must be handed down matters to some people who care about folk music.

It is one thing to cherish a music, to tap into its primal stuff, its source materials, explore its conventions, and ultimately use it to express your personal joy and sorrow so that other people can relate to it. It is quite another to experience being born black in America, to know that your great-grandparents were born into slavery, to experience the subtle (and less subtle) forms of racial prejudice that still permeate this culture. Music is more than an arrangement of sounds, and that experiential, ingrained knowledge allows the magnificent black guitarist Vernon Reid access to a level of blues that the magnificent white guitarist Eric Clapton simply cannot tap. Acknowledging cultural differences is not racism per se—and to say the blues properly belongs to the culture of black Americans and can only be borrowed by others is to state a fact.

On the other hand, blues has never been strictly the province of black folks. The seeds of the blues were born in Reconstruction, at a time when black culture was forcibly insulated and spiritually charged. The black music that anticipated the blues, the work songs and field hollers of slaves, was the result of a mingling of African and European styles; in fact, before the turn of the century there was little difference between the popular music of blacks and that of whites in the rural South.

As segregation forced black people to further separate themselves from white culture, a ballad style with its own code began to evolve—a form that in time came to be called the blues. But the wall between black and white was never impermeable; black musicians adopted the A-A-B structure of Celtic ballads—the first line was repeated, the third line was different—as the basic structure of the blues.

Early country—"hillbilly"—music was nothing other than white blues; Jimmie Rodgers had as much influence (arguably more) on black musicians as he did on white performers. In his useful *Encyclopedia of the Blues* (reissued in 1997 by the University of Arkansas Press) Frenchman Gerard Herzhaft points out that the first star of the *Grand Ole Opry* radio program was the black harmonica player DeFord Bailey, widely acknowledged as a blues musician.

Herzhaft also cites the example of "Mystery Train," popularized by Elvis Presley. Presley modeled his interpretation of the song on a recording by the blues artist Junior Parker, who had heard the song on a hillbilly record by the Carter Family, who recorded it as "Cannonball Blues" in 1927.

So it becomes apparent that Elvis was not the first white singer to sound "black"—Elvis sounded like Elvis; he grew up listening to black music as well as hillbilly singers and Bing Crosby—and that the blues isn't as pure a form as many purists would like to believe. In the years between the World Wars, most blues players were conversant with all kinds of popular music. Huddie "Leadbelly" Ledbetter was a particularly versatile musician—he had hundreds of reels, cowboy songs, and ballads memorized and could extemporize a blues to order on the spot.

✧ ✧ ✧

The better question than to whom the blues rightly belongs is whether the blues really exists anymore. It certainly seems to be an endangered species, or, to be more explicit about it, a decadent form. Blues, rigorously conceived and narrowly defined, is decadent in the same sense that late-nineteenth-century British literature is decadent—everything is a nod and a wink and nobody's really serious about the form anymore. It's the equivalent of a minstrel show.

That's not to say there aren't some vital blues performers—CeDell Davis, Junior Kimbrough, and Keb' Mo spring immediately to mind—or that the form itself is exhausted. There are people out there with the ability to fold hurt into music and to sing with eye-moistening conviction. There is still room for invention and delight, and anyone with talent and conviction can learn to approximate the sounds made by Robert Johnson, Charlie Patton, Muddy Waters, Elmore James, Albert King, B. B. King, T-Bone Walker, and others; perhaps a gifted few can even reinterpret or craft new songs faithful enough to the tradition to be called blues.

But there aren't many. By and large the blues has been removed from its original context and hijacked by artists who incompletely understand its cultural underpinnings. Archivists like Ry Cooder keep a respectful, sterilizing distance, while bar bands like Roomful of Blues or the Radiators roll over everything with a party bluster that effectively quashes whatever murderous intent the original artist may have had in mind. It may be great, exciting, cool music, but is it the blues?

No. "Blues" has become meaningless adjective; it no longer has currency as a noun when people describe the Fabulous Thunderbirds as a blues band and every thirteen-year-old guitar phenom from Shreveport as the next great blues player. Heavy metal kidnapped the blues and dosed it with crystal methamphetamine, and even the simpy San Francisco rock band Journey used to have a concert spot where they "jammed the blues" (and singer Steve Perry introduced keyboard player Greg Rolie as "one of the greatest bluesmen alive"). Blues has its own theme park—the Disneyfied House of Blues club chain.

Want more evidence that the blues is decadent? Albert Collins makes an appearance in the film *Adventures in Babysitting.* At the height of his popularity a few years ago, Robert Cray was opening shows for Huey Lewis and the News; and Son Seals complains that his audiences are primarily made up of beery frat boys who come to slum. B. B. King and Ray Charles are more spokesmen than artists.

This is perhaps not a disaster, though it may be difficult for some blues fans to reconcile themselves to the fact that the best way to hear the blues these days may be through Muddy Waters's records.

All these modern guitarists who bleed or splatter silver tones all over those big progressions may be excellent, big-hearted musicians, technical magicians who know how to twist and contort their guitar strings into eerie approximations of the human whelp, but the field they're plowing has been exhausted for quite some time. It's hard to accept the self-aggrandizing gestures of a Jimmy Rip or a Kenny Wayne Shepard after you've had long-dead Robert Johnson infect your nightmares with his nettling menace. Pain like that man's is consecrated and wild, and you don't have to be a blues purist to respect it.

Langston Hughes complained that white folks had taken his blues and "fixed 'em / so they don't sound like me." These days they don't sound like Robert Johnson much either.

1997

Luke the Drifter: The Way Hank Done It

It has always been such a romantic image: A Cadillac rolling through the icy West Virginia countryside in the first hours of 1953, with twenty-nine-year-old Hank Williams asleep, collapsed, dying while en route to a show in Canton, Ohio. Hank always said he'd never get out of this world alive and he was right; his weary heart gave out; the booze and the pills conspired to loose his soul from the frail and aching husk his body had become.

(To argue Williams more likely died before midnight seems uncharitable, though it is impossible to know for sure. Let's allow the legend to retain its symmetry; let's say it was early in the morning, not later in the evening. Let's round it off and not look too closely at the details.)

Hard living always came easy to Hank, and his easing out on a midnight ride might have seemed something of a blessing; he could have been racked by pain like Woody Guthrie or shot down like a dog like Sam Cooke or twisted in a steaming heap of rubber and metal like James Dean. When the angels came for Hank, the driver didn't even notice. Peace descended, the legend was fixed, and the death of Hank Williams was installed as one of those folkloric myths—like Robert Johnson's selling his soul to the devil—available to any writer, musician, or artist looking to evoke a cold, lonesome shiver or borrow a bit of the singer's sad, spectral mystery.

Hank Williams wrote your life. He wrote everybody's life. Or at least he sang it—in a voice too raw and mournful to make it on the radio today. And if he didn't have the transcendental culture-warping power of Elvis Presley—who recorded his first single for Sun Records eighteen months after Hank died—or the impossibly cool, seemingly unlimited artistic command of Frank Sinatra, Williams was at least the greatest country singer ever, possibly the greatest country songwriter ever, and certainly one of the greatest artists this country has ever produced.

✧ ✧ ✧

His recording career lasted only six years, from 1947 to 1952. And though only three of the thirty-three consecutive chart singles he released during that period failed to reach the Top Ten, the last months of his life were shot through with pain and tragedy. Williams was chronically bothered by a congenital spine problem that forced him to walk stooped and required the periodic use of painkillers; he was fired from the Grand Ole Opry in August 1952 because of his constant drunkenness and the resultant unreliability. He divorced his wife, Audrey, whom he had long suspected of cheating on him, and—seemingly on an impulse—married Billie Jean Eshlimar, the daughter of the police chief of Bossier City, Louisiana.

While Hank had money—he had made an estimated $200,000 a year from his recordings since 1949 and, in 1951, had signed a five-year, $1 million movie contract with MGM (he never lived to make a movie)—he still felt the need to exploit his marriage to Billie Jean, staging two "ceremonies" before paid-admission crowds in New Orleans' Municipal Auditorium. Hank was desperate in his last months, running, skeletal, and in pain.

It is ridiculous to try and imagine Hank Williams as an old man. He was ancient at twenty-nine. He was bad to drink; perhaps because of his back problems, he had been a drinker since his early teens. But for a few periods of self-enforced sobriety, he was a drunkard almost all his life. Had he not died that morning he would have died in six months or a year. He might have made it past thirty, but Hank wasn't a long-timer.

❖ ❖ ❖

Mercury Records used the occasion of what would have been old Hank's seventy-fifth birthday to issue a limited-edition, ten-CD box set called *The Complete Hank Williams*. And—as far as anyone can tell—it is complete, with 225 tracks, 53 of which have never before been released. It is virtually everything that Hank ever set down on tape, including television and radio appearances and a chilling apology to Washington, D.C., fans after he was forced by illness to cancel a December 1951 performance in that city. It is a ghost's voice, emaciated and wrecked, and listening to it one wonders how Hank was able to live another year.

❖ ❖ ❖

It was, by all accounts, a tortured life. King Hiram Williams was born on September 17, 1923, in the small town of Mount Olive. He always loathed his middle name (a misspelling of "Hiram") and was known as "Hank" from almost the beginning. For most of Hank's childhood, his father—a part-time farmer and long-time train engineer for the W. T. Smith company—was consigned to a veteran's hospital. Williams's mother, Lillie, was a nurse who—depending on the source—either gently encouraged her son's apparent musical gift or pushed him to perform.

In any case, Lillie exerted parental authority on her son well into his adult years and saw that he was exposed to church and gospel music. But Williams also studied other forms, most famously under the tutelage of a black blues singer named Rufus Payne—better known as "Tee-Tot"—who sang on the streets of Georgiana and Greenville, Alabama, where the Williamses lived for a few years.

While the legend insists that Tee-Tot was a huge influence on Williams, in reality it is difficult to say exactly what he learned from the street singer— possibly a few guitar chords and at the very least one enduring song, "My Bucket's Got a Hole in It."

Williams dropped out of high school and may have been playing on the streets (a la Tee-Tot) as early as 1934. By 1939 he had formed his own band, the Drifting Cowboys, and toured Texas and Mexico and made occasional radio appearances. In the early 1940s, he established a fair reputation as a singer in the honks around Montgomery, Alabama, and—except for occasional sorties into Mobile, where he would take jobs at the drydock when times got lean—he was able to support himself playing music.

In 1944, he married Audrey Mae Sheppard Guy, a woman he'd met during one of those stints in Mobile. There are those who believe that Audrey was Hank's muse—that she might have inspired both his simple, affecting love songs and his devastating portrayals of grief and heartache.

In any case, it was almost certainly Audrey who pushed Hank towards Nashville in 1946. He had already developed into a promising songwriter, with the giant Acuff-Rose Publishing combine handling his songs. Of the two men who lent their names to the company, Roy Acuff was one of Williams's musical heroes, while Fred Rose was an early believer in the young singer's potential. Rose was able to secure Williams a recording contract, first with tiny Sterling Records and, a year later, with the larger MGM.

But while Rose became Williams's producer, his more important influence on Williams was as a songwriting partner and mentor. Rose had been a Tin Pan Alley song craftsman, and he spent hours honing and refining Williams's ideas—to the point that some have argued Rose wrote more of Hank's songs than did Hank himself.

But Fred Rose alone could never had suffused that material with the plain, quaking poetry of Hank Williams's pain-bit voice.

✧ ✧ ✧

In 1948, Rose secured Williams a spot on the Louisiana Hayride in Shreveport, a kind of AAA farm team for Nashville's Grand Ole Opry. On May 7, 1949, Williams's "Lovesick Blues" reached the top of the country charts. It stayed there for sixteen weeks. Later that month, a son—Randall

Hank Williams, who'd grow up to be Hank Williams Jr.—was born. By the end of 1949 Williams was one of the stars of the Grand Ole Opry, and only Eddy Arnold was outselling Hank Williams as a country artist.

But just as his professional career was beginning to soar, Williams's personal life was in chaos. Audrey left him, taking their son. She divorced him later that year. The Drifting Cowboys drifted away.

He reconciled with Audrey and she divorced him again. He had an affair with a woman named Bobbie Jett—she had a daughter who now calls herself Jett Williams. He was fired from the Grand Ole Opry. He died.

It was over just like that.

All Hank Williams left behind is contained on these ten CDs; his legacy has an asking price of $170.

$$\diamond \; \diamond \; \diamond$$

It is a sad story. But life is filled with sad stories, and the reason Hank Williams is Hank Williams is not because he died like he died but because of what he did while he lived. He is at once as raw as Charlie Patton and Robert Johnson and as lithe as Frank Sinatra or Bing Crosby; his voice is light and supple and capable of illuminating corners of the lyric other singers wouldn't dare explore. His poetry—there is no other word for it—is plain yet deep, rich in nuance yet immediately understandable. Hank Williams was and is country music. He didn't invent it, but he opened up its themes and showed that it was possible to plumb the psychological depths of the troubled mind in something so apparently lightweight as a pop song. In a way, Hank Williams is the Daddy of all singer-songwriters; he was the first confessional pop singer. They say he could barely scribble out a letter, but he could write a song to crush your heart.

Once, when asked by a business reporter to explain the potency of his material, Williams put it this way: "It can be explained in just one word: sincerity. When a hillbilly sings a crazy song, he feels crazy. When he sings 'I Laid My Mother Away,' he sees her a-laying right there in the coffin. He sings more sincere than most entertainers because the hillbilly was raised rougher than most entertainers. You got to know a lot about hard work. You got to have smelt a lot of mule manure before you can sing like a hillbilly. The people who has [*sic*] been raised something like the way the hillbilly has knows what he is singing about and appreciates it."

Hank Williams was more than just a hillbilly singer. He has become one of our more useful cultural symbols—like Thomas Jefferson, Hank can be used to stand for anything; he gives comfort and legitimacy to all those who invoke his name. Lou Reed can write a song about him ("Pale Blue Eyes") with as much authority as Moe Bandy or Alan Jackson can sing about him. Whatever your argument, Williams has already made it for you—just pick the song that suits your situation.

A lot of the country music that comes out of Nashville these days doesn't sound much like Hank Williams, but there's hardly a hat in Nashville who won't tell you Williams was one of the one or two most important singers he (or she) has ever listened to. And they're not being disingenuous; they're right. Just because what they're doing can't be compared to what Hank was doing doesn't mean that his music doesn't matter to them, it's just that it is impossible for them to get out of the shadow of—as Hank Jr. sang—"a very famous man."

Nashville scorned Williams, and it is possible his ghost cursed that music-factory town. There hasn't been another like him. And the sincerity has leaked out of Nashville, to the point that the country music capital is a kind of synonym for cold-blooded professionalism.

No, Hank never did it thataway.

1998

Southern by the Grace of God: The Allman Brothers Band

Last I heard, the Allman Brothers were still touring—though they'd dropped Dickey Betts from the band. Legal action is pending.

The Allman Brothers Band persists, still playing dates and cutting records. Unlike some reconstituted rock 'n' roll bands, the ABB has managed to retain a couple of its key members—Gregg Allman and Dickey Betts are still at the heart of the group, and, if the dispatches can be believed, they are still a formidable live act. No doubt they want to concentrate on what is and what will be, leaving the what was for historians. Anyone familiar with the band's history would understand that.

The ABB has what might be called a tragic history—a couple of deaths, a long season of acrimony over a drug trial, allegations of financial mischief on the part of their record company, artistic and physical dissipation, a marriage to Cher, breakups and breakdowns and a slow spiral from the very top of their chosen profession to the minor leagues of rock.

Yet in 1971, distinguished by the twin lead guitars of Betts and the incomparable Duane Allman and the throaty, gritty vocals of organist Gregg Allman, it was possible to make a case that the Allman Brothers Band was the greatest rock 'n' roll band in the world.

◇ ◇ ◇

Even so, it is likely the band's members are not entirely happy that Capricorn, their old record label, itself raised from the dead in 1991, has just rereleased nine of their old records, the entire "classic" Allman Brothers catalog on newly mastered CDs. Sure, they will see some money—though not as much as label head Phil Walden, who no doubt needs the cash infusion the reissued CDs surely will bring—but the current version of the ABB is feuding with Capricorn, claiming the label cheated them back in the '70s.

For his part, Walden says that he is innocent and that the problems are largely the result of rumors that the bands' "advisers" have spread for years.

"I invite anyone to investigate my role in the Allman Brothers' success and then their lack of success, record sales–wise, in modern times," he said last year. "They dominated my life for a decade—I always did my best by them."

While the band itself might not be entirely pleased with the reissues, the rest of us can be grateful. It can be argued that a couple of the old records don't really serve the Allmans' legacy, but they do provide an occasion for reassessing that legacy. They were important—they are rightly considered the principal architects of what came to be called Southern rock.

Although Southern rock is perhaps best understood as a reaction to the excesses of late '60s psychedelia, the Allman Brothers were not simply loud, obnoxious boogie artists but subtle, intelligent musicians who—along with the Grateful Dead and Cream—pioneered the progressive, improvisational possibilities of rock. Their early work combines the earthy imperatives of Delta blues with the ethereal sky-crying of John Coltrane. They could stretch out and jam, but their jams only occasionally came across as self-indulgent or meandering.

They were less about flourish and expressionistic lyrics than about the insistent pulse of the music; they pushed rock beyond the parameters of the three-minute song without abandoning the integrity of the tune. Southern rock was provincial and reactionary and culturally conservative—like the rock 'n' roll of the '50s, Southern rock drew from black blues and white country and western styles and was entirely self-contained. The music existed not to make a point or send a message but to cause hearts to flutter and feet to move.

The Allmans believed in melody—and just when you thought they'd wandered off, they bring it back to that; clean, melodic country picking would cut through the great clouds of brewed-up, foggy noise.

When they were good, they were very, very good. And when they were bad, they were horrid. There is little reason to listen to several of the newly mastered CDs: *Enlightened Rogues,* originally issued in 1979, is just passable, though it features the novelty of "Blind Love," a song cowritten with the actor Don Johnson before he became famous for *Miami Vice. Wipe the Windows, Check the Oil, Dollar Gas* is a collection of outtakes that sounds as tired and perfunctory today as it did when it was released in 1976. *Win, Lose, or Draw*—originally released in 1975—is tepid and uninspiring. Depending on your point of view, *Beginnings* is either a cheat or a favor to the consumer—it's simply a repackaging of the band's first two albums (which are also being reissued by Capricorn). There are no bonus tracks, no enhanced liner notes. Still, there is enough on what is left to convert a few skeptics.

✧ ✧ ✧

Duane and Gregg were born one year apart, in 1946 and 1947, respectively, in Nashville, Tennessee. Their father died when the boys were young, and by the time they were in junior high, the family had moved to Daytona, Florida. Here they absorbed an eclectic range of radio music, including blues and country. By their teens, they were playing in local bands.

In 1965, they formed a four-piece group called the Allman Joys and cut their first record, a version of Willie Dixon's "Spoonful." A year later they moved to Hollywood, where they spent the next few years recording demos. They signed a record contact as part of a group called Hourglass. Around this time, Gregg claims to have met Jim Morrison of the Doors.

"He was standing in an alleyway outside the Whiskey A Go Go, wearing these black leather pants and drinking something out of a Heinz 57 vinegar bottle," Gregg remembered in the early 1980s. "He asked me if I wanted a drink and I said sure. I don't know what was in that bottle, but I woke up three days later, naked, in somebody's house who I didn't know."

Aside from the Morrison incident, little else exciting happened during their stay in Hollywood, and by 1968 Duane had moved back to the South, where he latched onto a highly lucrative gig as a session guitarist in Muscle Shoals, Alabama, playing on songs by artists such as Aretha Franklin, Wilson Pickett, Boz Scaggs, Delaney and Bonnie, and others. He supplied a slinky slide counterpoint to Eric Clapton's work on Derek and the Dominoes' "Layla."

But Duane wanted to front his own band, and soon he convinced Gregg to come home from California and form a band. They hooked up drummer Butch Trucks and created a Jefferson Airplane–style band called the Second Coming, which featured guitarist Betts and bassist Berry Oakley. Legend has it they jammed together and knew they had something special. They added a second drummer—Jai Johanny Johanson—and called it the Allman Brothers Band, a prosaic name that was itself a reaction to the then-conventional practice of giving bands surreal monikers.

Their debut album, with the similarly straightforward name, *The Allman Brothers Band,* was recorded in New York in 1969 and relies heavily on reworked, amplified country blues. (As Hourglass, the brothers prohibited themselves from playing blues standards—they were supposed to write their own songs.) While the album didn't cause much of a stir when released, it ushered in a new approach to American pop. Duane and Betts dueled with guitars, and if Gregg's singing sounds a little over-the-top, it wasn't long before he refined the style.

Idlewild South—their second effort, released in 1970—fulfills the promise hinted at on the first album. It features the gentle instrumental "In

Memory of Elizabeth Reed" and is marred only by Berry Oakley's hoarse shouting on the chestnut "Hoochie Coochie Man."

But the revelation is *Live at Fillmore East,* a two-record set (it all fits on one CD), originally released in 1971, that is considered one of the finest concert albums ever recorded. Here Duane and Betts stretch out on the classics "Statesboro Blues" and "Stormy Monday," reprise "Elizabeth Reed," and generally avoid self-indulgent overplaying. Every note stings, blisters, or applies sweet balm.

❖ ❖ ❖

Given the amplitude of Duane's talent, it is amazing that the band could continue after October 29, 1971. That evening Duane was riding his motorcycle through the waning light of dusk when a pickup cut in front of him. He hit the brakes, skidded, and crashed. He was twenty-four when he was killed.

The band continued on without directly replacing him, though they did add virtuoso keyboard player Chuck Leavell in 1973. Most of *Eat a Peach,* released in 1972, was recorded after Duane's death. Still, some consider it the Allmans' artistic high point. About half of the running time of the two-record set is given over to three live tracks, including an exhausting half-hour version of "Mountain Jam." Heard today, the live tracks seem superfluous, by and large inferior to *Live at Fillmore East.*

With Gregg falling deeper into a drug habit, Betts asserted himself on *Brothers and Sisters* and delivered the band's most commercially successful recording—a number one album in 1973. "Ramblin' Man" was the band's biggest single ever, and "Jessica" continued their habit of wistful instrumentals. Shortly after finishing recording—thirteen months after Duane's accident—bassist Oakley was killed in a spookily similar motorcycle accident a few yards from the spot where Duane was killed.

Already the band was disintegrating. In 1974 Gregg testified against their road manager, Scooter Herring, who eventually got seventy-five years in jail on a drug conviction. The rest of the band recoiled from the singer.

"He threw Scooter away just because he didn't need him anymore," Betts told *Rolling Stone* at the time. "There's not one person in this band who won't tell you anything different than that. That's why there's no Allman Brothers band. . . . There is no way we can work with Gregg again ever."

They did work together again—though it would have made a better story if it ended then and there. There were reconciliations and further breakups and, in between, even some decent music. Chances are Betts and Allman are sharing a stage together somewhere tonight.

They probably don't relish the situation; they probably don't appreciate the echoes from their own youth—because no matter how good they say this latest version of the Allman Brothers Band is, it can't compete with a band of ghosts.

1997

Up and Down with the Rolling Stones

In the northeast corner of the lobby of the New Orleans Hotel Inter-Continental, a member of the World's Greatest Rock 'n' Roll Band quietly reads. Charlie Watts is alone, protected from the attentions of the curious only by his thick book and his mild, professorial demeanor. In his quiet, immaculate clothes and trimmed, gunmetal hair, the delicate drummer could be a visiting anthropology lecturer or a Swiss accountant on holiday—anyone but a famous rock star.

He hears footsteps, and his eyes cut up from the page, over expensive, flashing platinum rims. He is obviously pained: Please don't, his eyes plead. Apprehension—a curtain of weary gray dread—falls for a moment. It lifts as he realizes his privacy will be respected; that the gentleman is obviously searching for someone else and he will be left alone. Rock's Bartleby—who'd prefer not, thank you—sinks back into his brave and stubborn insistence on normality, into his heavy book. Even after thirty-two years, Watts has yet to become acclimated to the rare air of celebrity.

Charlie Watts in the lobby is not the only, and perhaps not even the most visible, sign that the Rolling Stones are in town. A long black limousine has taken up residence a few feet from the front door, and British accents pipe in the elevator. There seem to be an inordinate number of shaggy, middle-aged men—folks who'd look more at home a few blocks away on Bourbon Street than in one of the city's poshest hotels—about. A young man with black curls falling around his shoulders, wearing a heather gray T-shirt bearing the familiar Stones logo—lips and tongue—wanders over to the concierge's station. For this tour, the tongue has grown spikes, it looks dangerous. Maybe that's just wishful thinking, maybe the Stones are just tired old rich guys traipsing around the world one more time, for one more big paycheck from the suckers. Maybe, but it doesn't feel like it. It feels, well, thrilling—cheap and raw—like it's supposed to feel.

This is puzzling.

Rock 'n' roll is supposed to be disposable party music, music for a doomed generation living under a nuclear shadow—it's nihilistic and self-destructive. Buddy Holly, Sid Vicious, and Kurt Cobain traced the perfect career arc: die young, stay pretty. As Neil Young sang, "It's better to burn out than fade away."

It's true that Mick Jagger, now fifty-two years old, has said things that might now be used against him—all across America writers are pulling out the cheeky "I'm afraid rock 'n' roll has no future" and "I'd rather die than be forty-five and still singing 'Satisfaction,'" quotes of twenty years ago—yet the Stones roll on.

But there is still some juice to these old geezers, something oddly appropriate about a fifty-year-old Keith Richards, finally grown into his death mask of a face.

"A lot of old blues players . . . have kept going until the day they dropped," he said back in 1978 when a writer asked if he thought the band could last fifteen more years.

✧ ✧ ✧

"We're in uncharted territory, that's for sure," Chuck Leavell, the band's primary keyboard player, says, his lilting Southern accent contributing a thoughtful cast to the words. "But when we're on stage, and I hear Keith do a little something different with a riff, when I see him start to smile and really get into it, when I see Mick come strutting by with all that attitude, I think that this really could be the best rock 'n' roll band in the world. On some nights, I think we are."

Leavell, it should be explained, is a quasi-Stone. While you may not have heard his name or seen much of him in the videos, he's an essential part—if not exactly member—of the band. He has played on all their recordings and tours since 1981. He's not part of the Rolling Stones, the legal entity that was set up by the band's original members—Richards, Jagger, Watts, retired bassist Bill Wyman, and the late Brian Jones—back in the '60s. For obvious fiscal reasons, that's a tough circle to crack—guitarist Ronnie Wood, who's played with the band for nearly two decades, only became an official member earlier this year.

But the Stones have always had a piano player in residence. Ian Stewart, "Stu," probably should have been a founding member of the band, but—at least according to legend—Stones manager Andrew Loog Oldham didn't think the heavy-set keyboardist fit in with the band's lean and angry image. So Stewart became an unofficial "sixth Stone" who served as the group's tour manager in addition to taking an occasional turn at the piano. It was Stewart who recommended Leavell to the band in 1981.

"Stu liked to play straight ahead, twelve-bar rock 'n' roll," Leavell says.

"He was a great player, a great rock, boogie-woogie player, but he didn't really like to play the slower, melodic things like 'Angie.' That's why the Stones have always worked with other keyboard players."

The Stones have, over the years, enlisted players as distinguished as Ian McLagan, Jack Nitzsche, Nicky Hopkins, and even "black Beatle" Billy Preston as second pianists. But since Stewart's death from a heart attack in 1985, Leavell has assumed the primary role. Now he executes the barrel-house rolls of "Honky-Tonk Woman" and gives "Brown Sugar" its saloon-meets-ragtime swing.

"Stu's death was just devastating to all of us," Leavell says. "His loss was as great a blow to the band as it was to me personally. Stu and I had become quite close over the years. . . . When I was auditioning for the band, I think it was finally his call. They had had all these piano players come into New York to audition and after it all they asked him. And Stu said, 'I quite like that boy from Georgia.'"

That boy from Georgia is actually a Tuscaloosa, Alabama, native, the youngest of three children of a comfortably middle-class insurance salesman and a piano-playing housewife who encouraged her son to "paint pictures" with the piano.

"I had some piano lessons," Leavell remembers. "But I really didn't have much discipline. I could pick out the notes, but I had a pretty good ear, so I really didn't learn to read music. I'd just kind of pretend to read and ask my teacher, 'Miz Jeter, how'd that go again?' maybe get her to hum a little bit of the tune so I could fool her."

Leavell also endured a brief junior high school trial with the tuba—"That's where I learned to read"—before moving on to guitar. It was, he says, the instrument of the moment, the instrument the singers played on a television show called *Hootenanny*.

"When I was thirteen I was playing guitar in a group, called the Misfitz, that did a lot of British Invasion stuff—we played a lot of things by the Animals, the Zombies and, of course, the Stones. We played 'Satisfaction' and 'It's All Over Now.' We played at the YMCA and before too long we had a spot on a local television show, a kind of *Tuscaloosa Band Stand* kind of thing."

He also did some session work in Muscle Shoals—he played on the 1968 hit "(Friend, Don't Take Her) She's All I Got" by soul singer Freddie North. By 1970—before he graduated from high school—Leavell had decided to make music his career.

"From there, there were two ways I could go," he says. "Muscle Shoals, of course, had a real healthy recording scene. But it was kind of closed there, it was real cliquish. Everybody knew each other and the same players played on every session. It would have taken me probably a couple of years to break in there, to really establish myself."

So Leavell went east, to Macon, Georgia, where he had heard that a man named Phil Walden was about to open a little studio and record label. Leavell stepped right into the nascent Capricorn Records operation, assuming keyboard duties on the label's house band. Another break came when he met Mac Rebennack, a piano player from New Orleans better known by the stage name Dr. John.

Leavell became "kind of a protégé" of Rebennack's, to whom he still remains close, playing in his band and on his albums. (It was at Capricorn that he also met his future wife, Rose Lane White, to whom he's been married for twenty-three years.)

Then in 1972, after the death of Duane Allman and just before the death of bassist Berry Oakley in November, Leavell was asked to join the Allman Brothers Band. He stayed with the band for four turbulent years, until they broke up in a riot of recriminations after Gregg Allman—to stay out of jail himself—testified against one of the band's roadies, arrested for drug trafficking.

Starting in 1976, Leavell and former Allmans Jaimoe Johnson and Lamar Williams formed Sea Level, a jazz-rock fusion outfit that released five critically well-received albums in the late '70s.

✧ ✧ ✧

So even though the forty-two-year-old Leavell can walk anonymously through the streets of New Orleans, most people have heard his music. He's played as a session musician on dozens of records, for artists as diverse as Welsh pub rocker Dave Edmunds, Hank Williams Jr., Aretha Franklin, flutist Tim Weisberg, doo-wop artist Dion DiMucci, Eric Clapton, the Black Crowes, country diva Kitty Wells, and French pop phenomenon Johnny Halliday. In between his work with the Stones, he has also worked on their various solo records, including Ron Woods's *Slide on It*. He's toured with the Fabulous Thunderbirds, George Harrison, and the Indigo Girls. Lately, he's branched out into producing—last year he recorded the bulk of former Allman Brothers guitarist Warren Haynes's debut solo album at his home studio.

But now he's with the Rolling Stones—and having fun.

"You should have been with us last night," Leavell says. "We went out, to a place called the Rock N Bowl, and Mick and Charlie were there. And it's just amazing, you know, 'cause these are guys I grew up listening to, wanting to be. And it was all cool. I mean, Mick, he handles the attention so well—he's been one of the five most recognizable people in the world for like thirty years or something, but he still manages to go out and live in the world. We just sat there, listening to Beau Jacques, and maybe people would come up to Mick and nod at him or say hello or something, but it was just real cool. A couple of girls tried to get him up dancing, and I think he wanted to do it, but in the end he decided he'd better not. But it was a blast to just hang around these guys."

✧ ✧ ✧

Leavell's wife, Rose Lane, has come over from Macon to catch this show. She doesn't travel with the band; the only Stones wife or girlfriend who still does that is Ron Wood's wife, Jo. But New Orleans is a great city to hang out in, and the guys have a five-day break. She wouldn't miss it.

Leavell obviously adores her. It's something you don't expect to run into, this rock 'n' roll domesticity. He's eager to talk about his kids—nineteen-year-old Amy and twelve-year-old Ashley—and the fifteen-hundred-acre tree farm he owns with his wife.

A dedicated environmentalist, Leavell admits he's a bit nutty on the subject of trees. When he's not working with the Stones or with other artists or on his music (he's hoping to land his own solo recording contract soon), Leavell serves as a spokesperson for the Georgia Forestry Association. He and Rose Lane were voted the American Forest Associations Georgia Tree Farmers of the Year in 1990, and the American Pulpwood Association named him Southeastern Forestry Association Activist of the Year in 1993. There's a whole string of forestry awards noted in his press bio.

"Most people are lucky if they have one thing they can be passionate about," he says. "I've got three—my family, my music and my trees."

He's comfortable in his role as a semi-Stone, and he's happy his role with the band has grown. While he's not the musical director—Keith Richards is—Leavell plays on every song and gives many onstage cues. And from time to time he's mediated musical disputes between the Glimmer Twins.

"During rehearsals, which are my favorite time with this band, they have these incredible tempo wars," he says. "Keith likes to drag a little, play a little behind the beat, while Mick likes everything a little quick. So it will go on for a while, and then I'll have to go, 'Guys, let's find the right tempo for this song.' And we'll get out a metronome and find the right tempo. They respect my role."

As for the very public rift that erupted during the mid-1980s between Jagger and Richards, Leavell says he sees signs of the bond strengthening.

"It's like a marriage," he says. "They went through that time that every marriage goes through, where you either split up or work through it. They've worked through it and it's made them stronger. There's still tension, sometimes a lot of tension, but artistically that's useful."

For Leavell, the Stones are the greatest rock 'n' roll band in the world—the "heavyweight champ"—because they understand and respect the music's Southern blues-based roots. It helps that his own roots are in the same tradition; he acknowledges a certain sympathy between Jagger and Richards and himself.

"While those guys are ten years older than me, it's like we went to different high schools together," he says. "We have the same musical vocabulary. I'm in the band because they wanted me to do what I do.

"This is a band that has always evolved, that's always understood that the music is the most important thing. It's not a band like the Allmans, a straight-up rock band where we were interested in virtuosity, in playing long solos; everything this band does is in the service of the song. They're not afraid to camp it up, to look silly on stage; they're into spectacle; they're into tongue-in-cheek."

And that's one reason, he thinks, the band has been able to survive for so long without becoming an oldies show—why it can survive the loss of a Brian Jones or a Bill Wyman and go on. The core of the band is Mick and Keith, and you can't discount shy Charlie back there hammering away like Thor. That's the heart, and the heart ain't tired—Jagger looks like a twenty-year-old leaping around up there. Richards seems ageless as Stonehenge.

And maybe Chuck Leavell is "expendable."

"Sure, some people worried that when Bill [Wyman] decided not to tour this time that maybe it wouldn't be the Stones," he says. "I worried about that. But then we got Darryl [Jones] and he's added a fresh kick to this band, something that Bill—no matter how great a player he was, and he was great—could ever have supplied.

"What it is, I guess, is that the whole is greater than the sum of the parts. Sure, maybe I'm expendable, but then I'm the guy being asked to play with the Rolling Stones."

In the hallway outside Chuck Leavell's suite high in the Hotel Inter-Continental, a drab little fellow looks momentarily startled. Then Charlie Watts lowers his eyes and smiles and nods in acknowledgment.

1998

Black Country Pride

In 1966, RCA Records released "The Snakes Crawl at Night," the first single by a young singer they billed as "Country Charley Pride." Written by Mel Tillis and Fred Burch, it was a was a straightforward, fairly typical country story song—a first-person narrative of infidelity, retribution, and justice. RCA released the single without a publicity photo.

So when Pride stepped out on stage in front of live audiences, he had his lines prepared: "Ladies and gentlemen, I realize it's a little unique me coming out here on a country show wearing this permanent tan."

It wasn't long before he could dispense with the disarming opener—within a couple of years Pride was one of the biggest stars in country music. From 1966 to 1990 the former minor-league baseball player recorded sixty Top Forty country hits—twenty-nine of which reached number one. He was named the Country Music Association's Male Vocalist of the Year in 1971 and 1972 and was the CMA Entertainer of the Year in 1971. He also won three Grammys. Today, at fifty-nine, he still occasionally tours and records.

Most people know who he is—Pride is the black country singer. To some, he might be the exception that proves the rule. For one of the things some people who don't care for country music are predisposed to think is that country music is illiberal and ignorant. A great many people who don't like country music probably object to it on purely political grounds—they don't want to be lumped in with the trailer dwellers, the rednecks, the unreconstructed racists who, they imagine, swoon over Faron Young and Tammy Wynette.

This is a ridiculous bias; country music is among the most democratic of popular music forms. It admits all voices, and it might be argued that fashion means less to country fans than fans of any other particular genre or even "serious music" listeners. No strain of American pop exists in a vacuum; Elvis Presley and Hank Williams—to name just two—were obviously and profoundly influenced by black musicians.

While RCA might have withheld Pride's publicity photos for fear that a black man might have been discriminated against by radio station program directors and disk jockeys, the success of "The Snakes Crawl at Night" was primarily due to Pride's resonant, supple baritone. Pride was like Jackie

Robinson in that it was ultimately his talent which determined the arc of his career.

On the other hand, Pride was unlike Robinson in that his success did not lead to record companies signing a flood of black artists. One could be forgiven for believing that Pride might be the only black American to make a significant contribution to the country music tradition.

✧ ✧ ✧

In a 1996 interview with the *New York Times*, Tony Brown, the president of a major country music record company, was quoted as saying, "Country music is basically white music. Why would black people want to sing all those straight notes. . . . Why would a black person want to be in a format that gives any white singer who tries to do a little curlicue or deep groove so much grief?"

All those straight notes? Anyone who has heard George Jones (or even Randy Travis) or Merle Haggard or Patsy Cline might find it difficult to understand how anyone intimately involved with country music could think of it as a genre comprised primarily of "straight notes."

The fact is that black musicians have made very significant contributions to country music from the very beginning. How can you draw a line between Robert Johnson and Jimmie Rodgers? Could hillbilly music have possibly evolved without the banjo—an instrument apparently invented in West Africa—or the fiddling styles of ex-slaves?

Consider that the first steel-string guitar recordings were made by Blind Lemon Jefferson and that black performers, songwriters, and producers have contributed to more than four hundred country chart hits. And recent surveys have indicated that black people may account for up to 20 percent of country music's audience.

In the early part of the century, rural people—black and white—listened to integrated string bands. Blacks and whites listened to the *Grand Ole Opry* broadcasts that began in the 1930s. A black harmonica player named DeFord Bailey was one of the first bona fide stars of the Opry. Bailey remained a part of the Opry for fifteen years, bearing with grace the occasional indignity—the Opry's publicity referred to him as the show's "mascot"—and became one of the most influential musicians in the country.

The Country Music Foundation and Warner Brothers have combined to produce a three-CD collection that attempts to document the contribution of black artists to country music. *From Where I Stand: The Black Experience in Country Music* stretches from Bailey—who is represented with three tracks—through Pride and beyond.

Some of the early tracks are obvious inclusions—the Mississippi Sheiks' "Sitting on Top of the World," Huddie Ledbetter's "Midnight Special"—while others, such as "Turkey Buzzard Blues," a vocal version of "Turkey in the Straw" by street musicians Peg Leg Howell and Eddie Anthony, and "Bill Cheatem," by the possibly pseudonymous James Cole String Band, are as revelatory as they are obscure.

The set's second disc focuses on the cross-pollination of soul and country styles that occurred in the '50s and '60s, as country and rhythm and blues artists adapted, crossed boundaries, and recorded pop songs in their own styles. Wynonie Harris took a cover of Hank Penny's country hit "Bloodshot Eyes" into the Top Ten of the R&B charts in 1951, while the do-wop group the Orioles enjoyed an R&B number one with their cover of Darrell Glenn's (and later Rex Allen's) "Crying in the Chapel."

Before Pride, Big Al Downing was perhaps the best-known (and certainly the most successful) black country singer—his version of "Down on the Farm," however, owes as much to Little Richard and Jerry Lee Lewis as it does to Porter Wagoner and Earnest Tubb, two white country artists he cites as important influences.

And then Ray Charles decided to revolutionize country music.

The importance of Charles's 1962 album *Modern Sounds in Country and Western Music* can hardly be underestimated; at the time country music was widely seen as the province of hicks. Charles—who had played with hill-billy bands in Florida before moving west and had a genuine love of the genre—interpreted the songs of Hank Williams, Eddy Arnold, Floyd Tillman, and Don Gibson (Charles's version of "I Can't Stop Lovin' You" was a number one single), and the resultant album topped the *Billboard* charts for fourteen weeks.

The Country Music Foundation was unable to license Charles's seminal recordings "I Can't Stop Lovin' You" or "Busted," and therefore had to settle for his high-energy rendition of Hank Snow's "I'm Movin' On."

The set's second disc also includes Ivory Joe Hunter's versions of "City Lights" and "He'll Never Love You," the Supremes' faithful cover of the honky-tonk weeper "It Makes No Difference," Bobby Hebb doing the Porter Wagoner chestnut "A Satisfied Mind," Dorothy Moore's "Misty Blue," and Al Green's startling take on Kris Kristofferson's "For the Good Times."

While Charles and other black singers largely adapted country music to their own styles, Charley Pride claimed the music as his own. There is a revealing anecdote in his autobiography: when a well-meaning Nashville type told Pride it was good to have a black in "our music," Pride smiled and replied, "It's my music too." When Pride was growing up in Sledge,

Mississippi, his mother favored Frank Sinatra, but his father listened to the *Grand Ole Opry*.

Pride was never interested in being anything but a straight-ahead country singer—his cover versions of Hank Williams's "Kaw-Liga" and "Lovesick Blues" are lovingly rendered. His voice is itself the embodiment of the country voice, solid yet capable of sliding in microtones, of yelping and hollering and yodeling when called upon to do so.

Although none of the black artists who followed Pride had anything approaching his kind of success, the third disc is in some ways the strongest of the three. Four of Pride's best-known songs are present, and there are also strong cuts from Stoney Edwards ("She's My Rock" and "Hank and Lefty Raised My Country Soul"), the Pointer Sisters (the 1974 hit "Fairytale"), and Aaron Neville ("The Grand Tour"). Professor Longhair's rollicking version of "Jambalaya" is included, as is a haunting version of Tom T. Hall's "How I Got to Memphis" by Otis Williams.

The high point of the set is the penultimate track, a terrifying, wracked, unpretty version of "There Stands the Glass," recorded by the late Ted Hawkins in 1994, forty years after Webb Pierce's hit version. It is a simply amazing performance, a chilling, scintillating *cri de coeur*.

It is exactly the kind of record that doesn't come out of Nashville anymore.

From Where I Stand is a valuable document in that it demonstrates that black people have always been involved with and engaged by country music. While it is true that the picture Nashville presents to the world is largely monochromatic, the music itself is available—and useful—to all sorts of Americans.

1997

Unthinking Blood: Ralph Ellison's
Juneteenth

We have been hearing rumors of and occasionally even reading excerpts from Ralph Ellison's famously unfinished second novel for the past twenty years or so. So it is not entirely a surprise that it has finally appeared—abridged and tightened and otherwise planed into shape by a literary executor. *Juneteenth* is now in the bookshops, a handsome edition with a sepia-toned jacket and a price of twenty-five dollars.

There is a helpful introduction by the executor, John F. Callahan, a professor of humanities at Lewis and Clark College in Portland, Oregon, and an even more helpful selection of Ellison's notes on the novel at the end.

Callahan makes no extravagant claims for his work; he merely has done his best with the materials at hand. Ellison began working on the follow-up to his first novel, the celebrated *Invisible Man,* in the early 1950s. He apparently envisioned a large, sprawling book published in three volumes. He made notes and drafts of the novel; he published the first excerpt from the book-in-progress in 1960. In 1966, a part of the novel was destroyed in a fire at Ellison's Massachusetts home.

After that, there were rumors that Ellison was reshaping and expanding his book, that it was changing, evolving into an impossibly ambitious project that—Callahan writes—was "multifarious, multifaceted, multifocused, multivoiced, multitoned."

The book was unpublished at Ellison's death and Callahan stepped in. With the help of Ellison's widow, he pulled a coherent book from more than 2,000 pages of typescript and printouts.

"Aiming, as Ellison had, at one complete volume," Callahan writes, "I proceeded to arrange his oft-revised, sometimes reconceived scenes and episodes according to their most probable development and progression. While doing so, I felt uneasily Procrustean: Here and there limbs of the manuscript needed to be stretched, and elsewhere a protruding foot might be lopped off, if all the episodes were to be edited into a single, coherent, continuous work."

As published, *Juneteenth* is a single volume, and the novel itself is just under 350 pages. After all the rumors, it is something of a pleasant surprise to discover that this *Juneteenth*—Callahan's *Juneteenth* perhaps, but the only *Juneteenth* we have—is compact and linear and readable. It is reminiscent of Joyce and Faulkner but it is also lean and economical and pointed. It is not the vast, encyclopedic epic we have expected—that Ellison might have intended—but it has its virtues. It is not sweeping, but personal. While it cannot be said to be a great book, it does remind one of Ellison's great humanity and command of language. It's not Callahan's fault that Ellison didn't finish the book; he did what he could. There is enough here for us to understand why—and to regret that—the book seemed to defeat Ellison.

✧ ✧ ✧

It seems strange to think that we have survived more than five years without Ellison; he died on April 16, 1994, with his critical and personal reputation intact. He managed to outlive his critics—those who thought *Invisible Man* was bourgeois and conservative and those from the '60s who thought Ellison insufficiently engaged with their struggle against white hegemony.

Ellison understood that race was simply another false idea, that the real stories were not black stories but human stories, that "blood and skin don't think."

This condition was nearly unique among the internationally famous black American writers who came to public attention after World War II. Ellison was always a better citizen than one might have expected, a fiercely intelligent man who lived much of his life in a segregated and hostile land. Despite an early acquaintance with socialism, he never succumbed to the gray lure of Marxism. Ralph Ellison always maintained a touching yet thoroughly pragmatic faith in democracy.

Ellison was at core an optimistic realist; he recognized that America's problems were not systemic and that with patience and love, tempered by a resolute insistence on the dignity of the individual, hearts and minds could be changed. Ellison understood that courage and persistent engagement were necessary for progress. He was, in his own words, "a novelist, not an activist," yet he was one of the great resisters of evil, a kind of national conscience who spoke in measured tones about both sides of the great divide without adopting a habit of protest or falling prey to the trap of identity politics.

He was well known because he wrote *Invisible Man*, a genuinely great book that recorded a black man's journey through post–World War II America, from South to North, from town to city. In the process the nameless hero moves from naive faith to bitter disillusionment, from academia to communism and finally to madness—to a coal cellar with a hundred lights burning, a place where he can enjoy his invisibility.

Yet if *Invisible Man* is taken as profound—and Ellison so wished it to be taken—it is also a great read, with stories full of tension and spirit and humor. It is richly textured, a story told largely in tongues, as Ellison accurately captured the voices of black sharecroppers and white Bourbons, of jive-spinning New York vendors and West Indian immigrants. It is funny. It sings with energy. It is a page turner. It is great.

Ellison was born in Oklahoma in 1914; his ancestors were black and Indian and white. His father named him Ralph Waldo Ellison and hoped he might become a poet; his mother recruited black people for the Socialist Party. He was trained as a musician, and his first ambitions were for the concert hall. He won a scholarship to Alabama's Tuskegee Institute, where he studied music until 1936, when a mix-up involving his scholarship caused him to travel to New York. There he met Richard Wright and became involved in the Federal Writer's Project.

Ellison was practically apprenticed to Wright from 1937 to 1941 (not incidentally the period in which Wright was writing *Native Son*). While Ellison still considered himself primarily a musician, he spent a lot of time hanging out at the Harlem bureau of the communistic newspaper the *Daily Worker*, where Wright wrote a weekly column. At the time, Wright also edited a magazine called *New Challenge*, and he encouraged the young Ellison write for it. Two of Ellison's most celebrated early short stories— "Flying Home" and "The King of the Bingo Game"—were first published in Wright's magazine.

After the publication of Wright's *Black Boy* in 1945, Ellison defended Wright against attacks from left-wing black intellectuals—including W. E. B. Du Bois—who contended that Wright's portrayal of black life was essentially bleak and brutish. Ellison published a famous response, titled "Richard Wright's Blues," which argued that Wright was heavily influenced by the musical form of the blues and that in *Black Boy* "the American Negro impulse towards self-annihilation and 'going underground' had been converted into a will to confront the world." That is perhaps the central theme of both *Invisible Man* and *Juneteenth*.

✧ ✧ ✧

Juneteenth is the story of a light-skinned Negro or white child named Bliss, who is raised by a black jazzman-turned-preacher named Hickman. As a child, Bliss is part of Hickman's traveling revival show, breathing through a rubber tube in a coffin until he hears his cue and rises from "the dead."

Later, the boy becomes a race-baiting senator named Sunraider, who employs the same kind of corrupt theatrics to mesmerize audiences. He uses the rhetorical and pyrotechnical tricks he learned from Hickman to galvanize segregationists, in much the same way Ellison appropriated Joycean stream-of-consciousness to enthrall readers. There are passages of unassailable brilliance, as when Old School sermonizing meets Huey P. Long-ish political rants. The spoken and unspoken mingle and charge through the reader's mind. Ellison blurs the lines between black and white, between the physical and the fantastic, between right and rationalization. It is a bravura performance.

Yet it cannot be considered a whole book—*Juneteenth* remains unfinished after all. It is evocative but not seamless, and we are left to wonder how things came to be. Perhaps the answers are somewhere in Ellison's sorted-through papers; perhaps they were burned up in the fire. Maybe they died with Ellison. Maybe he never solved his own riddles.

Juneteenth is tantalizing, frustrating, and ultimately half-baked. No doubt this is why Ellison never published it. What Callahan has fashioned is worthy—one would rather have the opportunity to read this version than not—but it ought not be taken for the real thing. This *Juneteenth* is a kind of shadow novel, an abridgment of a wild and unrealized dream.

1999

Hurting George Jones

Technical proficiency doesn't make a singer—any more than perfect grammar makes a writer or photographic precision makes a painter. The woods are full of ciphers with perfect pitch, reproducing cold notes as frequencies, nursing their precious instruments with honeyed tea.

Yet George Jones's station as the world's greatest living country singer—a title only the callow, the ignorant, and the willfully contrary bother to dispute—has almost nothing to do with his range or accuracy and everything to do with the emotive power of his phrasing and the tender-rough way he insinuates lyrics into the listener's head.

George Jones is all damage and heartbreak and brave grim survivor smiles. His voice starts in his sinuses and sticks in the listener's chest like an ax. When he's right—and maybe even when he isn't quite right—Jones wounds, nearly cripples, his audience. His is a voice that sounds like a kazoo in a deep cave; the round, brown baritone blossoms then careens into an excitable, raw-nerve tenor—the paper reed bleats and sometimes the pitch wavers but the end result is devastating: This is hardcore.

The new album, the post-crash album, is almost worthy of the legend. Jones's first release since the vodka-fueled March 1999 car crash that left him unconscious for eleven days and nearly killed him is called *Cold Hard Truth*. It is a genuine petty miracle of a record, full of heart, a piercing, resonant reading of a solid batch of songs. It can be considered a semiautobiographical song cycle, and had Jones perished in that car wreck, it would have seemed an eerily prophetic record. One can't help but wonder if the accident itself—Jones got drunk and plowed his Lexus into a bridge abutment, he's since pleaded guilty to DWI—contributed to the overall effect.

It is always difficult to separate a living legend's biography from his product, but in this case the question concerns not the added poignancy provided by the near-death experience but the fact that Jones's accident prevented him from performing the usual Nashville prerelease ceremonies—the vocals on the record are all "scratch" vocals, recorded live with the band, not the cleaned-up pitch-corrected overdubs Jones was planning to record. There is an appealing roughness, an insouciant temper, that pervades the record—there is none of the spoiling carefulness that mars so many Nashville productions.

If it isn't a genuinely great record, it's because some of the material is less than equal to the star's performance—though "Choices," the first single, is perhaps the best song Jones has tackled since "He Stopped Loving Her Today" nearly twenty years ago, and the title song is an absorbing ballad. The rest of the material is simply top-notch Nashville, which is to say that at times it seems hedged and crafty and overt. (But that's what country music is these days, and not even George Jones can redeem an industry Disneyfied decades ago.)

✧ ✧ ✧

Perhaps no one in this age of celebrity confessions has told as many stories on himself as George Jones. *I Lived to Tell It All,* Jones's 1996 biography, as told to veteran Nashville Boswell Tom Carter, is a plain-spoken yet lurid look at the dark life of one of the world's worst addictive personalities. It is replete with bad behavior, pills, cocaine, bar fights, gunplay, comebacks, relapses, bankruptcy, homelessness, broken marriages, failed parenthood, trashed hotel rooms, missed concerts, and a washroom encounter, with Porter Wagoner, that probably should never have been publicly aired.

Jones has been through it all; he's suffered and striven and brought more misery down around his own head than most civilizations could stand. But he never fired a shot at Tammy Wynette. Or so he claims.

Born in East Texas in 1931, George Jones rose out of Beaumont and Houston honky-tonks as the spiritual heir of Hank Williams and a vocal ringer for Lefty Frizzell or, if he chose, Roy Acuff or Bill Monroe. His childhood was appropriately rough—when he was sixteen, Jones ran away from home after a particularly fierce beating at the hands of his father, an itinerant laborer named George Washington Jones.

He ended up in Jasper, Texas, singing on a local radio program for a few months before returning home to Beaumont to join a husband and wife vocal duo who sang on that city's KRIC. In 1949, Jones met Hank Williams, who was visiting the station to promote a new single. Williams reportedly told the young singer to "sing like George Jones."

In 1950, Jones married his first wife, Dorothy, and soon went to work for her father as a house painter. The marriage collapsed in less than a year, and Jones was briefly jailed for failure to support his young wife. After the divorce was final, he enlisted in the marines in 1951, expecting to be sent to Korea.

He never made it overseas. Instead he was stationed at California's Camp Pendleton, where he continued playing in bars. He was discharged from the marines in November 1953 and returned to Beaumont where he was almost immediately signed by local record producer Harold W. "Pappy" Dailey to fledgling Beaumont-based Starday Records.

Jones's first single, an upbeat, self-penned number called "No Money in This Deal," was released in early 1954 to thunderous indifference. Starday released four more singles that year, none of them receiving much attention. Then, in the summer of 1955, not long after Jones had married a Houston carhop named Shirley Corley, Starday released a song cowritten by Jones and a childhood friend called "Why, Baby, Why." It shot up the country charts, peaking at number four. Jones's version of the song might have gone even higher had not a cover version been rush-released by established stars Webb Pierce and Red Sovine. Pierce and Sovine's "Why, Baby, Why" went to number one.

The success opened a few doors for Jones—most importantly, Dailey secured the singer a spot on the Louisiana Hayride in Shreveport, where he shared the billing with Elvis Presley. "Why, Baby, Why" was the start of an impressive string of hit singles—Jones reached the Top Ten with regularity in 1956 with such singles as "What Am I Worth" and "Just One More."

(Yet a series of rockabilly singles Jones recorded about the same time— as "Thumper" Jones—did poorly.)

In August 1956, Jones joined the cast of the Grand Ole Opry and his first album was released. The next year, Starday signed a distribution deal with Mercury. Jones's records began appearing under the Mercury label and Dailey began recording Jones in Nashville studios. The hits continued uninterrupted, and in the spring of 1959, Jones's biggest hit to date, the boogie-driven "White Lightning" (written and originally recorded by J. P. Richardson, "the Big Bopper," another Pappy Dailey protégé) spent five weeks at number one.

His next big hit, the ballad "Tender Years," came two years later. It spent seven weeks at number one and marked a change in Jones's artistic direction—the smoother production and bigger arrangement anticipated Jones's later success as a helmet-haired "country-politan" balladeer.

Pappy Dailey became a staff producer for United Artists Records in 1962 and brought Jones along with him to the label. Jones's first single for United Artists, "She Thinks I Still Care," was his third number one hit. *Billboard* magazine named Jones its Favorite Male Country Vocalist. In 1963, Jones began performing and recording with Melba Montgomery. Their first duet, "We Must Have Been out of Our Minds," peaked at number three in 1963, and although they never had another Top Ten hit, their voices blended extraordinarily well, with a rough bluegrass edge that was a refreshing alternative to the increasingly slick Nashville sounds of the '60s.

Jones changed record labels again in 1965, following Dailey to Musicor, where he recorded almost three hundred songs in five years. Not surprisingly, Jones cut a lot of mediocre material in this period, along with a few bona fide classics such as "Walk through This World with Me" and "A Good Year for the Roses." While he consistently put singles in the Top Ten, he was not at his artistic peak during this period—partly because his personal life was in a shambles.

Always a drinker, Jones's behavior was becoming increasingly erratic. He began missing performances and Shirley filed for divorce in 1968. In the aftermath of the broken marriage, Jones moved to Nashville for the first time, where he met Tammy Wynette, the most popular new female vocalist in country music. She was having trouble with her own marriage to songwriter Don Chapel.

✧ ✧ ✧

Jones and Wynette were married on February 16, 1969, a move that led directly to his breakup with Dailey. Jones, unhappy with most of his Musicor recording, blamed Dailey for the assembly-line production and the weakness of much of the material. He was also frustrated that he was unable to record with his new wife—neither Musicor nor her label, Epic, would allow one of their artists to sing on a record released by a rival label.

In 1971, Jones severed ties with Dailey and Musicor, in the process signing away all rights to the huge vault of Musicor recordings. This allowed the label to continue to release albums of "new" George Jones material deep into the '70s, long after he joined Wynette on Epic in 1971.

Jones and Wynette, dubbed the King and Queen of Country Music, became the genre's biggest stars in 1971, selling out concerts as a duo and racking up Top Ten hits together and separately. Jones—previously known as a short-haired, redneck, honky-tonk hero—had successfully recreated himself as a smooth, sophisticated balladeer with a shock of styled hair.

Jones's new producer was Billy Sherrill, who had been working with Wynette. Sherrill was known for lush, string-drenched productions and had the reputation as a despot in the recording studio. Musicians—including singers—were there to follow his direction. Jones and Sherrill had some problems at first, but with the commercial success of Sherrill's singles, they soon developed a comfortable working relationship. And Jones's phrasing retained its wrenching, tortured bite.

By 1972, the Jones-Wynette marriage had become something of a public soap opera, with the pair seeming to communicate largely through their singles. Jones was heavily into cocaine abuse and was drinking as heavily as ever. Wynette filed for divorce in 1973, then withdrew her petition as the couple marked their reconciliation with the number one single "We're Gonna Hold On."

In 1974, Jones released "The Grand Tour," a devastating picture of a broken marriage, which became his first number one hit since "Walk through This World with Me" seven years before. The follow-up was a Sherrill composition, "The Door," which ended—literally enough—with the sound of Sherrill's office door closing. A few days after that record also hit number one, Jones recorded "These Days (I Barely Get By)" with lyrics by Wynette. She left Jones two days later; by the end of the year they had divorced.

◇ ◇ ◇

Still, the couple continued to record and tour together, though the late '70s were a tough time for Jones. His health was bad and his records weren't selling, and he became notable for his drunken, drug-fueled rampages and his fondness for shotguns and pistols. In 1979 alone, he missed fifty-four shows—cementing his nickname "No-Show" Jones.

After the moderate success of a couple of novelty songs featuring, respectively, Johnny Paycheck and James Taylor in 1978, Jones decided to record an album full of duets, *My Very Special Guests,* in 1979. He didn't show up at the sessions, however, and had to overdub his vocals after his partners recorded theirs.

A few months later, doctors told Jones that he had to quit drinking or die. He checked into a rehab clinic—and left, uncured, after a month. His weight fell to about a hundred pounds. His cocaine addiction was a bigger problem than his drinking.

So he mounted a comeback. In 1980, he recorded "He Stopped Loving Her Today," perhaps the most moving country song ever recorded. And that set off another string of Top Ten hits and number one singles; they ran through 1986. Jones was arguably as popular through the '80s as he had been in the '60s.

Yet he never really broke free of his demons. In 1982, Jones was caught on camera, veering his car drunkenly through the streets of Nashville with the police in pursuit. Though his 1983 marriage to Nancy Sepulvalda helped a bit—Jones claimed he managed to detox and had shed himself of his addictions by the end of 1984—there is the troubling business of that car crash.

Jones's streak seemed to run out around 1987, when the country charts came to be dominated—ironically enough—by a slew of young artists who had been greatly influenced by Jones. As Randy Travis, Keith Whitley, and

Dwight Yoakum ascended, Jones's lights faded. He kept recording, but nothing clicked.

He moved to MCA in 1991, released a string of lackluster albums that didn't sell.

Cold Hard Truth is Jones's first record for Asylum Records, and the liner notes indicate the record company has a bit of faith in Jones yet. Keith Steagall is a tasteful, unobtrusive producer who knows enough to keep the focus on Jones's remarkable, grief-toting voice. It is a great comeback, at least in an artistic sense. As willfully moronic, self-destructive, mean, and ugly as Jones has been throughout his unfathomably long career, it seems a graceful gesture.

It is how we'd like to remember George Jones, rough yet tender, a man besieged by ancient, indefatigable ghosts that defy explanation. The notes clench, then open, spreading slowly, climbing and beginning to ring. It is the voice of a fallen angel, the voice of a busted man hanging onto the one shimmering, inestimable, inexplicable gift he's ever had given to him. It is the voice of a man in unrelievable, exquisite, shattering, and transfiguring pain.

1999

Dear Welty

It is an odd thing about genius; it tends to erupt in unlikely places. Why should Mississippi be such fertile territory for writers? Maybe Faulkner is explicable, the inevitable Southerner, Yoknapatawpha County's gloomy God—maybe someone had to be Faulkner. But what about these others? What accounts for the existence of a Larry Brown, the fireman who took to writing because he thought it might be a good way to earn some extra cash; or Willie Morris, the Southern Icarus; or wild-blooded Barry Hannah? How could a commercial colossus like John Grisham arise from the same Oxford hills as Count No-count? Why Donna Tartt or Beth Henley or Lewis Nordan? Why Will Percy and his nephew Walker and the neighbor boy Shelby Foote? Why Richard Wright?

Richard Ford contends his writing life is perhaps the most unlikely, but unlikelier still seems the story of "Miss" Eudora Welty, who, truth be told, might be the most enduring Mississippian, or at least the most readable enduring Mississippian. At nearly ninety years old, she is again in vogue, and it is likely that her books will still be in print ninety years on.

In September, the prestigious Library of America will issue two volumes of her work, *Stories, Essays, and Memoir* and *Complete Novels,* that will collect most of Welty's published work over the past fifty-seven years. Sally Field has optioned the film rights to Welty's Pulitzer prize–winning novel *The Optimist's Daughter.*

While her excellence was not immediately perceived by the world at large, the publication of Welty's first collection of short stories in 1941 did draw at least one remarkable notice. Soon after the volume was published, a letter arrived at Welty's Jackson home bearing a Hollywood postmark.

"Dear Welty," it began. "Who are you? Will you tell me? How old are you? Where do you live?" It was signed "William Faulkner."

It took years for the rest of the world to notice what Faulkner so readily apprehended—that this slender Southern flower had the voice and vision of a true artist. While in the past twenty-five years or so Welty has been showered with honors, including Pulitzers and a presidential medal and more writers' awards than can be recollected, for long stretches she was without a publisher or an audience, often dismissed as a "womanish" writer or misperceived as a hobbyist, a nice old white lady who wrote short stories.

How it is possible that anyone could read, say, *The Robber Bridegroom* or *The Optimist's Daughter* and still disbelieve in Welty's power is a mystery. More likely Welty's critics were ignorant of the quiet magic in her words. Welty is a fearless writer; like Faulkner, she has a prodigious gift for imagining the minds of characters whose backgrounds are wholly different from her own. A product of a culture where, growing up, her only contact with black people came from her encounters with her family's servants, she nonetheless was able to enter the consciousness of an elderly black woman exhausted by life. She could reconstruct the bitter inner murmurings of a racist assassin drawing a bead on Medgar Evers or imagine the hopeless loneliness of a traveling salesman during the Great Depression. She has turned her imagination on all sorts of hearts—some soft and admirable, others knotted with hate—and rendered them all in human shades.

As a writer, she is, above all, generous with people.

✧ ✧ ✧

Eudora Welty was born in Jackson, Mississippi, on April 13, 1909, into a genteel family that prized learning. According to family legend, as a child, Welty's mother, Mary Chestina, was trapped on the second floor of a burning house; she refused to leap to safety until she had tossed her entire twenty-four-volume set of Dickens out the window to safety. Her father, Christian, was a director of the Lamar Life Insurance Company.

Eudora Welty never married and has lived most of her life in a rambling Tudor house her father built in 1925. While there are reports she has grown physically feeble, a neighbor of hers reports that her cornflower eyes twinkle and that she is alert and quite good company. She still entertains occasional visitors.

She might have had another kind of life. For a time she considering living amongst the svelte and terrifying women of New York; she prepared herself for a career in advertising, first at the Mississippi College for Women, then at the University of Wisconsin, and finally at the graduate school of business at Columbia University. But she found that work and that city uncongenial. Of her time in New York she has said that she felt trapped in "an iron cage of guilt" and that she considered any pleasure she derived from living in the city purchased with her mother's deprivation. Sending her to school had been a financial hardship. And so, though she loved the jazz clubs and the galleries of New York, she came home to Mississippi in 1931 soon after her father was diagnosed with leukemia.

In her 1984 memoir, *One Writer's Beginnings,* Welty described the scene with powerful restraint. As her father lay dying, the doctor decided to attempt a blood transfusion. Welty's mother insisted on being the donor and so was lying on a cot near her husband's side, with a tube running from her arm into his.

"All at once his face turned dusky red all over," Welty writes. "The doctor made a disparaging sound with his lips, the kind a woman makes when she drops a stitch. What the doctor meant by it was that my father had died."

✧ ✧ ✧

Back at home, Welty—who had ambitions to be a writer but was sure she'd never be able to make a living writing stories—took a job at the local radio station WDJX while serving as a "social news correspondent" for the Memphis *Commercial Appeal.*

Then she took a job as a publicity agent, junior grade, for the Works Project A. She traveled all over Mississippi taking photographs of the people who occupied that poor state, first with a simple Kodak Brownie, later with a Rolleiflex. (One hundred of these photos were collected into the book *One Time, One Place,* published by Random House in 1971 and reprinted by the University of Mississippi Press in 1996.) Welty's most famous photograph is an image of an old black woman in a tattered dress with a face seemingly imbued with a kind of heroic dignity and patience—an image not unlike the ones she was later to manufacture with her language.

She published her first short story, "Death of a Traveling Salesman," in 1936, in *Manuscript* magazine. The *Southern Review* accepted one of her stories. By the end of the decade, she was publishing fairly regularly in general circulation magazines such as the *New Yorker* and *Atlantic Monthly.*

About this time she drew the attention of a young Irishman, Diarmuid Russell, son of the poet George William Russell. Diarmuid had recently cofounded a literary agency in New York, and he wrote to Welty, hoping to sign her as a client. Welty quickly agreed and soon the two had established a relationship that provided the fundamental support of Welty's creative life until Russell's death in 1973. While Russell conceded that he could not always sell Welty's work because it was too subtle and "oblique" for a mass audience, he understood she possessed an original, unique voice that was not to be bent to commercial purposes.

Russell encouraged her to write as she pleased, regardless of fashion, and helped find her sympathetic editors like Mary Louise Aswell at *Harper's Bazaar.*

Then, in 1941, her first collection, *A Curtain of Green,* appeared, attracting at least William Faulkner's attention and initiating a serious writing career.

The next year saw the publication of her novella *The Robber Bridegroom*, and in 1946 she published her first full-length novel, *Delta Wedding*.

Her books were not huge sellers, but they were generally well-regarded, and she could always make a little money by publishing a story in a magazine. She won a few literary prizes. She was living in what she has described as a "dream world."

❖ ❖ ❖

In the 1950s, the dream began to disintegrate. Both of Welty's younger brothers—Edward and Walter—had developed debilitating arthritis, and her mother, already afflicted with cataracts, suffered a broken hip and a stroke in rapid succession. For the next fifteen years, Welty all but ceased writing in order to care for her family. She published next to nothing, despite Russell's pleading and her encroaching poverty.

Walter died in 1959. Welty's mother died in January 1966; her brother Edward, four days later.

In 1972, she published her masterpiece, *The Optimist's Daughter*, a book about a young woman who must contend with her dying mother's brutal verbal abuse. It won her the Pulitzer prize and made her, at sixty-three, an international sensation.

And so for more than a quarter of a century she has lived as she pretty much always has, receiving guests in Jackson and now and again venturing out into the world. A fragile-looking little woman with a skeleton of steel, she has not published much since, especially not since the memoir came out in 1984, but she still goes for a daily drive around Jackson with her caretaker, still sees her brothers' children when they come to visit. A couple of years ago a group of French people came to Jackson to induct her into the *Legion d'honneur* in a ceremony held in the Old Capitol building.

"We start from scratch, and words don't; which is the thing that matters—matters over and over again," she once wrote by way of explaining herself. "For though we grow up in the language, when we begin using words to make a piece of fiction, that is of course as different from using even the same words to say hello on the telephone as putting paint on canvas is. The very leap in the dark is exactly what writers write fiction in order to try."

Which is another, more modest way of saying it: Miss Eudora is a miracle.

1998

Walker Percy: Keeping Quentin Alive

In a 1989 interview, Walker Percy remarked that he didn't "like to be described as a Southern writer."

Percy's reluctance to be typecast is understandable, and not just from the perspective of the artist who hopes to transcend regionalism and speak to the world. Aside from Faulkner, the academic factories of the Northeast—where literary taste is manufactured—tend to either ignore or ghettoize "Southern" writers, preferring instead to canonize the coolly understated and delicately filigreed prose of a Henry James or the postmodern fireworks of a Pynchon or DeLillo. To be a Southern writer is to be shunted into the elective courses, away from the mainstream of Melville, Hawthorne, and Mark Twain.

"The danger is," Percy told his frequent inquisitor Lewis Lawson, "if you're described as a Southern writer, you might be thought of as someone who writes about a picturesque local scene like *Uncle Tom's Cabin, Gone with the Wind,* something like that."

Percy ferociously sought to evade labeling, stressing the existential and philosophical aspects of his work. And even casual readers of Percy's novels are likely to recognize that the author's style and subject have more to do with the Christian existentialism of Søren Kierkegaard and Gabriel Marcel than with Allen Tate, Robert Penn Warren, or (for gosh sakes) Erskine Caldwell and Margaret Mitchell.

Yet Percy, despite his protestations, was a consummate Southerner and hence a Southern writer. From his earliest undergraduate attempts at fiction to his final novel, 1987's *The Thanatos Syndrome,* Percy was clearly absorbed by the South and Southern themes. How could he have been anything else?

✧ ✧ ✧

While the facts of an artist's life may or may not be significant to the condition of his mind (where someone comes from may have little to do with where one is headed; after all Jerry Jeff Walker is from upstate New York), in Walker Percy's case the facts argue for an inevitable Southernness. This is made clear by the most recent biography of Percy to appear, a work by Father

Patrick Samway, whose previous books include a biography of Faulkner and who compiled and edited *Signposts in a Strange Land* (1991), a posthumous collection of Percy's nonfiction. Samway has elected to concentrate on what is patently demonstrable in the aptly named *Walker Percy, A Life* (1997); there is no radical reinterpretation of Percy's work and no speculation about the author's private life. Samway's strong suit appears to be doggedness; he roots out the facts with such precise tenacity that those unfamiliar with Percy's work (or inoculated against its charm) are likely to find it dull.

Others are likely to find this dullness a virtue; Samway delivers exactly what he promises, a detailed account of the life of this most reluctant Southerner. While there have been other biographies of Walker Percy—most notably Jay Tolson's *Pilgrim in the Ruins* (1993) and Robert Coles's *Walker Percy: An American Search* (1978)—most of them were less straightforward than Samway's and focused more on the writer's work than on his life.

University of Florida history professor Bertram Wyatt-Brown's 1994 study of Percy's family—*The House of Percy: Honor, Imagination, and Melancholy in a Southern Family*—went back to the sixteenth century and lavished detail on the family's antebellum days in Philadelphia. While it was as fascinating as it was impressive, it wasn't a definitive biography of the author.

Samway's book complements these earlier efforts nicely. Though he's no stylist and has a tendency to repeat—and contradict—himself, one feels confident of the facts he presents and doesn't mourn the scandals (surely there were scandals?) that might have been invented.

Reading Samway's book, one is convinced that Walker Percy earned the Southernness he worked so hard to overcome.

✧ ✧ ✧

Percy was a Southerner both by birth and by temperament. He was born in Birmingham, Alabama, in 1916 and lived there thirteen years before moving with his family to Athens, Georgia, where his father promptly committed suicide, continuing a gruesome family tradition; his grandfather, after whom Walker was named, also killed himself. The next year, Walker Percy's first cousin, once-removed, "Uncle" Will Percy (1885–1942)—the Mississippi poet and memoirist—invited the bereft family to move to his plantation in Greenville, Mississippi. There Percy finished his last three years of high school and made the acquaintance of one Shelby Foote, who would grow up to become a novelist and perhaps the leading historian of the War between the States.

He enrolled in the University of North Carolina—where he was placed in remedial freshman composition after writing a paper that described the Mississippi River in a convoluted, Faulknerian syntax with minimal punctuation.

From there he attended medical school at Columbia University in New York City, where he contracted tuberculosis while working as a physician at Bellevue Hospital. He spent nearly two years recovering from the disease at a sanitarium in Saranac Lake, New York.

As Percy himself recognized, his bout with tuberculosis was not without its compensations. During his long convalescence, he dipped deeply into the French existentialists—especially Jean-Paul Sartre and Albert Camus—as well as Tolstoy, Dostoevsky, and Thomas Mann. While Percy regretted not serving in World War II, his illness kept him out of the army.

After his 1946 marriage to Mary Bernice ("Bunt") Townsend, Percy lived briefly at what had been his Uncle Will's summer retreat near Sewanee, Tennessee, before moving to New Orleans's Garden District. After Percy's first novel, *The Moviegoer*, was published in 1961, he moved across Lake Ponchatrain to what would become his permanent home, Covington.

❖ ❖ ❖

Not only did Percy live in the South, all of his major characters are Southerners and—allowing for the occasional sortie to Manhattan or New Mexico—all his stories are set there. Percy vigorously resisted the influence of Faulkner—as a young man he refused to enter Faulkner's home in Oxford, Mississippi, preferring to wait in the car while his friend Shelby Foote visited with the great man. (Faulkner, who'd been persona non grata at Uncle Will's house since showing up drunk on the tennis courts, came out to the car to chat with young Percy before the pair left.)

Percy admired Faulkner's work but hated the thought of becoming him. In *The Moviegoer*, Percy creates a character named Sam Yerger, a kind of professional Southerner based on the public perception of Faulkner. He also told his interviewer Lawson, "I would like to think of starting where Faulkner left off, of starting with a Quentin Compson who didn't commit suicide. Suicide is easy. Keeping Quentin Compson alive is something else."

Just as Quentin Compson felt burdened by his Southern heritage and the obligations pressed by history, so Walker Percy (and every other writer who lives in the South) must feel burdened by William Faulkner and what critics call the Southern literary tradition.

So Walker Percy, the descendant of Will Percy and several nineteenth-century women writers, attempted to divert critics from the Southern influences in his work. He might even have believed that he had more in common with Martin Heidegger and all those theologians who came muttering out of the Black Forest all those years ago than he did with loud and loutish Count No Account, barefoot and slovenly drunk on Uncle Will's tennis courts.

It is easy for the literal-minded to indict Percy on charges of noblesse oblige paternalism and sexism; his black characters and female characters are usually easy to type and seemingly less advanced than his white Southern men. Yet Percy filters his ideas through these same white Southern men who are neither angels nor beasts, despite their collective tendency to think of themselves in these terms. Percy's heroes aren't good role models, and his Feliciana—the fictional realm where his later novels are set—isn't Paradise; in fact, it may very well be doomed. Walker Percy was not politically correct before not being politically correct was chic.

Again and again, Percy returns to the Southern notions of class and honor. In *The Moviegoer,* he has Binx Bolling's Aunt Emily say it plain: "I am not ashamed to use the word 'class.' I will also plead guilty to another charge. The charge is that people belonging to my class think we're better than other people. You're damn right we're better. We're better because we do not shirk our obligations either to ourselves or to others. . . . we live by our lights, we die by our lights, and whoever the high gods may be, we'll look them in the eye without apology."

✧ ✧ ✧

While Percy felt free to parody that kind of pride, it is not difficult to believe he secretly subscribed to this kind of chivalric code; as a serious Catholic, Percy considered slavery America's original sin and thought that racial prejudice could be overcome by the strict and honest application of Christian doctrine. For Percy it was simple—those who hated people for the color of their skin not only were wrong, but knew in their hearts they were wrong. What made the difference was not race, but honor.

While Percy made comedy from Southern manners, he also recognized their value. In the end, there is a utility in Southern indirectness and courtesy; the rationalizing Yankee is nearly always depicted as a dehumanizing force. The alternative to living gracefully, to indulging petty kindnesses, is a kind of living death. Walker Percy preferred a world where "people still stop and help strangers."

Percy could use an existential term like Marcel's "intersubjectivity" without blushing or seeking to subvert the idea with irony; his novels really aren't as difficult as he sometimes pretended. They speak to the heart.

In the end, his work evades nothing: the hard questions are wrestled, the past is remembered and afforded what it is owed. Even Percy's own evasiveness about his essential Southernness is in keeping with the Southern character.

1997

Miller Williams

So much for journalistic objectivity—Miller Williams is a pure poet and a dear friend, and I only wrote this story, for our newspaper's "High Profile" society section, after some coaxing. I'm just glad Miller wasn't unhappy with the way it turned out.

You go through your life, living, working, doing the things you must and the things you should and some things you merely wish to do, and then one day, for reasons that may be totally beyond your control, the earth shudders. There is a crack in the sky, a hiccough in television waves, a wrinkle in the firmament. Things change.

And while you know this, you can't help but feel the subtly shifted paradigm in your blood and bones, even as you live more or less the way you have always lived, the way you lived when you were poor and struggling, the way you lived when you discovered yourself solidly middle-class.

You still climb up on the stepladder to spray Kilz on the ceiling where it has begun to stain, yet you know that the world regards you differently than it did before—you know that there are people, maybe millions, who know your name, who heard you read your poem on national TV. It lasted for a little less than three minutes, about as long as one of your famous daughter's ballad songs, about as long as it takes to clean a good-sized trout or listen to the top-of-the-hour newscast on public radio. Odd how that such a little thing, a few breaths, a few crisply enunciated words into a microphone, could seem to make so much of a difference in the way the world reacts to you.

❖ ❖ ❖

On December 3, 1996, Miller Williams received a phone call from a reporter at the *Washington Post*. She had heard from a source that President Bill Clinton had selected Williams, an old Arkansas friend, to write and read the inaugural poem.

Williams hadn't heard this—and said so. It seemed at least presumptuous to talk about a thing that mightn't happen. But the reporter insisted she was sure of her sources, wouldn't the poet consider granting her an interview?

"Mr. Williams," she said, "trust me."

The story ran in the *Post* the next morning—without any comments from Williams. Before noon, there were calls from the *Today Show* and the *San Francisco Chronicle*. Before nightfall, the invitation itself had been extended. Williams hung up the phone and looked at his wife, Jordan.

"I've been invited to write the inaugural poem," he said.

"My God. What am I going to wear?" she said.

✧ ✧ ✧

Understand, Miller Williams was famous before he read the poem on television, but famous only in the limited way that poets can be famous in America.

That is to say that while a lot of people knew his work, a few more knew his name, and he had earned the respect of his peers, it wasn't anything like celebrity. You couldn't even reliably find his books in the Fayetteville Barnes and Noble. In 1976, he won the Prix de Rome for Literature of the American Academy of Arts and Letters, which meant an expense-paid year in Rome with no specific obligations.

He has published about thirty books, collections of poetry and translations of foreign poets' work and textbooks and even—with James A. McPherson—a history of America's railroads. A volume of short stories is on the way as well as a new book of poetry.

Williams has served as Visiting Professor of U.S. Literature at the University of Chile and Fulbright Professor of American Studies at the University of Mexico. For seven years he was a member of the poetry faculty at the Bread Loaf Writers' Conference. He has represented the State Department on reading and lecturing tours through Latin America, Europe, and the Middle and Far East. He has published stories, translations, poems, and critical essays in most of the seminal journals and mass circulation magazines in the United States and others in Canada, Latin America, and Europe. His poems have been translated into many languages.

Harvard has honored him with the Amy Lowell Award for poetry. He has been presented with the New York Arts Fund Award for Significant Contribution to American Letters, has won the Henry Bellaman Poetry Prize, the Charity Randall Citation for Contribution to Poetry as a Spoken Art, the John William Corrington award for Literary Excellence, and the Academy Award for Literature of the American Academy of Arts and Letters, and has been named Socio Benemerito dell' Associazione of the Centro Romanesco Trilussa in Rome. In 1990, he won the prestigious Poet's Prize. He has won almost all of the important prizes poets can win; the few he hasn't are still within his grasp.

Still, Williams realizes that in the poetry business—as in some other businesses—it is difficult to win some of the big prizes without being located on one of the coasts.

"I would rather live in Arkansas than win any prize on earth," he says. "I think of myself as an Arkansawyer, but not an Arkansas poet. And I'm gratified that my poetry has won so many of the big prizes."

One could fill up columns and columns with Williams's awards and accomplishments—he started the University of Arkansas Press and was its director for seventeen years as it earned a national reputation for excellence. One could spend paragraphs on the cluttered walls of his modest but not small house in Fayetteville; every painting, every photograph has a story. Miller Williams has a lot of friends, many of them celebrated people themselves—actors, musicians, writers, presidents.

He is former president Jimmy Carter's "poetic mentor." He traveled with country singer and songwriter Tom T. Hall in his tour bus. If for some reason you want to connect Bill Clinton to the Chilean poet Pablo Neruda, you can do it through Miller Williams. One of Williams's closest friends and comrades in the civil rights struggle is George Haley (brother of the author Alex Haley), who was chairman of the Postal Rate Commission under George Bush and remained on the commission until Bill Clinton appointed him U.S. ambassador to the Republic of Gambia.

Williams can tell you about the time he and Jordan spent the night dancing with John Ciardi and his wife at Ralph Ellison's apartment in Harlem and how Ellison insisted on walking the four of them to their car because he didn't want four white friends of his on the Harlem streets after midnight without a black presence to vouch for them.

News of Willie Morris's recent death reminds him of the time he saw Eudora Welty at a reception in New York. "Everyone else was dressed for Sunday morning church and she was in a wash dress and a shapeless cardigan sweater with what seemed to be kitchen slippers," Williams remembers. "And she was treated with such awesome respect by everyone that all of us felt terribly overdressed."

There is too much. You can't confine a man like Miller Williams to newsprint. It hurts to try. Sure, Williams read a poem on television and 150 million people probably heard and saw him; sure, his daughter Lucinda is perhaps the most critically acclaimed singer-songwriter working in popular music today (he's equally proud of his other children: Robert, who drives a truck in New Orleans and plays piano in a jazz band, and Karyn, a nurse and an autoharpist with the Family Reunion String Band in Indianapolis), but the thumbnail biography is insufficient.

Miller Williams is someone to go to dinner with, to have a drink with, to listen to—oh, the whole tone of this story so far is wrong, but it is all we have.

Maybe what you need to know most about Miller Williams is this. About a month after he returned to Fayetteville after reading the inaugural poem, he encountered a man of about sixty in Collier's Drugstore.

"Are you Miller Williams?" the man asked.

"Yes, sir," Williams responded.

"Well, I just wanted you to know I didn't watch the inauguration—I'm a Republican businessman—but I read about you and your poem in the *Wall Street Journal*. I was skeptical but the poem was there so I read it. Well, I want to tell you, I took it home with me at noon that day and I said to my wife, 'Honey, I understood a poem.'"

"Sir," Williams said, "I'd rather hear that from you than from a hundred English professors."

Williams's poems are constructed of plain words; they aren't obscure or ambiguous. They mean what they say.

"It is almost inexpressibly important to me that my poetry be accessible to anyone who cares to read poetry, whatever their station in life, whatever their background," he says. "At the same time, I want to write poetry that acquits itself as serious poetry to those in an academic position to make that judgment."

His longtime friend Tom T. Hall is impressed by Williams's poetry's simple yet evocative power.

"Miller is a great storyteller, a master teacher, a brilliant poet, but most of all a wonderful, reliable friend," Hall says.

Miller Williams is a conciliator, a teacher, a role model—a wise man.

"I think that Miller's attitude towards contemporary poetry, in general, is something us younger poets could learn a lot from," Marck Beggs, the poet who serves as director of the Master of Liberal Arts Program at Henderson State University in Arkadelphia, says. "He is generous in his praise and careful in his criticism. He seems to exist outside all the internal bickering of the current poetry scene."

✧ ✧ ✧

Williams turned sixty-nine years old on April 8, 1999. He is fit, trim, with gray-blue eyes that dance and spark behind his professorial glasses. He seems perpetually on the verge of laughter, and he has something of the toned, alert intelligence about him. He dresses well, with caps and vests, and one senses that he knows damn well he is a handsome man, though he calls himself "just an Arkansas hillbilly."

He was born in Hoxie, one of six children. His father, E. B., was a Methodist preacher, an early integrationist who sought to organize sharecroppers in the Southern Tenant Farmers' Union. They moved about frequently—to Fort Smith, Booneville, Paragould, and Russellville. Miller began writing early and found himself especially drawn to poetry.

When he entered Hendrix College he fully intended to major in English.

"But a psychological evaluation indicated I had no verbal aptitude," Williams says. "I was told I'd embarrass myself and my family."

So he went into science. He studied hard and well and ended up doing graduate work in zoology, teaching high school and then college biology. He married young, had a family, and went to work selling appliances for Sears and college textbooks out of his car's trunk. But he always wrote poetry.

In 1950, teaching biology at Millsaps College in Jackson, Mississippi, Williams hosted a poetry show on television (can you imagine such a thing these days?) and had poems published in the *New York Times*. He imagined that he might live out his life as a scientist-poet, like the pediatrician William Carlos Williams or the novelist Walker Percy, who was trained as a physician.

But in 1961, he met John Ciardi, the poet who would become his friend and mentor. Ciardi invited Williams to the prestigious Bread Loaf Writers' Conference in Vermont. There he met Robert Frost and discovered a kind of community of poets he suspected existed but had never before encountered. The next year Williams joined the faculty of Louisiana State University in Baton Rouge—as an English professor.

His poems are still shot through with science; his training has lent his work a kind of epistemological skepticism, a distrust of certitude that nonetheless acknowledges the role faith plays in human pursuits. A new poem, "After All These Years of Prayer and Pi R Square," illuminates Williams's synthesis of these two seemingly antithetical paths of intellectual striving:

> *How sweet a confusion that science, that creed of the creature,*
> *that earthly philosophy of numbers in motion,*
> *distrusted by rabbi, sheik, and preacher*
> *who have clothed its nakedness in flame,*
> *should quietly introduce us to the notion*
> *of something weightless within us wanting a name.*

"I don't know of any poet who can express more clearly and beautifully the humorous and serious thoughts of this modern world," former President Jimmy Carter says. "Miller Williams has been an inspiration to me."

✧ ✧ ✧

For more than thirty years, Williams has been primarily, professionally, a poet, but even poets have to eat. So he taught as well, building a reputation as a genuinely great classroom instructor.

In 1980, the University of Arkansas Board of Trustees established the University of Arkansas Press and named Williams its founding director. He gave up teaching in 1983 as the press grew to consume more of his time. When he retired from the press two years ago, he decided to rededicate himself to teaching. It has been a delightful "rediscovery."

"I wasn't deciding what I was going to do all day," he says. "I was going to the press to find out what problems I had to deal with. Administration is not a proactive profession—it is a reactive profession. I think whether one is managing a shoe store or serving as president of the United States, one is reacting to what happens all day. Now as a writer and teacher, I'm being primarily proactive."

Though the adjustment has been more difficult than he expected, Williams is enjoying his students.

"That break was good for me," he says. "I had those years off, so I didn't burn out in the classroom. Right now, I'm teaching three hours a day, but I'm spending more hours a day doing what the university is paying me to do than when I was at the office eight hours a day. And I'm enjoying it so much."

Williams is happy; he works out daily. He still writes his poems in longhand, on a yellow legal pad, with a worn square of oak resting on his lap as a desk and his dog Bubba at his feet. He is working as hard as ever, maybe harder. Things have gotten back to normal, but things are not quite the same.

"I feel better, physically, than I ever have in my life," Williams says. "I am more at peace with myself in the world than I have ever been in my life. I wouldn't go back a year and certainly not thirty. I'm probably one of the luckiest people on earth when I look at the way I'm privileged to live, as what Americans call middle-class, when I realize to how many people this is unimaginable luxury. Also the wife I have, the children I have, the grandchildren, the dogs—if I were writing a play to star in, I couldn't cast it any more marvelously than this play has been cast."

1999

Lucinda Gives 'Em Hell

I love Lucinda Williams—to the point that I found it hard to talk
to her. I understand she has since let her hair go back to blond.

Austin, Texas: to a bunch of musicians, writers, and record industry
types, 11 A.M. can come pretty early in the morning—especially after a night
consumed in the clubs along Sixth Street, feeling the mathematically precise
microbursts of fifty-four-year-old Jeff Beck's Stratocaster popping like angina
in their concave rock 'n' roll chests. Who turns out to hear a speech the morning after an expense-account-funded death march through the dark and terrible nightclubs of America's hippest music city?

But improbably enough, they turned out. More than a thousand people,
maybe more than that (the *Austin American-Statesman* said it was probably
the largest crowd ever for one of these speeches), crammed into a ballroom
in the Austin Convention Center—a room that seemed as long as a city block
and as wide as a basketball court—to hear Lucinda Williams deliver a keynote
speech at this year's South by Southwest Music and Media conference. And
if they were expecting yet another eulogy for the dying business of rock 'n'
roll, they must have been a little disappointed. Williams didn't seem the least
bit distressed.

By now, you probably know Lucinda Williams—at least you've heard the
name—a singer-songwriter with a reputation for stubbornness and quality.

❖ ❖ ❖

She was born in Lake Charles, Louisiana, on January 23, 1953. She is
the daughter of Fayetteville poet Miller Williams, director emeritus of the
University of Arkansas Press. She grew up in Vicksburg and Jackson and
Baton Rouge and Macon and Atlanta and Santiago, Chile, and New Orleans,
and finally she dropped out of the University of Arkansas in Fayetteville and
began the career of an itinerant musician, playing in bars and coffeehouses
in Austin, Nashville, Houston, and Greenwich Village.

For a while, she called herself simply "Lucinda" and sang Howlin' Wolf.
Her first album, *Rambling*, was pretty much straight roots music (more blues

and country than folk, but you could hear the skeins twisting around each other) and pretty much gorgeous. She got $250 to record it.

Her second, *Happy Woman Blues*, announced the arrival of a potent pop country songwriter. She made $400 for that one. But it was *Lucinda Williams,* her third album, recorded for Rough Trade, a British label that specialized in punk and ska acts, and released in 1988, that established her as an artist of the first rank.

While you couldn't exactly call *Lucinda Williams* a commercial hit, it earned her a small but intensely loyal (and somewhat obsessive) following and a burgeoning reputation as a "musician's musician." But Rough Trade folded soon after the album was released, leaving her without a record company. RCA snapped her up, but when they presented her with sugary, radio-ready mixes of her songs, she told them "no thanks" and walked out on Elvis Presley's old label.

Her proud father tells the story this way: "One of the RCA executives stood up and said to her, 'Young lady, no one has ever walked out on an RCA contract,' and she said, 'Well, you can't say that any longer, now can you?'"

She eventually landed at Chameleon, another tiny independent label, and the RCA songs showed up—mixed her way—on her 1992 album, *Sweet Old World,* a collection of trenchant songs about longing, love, death, and putting the bad past behind you.

In 1994 Mary-Chapin Carpenter had a hit off "Passionate Kisses," Lucinda Williams's rollicking, pop smart centerpiece that included the defining lyric "Is it too much to demand? I want a full house and a rock 'n' roll band." Williams got a songwriting Grammy and a house two doors down from Emmylou Harris out of it. Patty Loveless recorded her "The Night's Too Long." Tom Petty covered "Changed the Locks" off *Sweet Old World.*

Then everyone settled in to wait for the next album. It took awhile—that wasn't all or even mostly her fault, by the way—but when it finally arrived it was gorgeous.

✧ ✧ ✧

Car Wheels on a Gravel Road is everything Williams's fans could have hoped it would be. It is a work of art that makes all the speculation about commerce and record company intrigue seem silly.

It is replete with grace and a kind of tough magic. It rocks. It induces shivers. It bleed and moans and cracks a wry grin as it brushes its hair back from its eyes. Oh, my baby.

It wasn't a huge seller—last year it peaked at number sixty-five on the *Billboard* charts—but it was the album of the year in the *Village Voice*'s prestigious *Pazz and Jop* poll of music critics nationwide. It was also voted the top album by an organization called the National Music Critics Association. It got four and a half stars in *Rolling Stone* (the rumor is that the reviewer, Robert Christgau, wanted to give it the maximum five stars but was talked out of it by an editor who was nervous about anointing the album one of the best of all time).

◇ ◇ ◇

A little less than a year later, she is the certifiable critics' darling, brandishing her Gibson guitar as a shield as she takes the stage to talk with the critics and the label execs and the struggling hopeful artists who swarm to South by Southwest. With her new black spiky bangs making her look like Chrissie Hynde's little sister, she takes advantage of the opportunity to sing a few songs and, in between, to talk simply and straightforwardly about something as corny and unfashionable as artistic integrity and the increasing irrelevance and looming obsolescence of the star-making machinery behind the popular song.

"I don't think major labels are working anymore," she says. " I really don't."

There is wild applause—you can tell the record company folks because they're the ones not clapping, not even smiling.

"Every one of the young, unsigned bands here this year probably thinks that this could lead to a record contract, " she says. "But that doesn't mean what it used to mean because these days, rather than developing artists, investing in them, nurturing them, the few record companies that are left standing after the latest round of consolidation function like banks."

If they think an artist is worth the commercial risk, they might loan them the money to tour. They might promote an album they think has the potential to make them money. Then again, they might record a band cheap, sell a modest but profitable amount of product, then cut the kids loose—advising them they ought to be thankful for their perfect one-hit wonder career trajectory.

Not that there's anything wrong with being anonymous or without a record deal these days.

"I was gonna call my little speech 'Why I Don't Want to Be a Star,'" Williams says. The audience laughs, even the industry types. Last time they checked, *Car Wheels on a Gravel Road* was back on the *Billboard* charts at number 156. (She got a bump from the Grammy Awards, where *Car Wheels* won Best Contemporary Folk Album, an absurd category for what was essentially a rock 'n' roll record, but never mind.)

These days you might not need a record company, especially if you're Lucinda Williams. These days you don't have to sell a million copies to live well enough, to put your music out, to do what you always wanted to do. Williams knows that Mercury—her record label—will defer to her as long as she puts out records that do as well as *Car Wheels*.

Critical adoration can't save your career—Nashville fire starter Robbie Fulks got dropped by his record company last year; heck, the great Van Morrison once got dropped from his—but coupled with modest commercial success, it shifts the balance of power in the artist's favor. Williams smiles like she's just beginning to realize this; she's got a history of being thought of as difficult and demanding—just as she once walked away from a major record deal because they wanted to tinker with her songs, she won't elide verses for *Good Morning, America*. She can get away with this because she's not interested in becoming a star. She could walk away from it all; she'd still be able to make her music. She'd find a way to put records out. And her fans would still find her.

"I can't be easily swayed by illusions of grandeur. I think it's important to keep your power—don't let anybody take your power away," she says. "You need to maintain your beliefs. You have to be willing to walk away from it all."

Later, after the speech, Williams admits that she's thinking about maybe starting her own label, something akin to Steve Earle's E-Squared, that she's not as disciplined about writing as she should be, and that while the critical adulation, the Grammy, and the sold-out shows feel a little like vindication, that's no more real than the corporate shuffle. They can't take her power. Nobody else is doing them like that these days; despite "Passionate Kisses" and a couple of other tracks, Williams is not a songwriter who gets her songs cut a lot in Nashville.

"They've got a thing about body parts in Nashville," she says.

She's too raw for country radio, with a hillbilly voice that can sound like ripping silk or the loneliest she-coyote in the world. She ain't pop either. She's simply good.

With her trademark way of imbuing simple words with a real, tough sensuality, Williams is what they used to call an "integrity artist," someone who you want on your record label as much to advertise your good taste as to make you money. Bob Dylan was such an artist for a long time (maybe he still is); his sales figures were a closely guarded secret at Columbia during the 1960s. Other artists might want to sign with your label because you've got a Lucinda Williams or a Bob Dylan there.

So she figures it's safe for her to rail against the corporate world—they can't do a thing to her. They can't do a thing to anyone who doesn't buy into their view of the music business.

"I'm the same person I was when I started singing in Austin in 1974," she says. "I won't change. You can't change me."

Which begs the question: Who would want to?

1999

Storyteller: Tom T. Hall

Tom T. Hall was my father's favorite singer and one of the biggest influences on my writing life. I told him that, and I'm glad I did.

A case might be made that Tom T. Hall is the greatest country songwriter of his generation. Some people think so. Some people cannot help but be amazed by his command of simple language, his journalistic eye for detail, and his calm, conversational singing voice that never undercuts the integrity of the song.

"Integrity" is perhaps the right word to describe Hall's songs. There's nothing false or cheap about them. They're rugged products, American-made and sturdy. Hall's words are plain but never trite; his melodies meander naturally, finding their own pace, their own feeling. His best melodies seem utterly timeless; it is impossible to imagine them ever not existing.

Some people think the subtitle of the 1993 box-set retrospective of Hall's work—*Storyteller, Poet, Philosopher*—isn't the least bit hyperbolic. Some people think that his latest album, 1997's *Home Grown,* may be the best country album you'll never hear on country radio.

So some people might be relieved to know that Hall doesn't consider himself retired, despite a quote attributed to him in the text of Robert K. Oermann's wonderful essay that accompanies the box set: "Miss Dixie [his wife, Iris] says I'm not to use the word 'retired.' I don't see what's wrong with it."

Well, it's a relative term, Halls says from his office in Franklin, Tennessee. It's not like he's not keeping busy. He's just not out there trying to whip a single up the charts, playing county fairs, and cutting promos for the DJs to play during station breaks: "Hi, this is Tom T. Hall and you're listening to . . ."

No, it's a little different, but it's a whole lot the same. Put it this way: Hall isn't worried that you haven't heard his latest record on the radio. He isn't worried about the charts or about who's number one this week. Been there, done that.

"I'm just coming off the playing field; I'm not competing with the young boys and girls who are doing whatever they're doing," Hall says. "Nobody knows what retirement means unless you're with some corporate thing where they give you a watch. I wanted to do it in my mind; I wanted to dull that competitive edge. You see these baseball players hanging on, going to play in Japan. . . . I'd like to be one of those guys who says, 'OK, that was fun; now you guys can have it.'

"It didn't mean I was going to go lock myself in a room. I've got a lot of things I want to do."

At sixty-one, he's just finished writing his first screenplay and he's preparing to make his long-delayed acting debut. It's just a little "el cheapo" TV movie for the Nashville Network, but they asked and he was interested. Write the thing; play the old man; maybe sing a little through his nose. It was fun; he enjoyed it.

"If the phone rings and it's something you'd like to do, you go do it," he says. "It's fascinating what comes across the desk."

These days he has time to consider interesting offers like that.

"When I was hot I had offers—John Boorman wanted me to play the guy in *Deliverance* who plays the guitar for the retarded banjo player. Then they shoot me and I float down the river. I said I think I can handle that. But they wanted me for six months."

And when Tom T. Hall was hot, he didn't have six months.

What he doesn't want to be is hot again. While Hall downplays his celebrity—he doesn't care much for celebrities, to tell the truth—there was a time when he was big-time famous, a star. He's comfortable enough now, with his fans and his opportunities, the chance to make music without compromises.

For instance, *Home Grown,* the album that some people like so much, wasn't really designed for radio air play. What happened was that Mercury Records—bless 'em—gave Hall a bit of money and told him to go make the record. Never mind that he'd never produced an album before.

Hall did what he wanted—he rented a studio, recruited some of the "best acoustic musicians in the world," and turned them loose on the material.

"Radio is not going to play this album; we know that," he says. "There's an idea that everything these days has to be 'radio friendly,' so I came up with the term 'radio hostile' to describe what we were doing.

"So many of the older guys go in knowing that radio is not going to play 'em and they end up beating their brains out trying to sound like '90s guys. I thought, 'Why do that?' It just irritates me, my fans, doesn't fit in with my music or anything. Now that approach doesn't assure you of any kind of success, but it's something you're proud of and maybe you get rid of a few [records] and pay the bills. I love the album; I really like it."

It is a likable album, a throwback to the days before country music was the province of big hats playing mollified rockabilly. The first track, "Bill Monroe for Breakfast," is a hard-picked bluegrass number that features one of the longer fade-outs in memory. "Local Flowers" (written by Hall with Miss Dixie) has the grace of a Carter Family classic, and "The Way I've Always Been" is one of Hall's most affecting lyrics.

Some people think it is the best country music album released last year.

✧ ✧ ✧

He was born May 25, 1936, in a log cabin behind his grandfather's house in Tick Ridge, Kentucky, seven miles from Olive Hill. His father was a preacher who worked making bricks in a factory. Hall grew up poor but apparently dreamy, a barefoot boy who picked up a guitar when he was four years old and wrote his first song a few years later, after he overheard neighbors arguing.

"I heard him say to her, 'Why haven't I been good to you?' and I thought to myself that sounded like a country song. Now at the time I didn't know anything about writing songs; I didn't know anybody really wrote them. I thought they had a big warehouse somewhere and whenever they needed some new songs they'd just go in there and pull a few out. So I just made it up as a joke."

But soon he ended up singing the song for family and friends. When they asked where he'd heard it, young Tom T. Hall told them he heard it on the radio.

You can't listen to Hall's music without gleaning some biographical details. Even if the names are changed, all the songs sound true. They are true, even if the facts have faded. The man who ran the bar while "watching *Ironsides* on TV" in "Old Dogs, Children, and Watermelon Wine" is real, as is the kid who bums a ride in "The Hitchhiker" and the widow in "The Ballad of Forty Dollars."

Hall writes what he knows—what he has heard, seen, and experienced. Some of his songs started out as his father's stories, some of them he's lived. "Salute to a Switchblade" came out his army experiences in Germany.

Almost all the songs are autobiographical to some extent; that's the way Hall has always worked.

"A long time ago, Stonewall Jackson, the country singer, lived down around the corner from me out here in Williamson County," Hall says. "I had a little small house there. I hadn't made any records at that time; I was just writing. He said, 'Tom T., I'm going to do me a prison album; write me a song. I said, 'Well, OK.' So I go home and I tell Miss Dixie, 'Stonewall Jackson wants me to write him a prison song. I've never been in prison.' She said, "Well you been in jail, write about that.'"

While Jackson never got around to recording that album of prison songs, Hall's "A Week in a Country Jail" became a number one country hit in 1969.

"It went to number one and I began to think, 'Hey, maybe people care about where you've been and what you've done.' So I started writing more like that. That got me into—God forgive me for this cliche—but like all writers, I have to write about what I know."

Similarly, one of Hall's biggest hits (and finest songs), "The Year That Clayton Delaney Died," is a true story. The real Clayton Delaney was named Floyd Carter, and he was the most important musical influence in Hall's life. He died in 1949, the same year as Hall's mother.

"He played the honky-tonks in southern Indiana after World War II," Hall remembers. "Then he got sick; he got TB or he got lung cancer—back in those days the doctor would come in and say, 'This man is dying,' without the benefit of diagnosis. In those days people didn't hang around doctors. So whatever killed him—he was about nineteen years old."

That marked the end of Hall's childhood. At fifteen, after his father was wounded in a hunting accident, he dropped out of school and got a work permit.

✧ ✧ ✧

But Hall wasn't ready to resign himself to the drudgery of factory work. He joined a bluegrass band and started playing on the radio in Morehead, Kentucky. He later got a job as a DJ. In 1957 he joined the army for a three-year hitch, was shipped to Germany, where he ran into Elvis in the PX, and wrote a couple of songs that would have been hits had Hall recorded them.

"I figured out that in the course of a three-year enlistment the average GI would drink something like three thousand gallons of beer, so I wrote a song about that. I also wrote 'Gausthaus Rock,' which was a really big song over there—people were playing it for years after I left. I didn't know anything about copyright or anything back then, so I guess they're both in the public domain, but those were some big songs.

"That's when I figured out I could write songs. I figured if I could write for GIs I could write for the general public," he says.

But when he came home after his hitch, he didn't immediately move to Nashville to pursue a writing career. He went back to his DJ job in Morehead.

"I was pretty fatalistic about it. I thought if I was any good they'd come and find me. That was naive, but that's what I really believed."

And that's sort of what happened. A friend took a tape of Hall's material to Newkey's Music; they listened and offered Hall a nine-to-five job writing songs. On January 4, 1964, Hall moved to Nashville with less than fifty dollars in his pocket.

It didn't take him long to become one of the top songwriters in what was then a fairly cozy industry. In 1967 he began to record on his own, scoring a modest hit with "I Washed My Face in the Morning Dew," a protest song that sounded more like Bob Dylan's "Blowing in the Wind" or Pete Seeger's "If I Had a Hammer" than the lush "violins and voices" productions in vogue in Nashville at the time.

In 1968, Jeanne C. Riley recorded Hall's "Harper Valley P.T.A." It went on to sell six million copies, win a Grammy, and inspire a movie and a TV series.

Hall never recorded the song (which was remade in 1996 by Billy Ray Cyrus)—in fact, he's never recorded any of the songs he's written for other artists. It's a quirk of his, maybe a manifestation of his humility. Some people think his original recording of "Margie's at the Lincoln Park Inn" cuts the version that Bobby Bare took to the top of the charts in 1969. Some people would rather hear him sing "Itty Bitty" than listen to the Alan Jackson record.

But then, some people have a thing for Tom T. Hall.

✧ ✧ ✧

Because his songs sound effortless, unforced, there may be a tendency to downplay the craft, the talent, the genius involved. Some of Hall's songs sound like they've been around forever; they sound like folk songs, passed down from generations. Some are topical—Hall is one of the few pop songwriters who has ever been able to write about politics without sounding heavy-handed or didactic. He likes to say he is a witness, not a judge.

To that end, he used to wander around, putting himself in a position to overhear snatches of conversation, real people rubbing up against a sometimes hard world. We wear ourselves out on the world. Sometimes it's wise to take a step back.

Hall's written a few books—including the novel *The Laughing Man of Woodmont Cove* and a short-story collection called *The Acts of Life*. He wrote a children's book, too, and was going to write another one, but the publishers objected to what they perceived as gender stereotypes.

He seems more bemused than angry as he tells the story: "There are two scenes they objected to. In one, the little girl goes into her father's toolbox and steals a screwdriver for this adventure. In another scene, the children are sitting in the kitchen with their mother on Saturday morning making pancakes. They sent me back a letter asking why it had to be the father's toolbox, not the mother's. And they wanted to know, if the children and their mother were in the kitchen, where was the father? They threw me out of the children's book business. At first I thought it was a joke."

He manages to be philosophical about it.

"Oh well, I haven't done a cookbook, but I've done just about everything I've wanted to do," he says. "It's all right to be ambitious, but you've got to know what time it is, too. The other day I was listening to 'I Washed My Face in the Morning Dew.' Now I've got a line in there that says 'they were laughing at a poor crippled man.' Well, I got to thinking and, wow, I'm glad I wrote it back when I did. Man, how would I ever work in 'ambulatory-disadvantaged' if I wrote it today?"

1997

Fay Jones: Making Space Sing

Fay Jones was one of the gentlest, most impressive men I have ever met. This is an abbreviated and revised version of an essay written before he retired from the active practice of architecture in 1997.

Dickson Street in Fayetteville gives up few clues to the proximity of the architect. In front of a two-story brown-brick building that houses Underwood's jewelry store, there is a geometric, sawed-steel sculpture set off from the sidewalk.

As solid and unspectacular as a two-thousand-dollar suit, the building fits into the street without calling attention to itself. An upstairs window frames a skeletal model, a clatter of sticks in rhythm. On an upstairs wall, small metal sans serif letters spell out "EUINE FAY ONES."

Dropped *J* notwithstanding, behind the door, down a short hall, Fay Jones is waiting, unprotected by staff, in his purple Alexander Julian shirt, pressed khakis, and loafers, his back to a windowful of glacial blue Arkansas sky.

✧ ✧ ✧

Two intractable American ideals have their confluence in Jones. First is the Emersonian idea of the self-reliant individualist who develops a personal philosophy about his work and holds to it, even when others in his field are heading in an entirely different direction.

The second is as simple as the idea of craftsmanship: the scrupulously designed and carefully crafted single-family house in a setting in balance with its natural surroundings. Unlike some famous architects, Jones never designed buildings to comment on other buildings, never used architecture as an avenue for expressing abstract ideas or promoting a philosophy. He designed buildings—houses and sacred places—to be occupied by people.

He has said that it was never his goal to become a nationally known architect, that he simply tried to do a good job of solving whatever problems he encountered.

While Jones makes no extravagant claims for his buildings, his work supplies evidence that we are more than animated coagulations of blood and bone and flesh; it argues for the transcendental possibilities of the human soul.

❖ ❖ ❖

Fay Jones was born in Pine Bluff, Arkansas, on January 31, 1921, and his family soon moved south and west to El Dorado, where his parents ran a restaurant.

As a boy growing up in the Great Depression, Jones discovered an affinity for art, drawing his high school mascot on the backs of his friends' jackets. He also found himself building, in an almost intuitive fashion, tree houses and lean-tos. He used whatever scrap material he could gather and put things together as they fit. He built increasingly elaborate tree houses, including one in a giant oak, equipped with a brick fireplace and roll-up doors and screens. While this early Jones building was lost when a spark from the fireplace set it afire, he built several others.

He never imagined he might be able to combine his two avocations into a career—no architects practiced in El Dorado in those years and most buildings were built in a rudimentary, straightforward way.

Then, in 1938, Jones went to a Saturday movie matinee that included a Popular Science short about Frank Lloyd Wright's nearly completed Johnson Wax building in Racine, Wisconsin, with its Pyrex glass partitions and curving brick walls. It made Jones think of Flash Gordon or Buck Rogers. He realized he wanted to become an architect, and he knew which one he most wanted to meet.

He went to the University of Arkansas fully intending to pursue this goal, but when he got there he found there was no school of architecture, just some classes offered in the school of engineering. He enrolled, but in 1941, a month before the Japanese attacked Pearl Harbor, he withdrew from the university and joined the navy, becoming a pilot.

While still a naval officer, Jones met and wooed Mary Elizabeth "Gus" Knox, a Hot Springs native, who still keeps his office books. After the war, Jones returned to the University of Arkansas, the first student to sign up for the newly created architecture program started by John Williams, a recent graduate of Oklahoma A&M.

It wasn't long afterward that Jones managed to meet his favorite architect. It's the sort of story that—coming from anyone other than this surpassingly modest man—might be dismissed as self-mythologizing.

It was in the spring of 1949, the year the American Institute of Architects had at last selected Wright to receive its highest honor, the Gold Medal. It was to be presented to Wright during the AIA annual convention, which was to be held that year in Houston—driving distance for Williams and a group of University of Arkansas students. Even though they couldn't afford to register for the convention, they drove down to hang around the periphery of the convention, hoping to draw some "informal contact" with some of the architects.

Jones remembers that one of the buildings in Houston the architecture students wanted to see was the Shamrock Hotel, a brand-new structure that had been featured in *Life* magazine. It was a skyscraper on the outskirts of town, and while it wasn't hosting the architects' convention, it threw a lavish grand opening party the same week, complete with Hollywood stars like John Wayne, Pat O'Brien, Dorothy Lamour, and Robert Preston.

On the eve of the convention, the officers of the AIA decided to hold a private reception for their Gold Medal honoree at the Shamrock. And Jones and his fellow students "and half of Houston" decided to drive out to see what the fuss was all about.

Jones and company more or less sneaked into the reception, then thought better of it and retreated into a back hallway. Just then a set of padded doors burst open and a small man wearing a cape and a porkpie hat emerged.

While the students pressed against the wall of the narrow hallway to give Frank Lloyd Wright and his entourage plenty of room to pass, the great man walked up to them, stuck out his hand, and introduced himself.

"I said, 'We know who you are, Mr. Wright; we're architecture students from the University of Arkansas,'" Jones remembers. About that time an AIA official came out to fetch Wright back to the party.

But Wright said he intended to take a look around the building. He took Jones by the arm and announced that he was going to take these architecture students on a tour of the building.

"I was kind of like his Charlie McCarthy, his prop," Jones remembers.

✧ ✧ ✧

After graduating from the University of Arkansas, Jones accepted a fellowship at Rice University in Houston. From 1951 to 1953, he taught architecture at the University of Oklahoma, where, through the intercession of department chairman Bruce Goff, he encountered Wright again at a small faculty dinner. Wright invited Jones to visit his Taliesin West complex near Phoenix, and during the school's Easter break, Jones made the drive.

Soon the invitation was expanded as Wright invited the entire Jones family, which then included two daughters, to spend the summer with Wright and his Taliesin fellows at the Taliesin complex in Green Spring, Wisconsin.

From 1953 until Wright died in 1959, Jones and his family spent the summers with Wright and the Taliesin fellows.

Unlike most of Wright's students, Jones was already an architect, so he spent relatively little time on the domestic chores to which Wright routinely assigned his apprentices. Instead of hoeing fields or washing dishes, Jones worked in Wright's drawing room. His first summer there he worked on the plans for the Price Tower, a charmingly absurd skyscraper Wright built in the small town of Bartlesville, Oklahoma.

Jones says he never experienced the famous Wright temper or the egotism other former students have reported. Instead, he was impressed with Wright's gentle charm and prodigious talent as well as the intellectual atmosphere Wright cultivated at Taliesin.

It was Wright who convinced Jones to return to Arkansas. Jones lamented that he missed the hills of his native state and that, though he enjoyed his colleagues at the University of Oklahoma, he felt dislocated.

"Why not go back to Arkansas?" Wright counseled. "It is not as spoiled as the rest of the country. You can build there."

So, in 1953, Jones returned to Fayetteville, to teach and to "test his ideas in the real world." He expected to remain primarily a teacher, to practice during summers and breaks, maybe build a house or three every year.

It wasn't long before Jones's work was noticed in several national publications, including *House Beautiful.* National recognition brought Jones letters of inquiry from all over the country. During his more than forty years as a working architect, Jones designed approximately two hundred houses. While many of the early ones are concentrated in the low hills of Fayetteville, his architectural stature soon brought him inquiries from all over the country.

Yet there is Arkansas in most of his work—at least most of his projects would seem at home here. When he came back, he says, he began to develop some ideas about the kind of architecture best suited to a place like Arkansas. He says he looked around and discovered the things that seemed most honest to him were "the barns." They seemed to be at home with the rolling Ozark landscape.

Jones began to strip away layers of his formal education, to look at the things that were most natural and basic. All his training had taught him to fit buildings to the contours of the land—to think about things like orientation and sun control. And he thought about building with indigenous materials, about solving whatever particular problems the site presented with the most straightforward solution.

Jones decided if a building was responsive to its surroundings then it naturally fit the region. He combined an engineer's precise geometry with an especial concern for the building's integrity with its environment. He took what he found useful from Wright, but never slavishly followed the master's dicta.

In 1958, the year before Wright died, Jones invited him to Fayetteville to speak. He says he dreaded Wright's judgment when he took the old man to look at the house Jones had designed and built for himself.

Wright looked at the house, then told Jones, as he moved his hands back and forth horizontally, "I always seem to do it like this."

Then the old man chopped his hands up and down vertically. "You do it like that. Do more of that. I like the drip."

✧ ✧ ✧

Jones's buildings evoke something of the spirit of Wright, yet it would be wrong to cast him as an inheritor of the Wright style. Jones's work has sometimes been described as "Ozark Gothic," an allusion to the classical elements apparent in much of his work, especially his ecclesiastic buildings such as Thorncrown and Cooper Chapels.

"Jones' architecture begins in order and ends in mystery," Robert Adams Ivy Jr., an architect and architecture critic, writes. "His buildings, which employ rock-solid materials arrayed with geometric precision, inevitably connect one specific place with natural laws and ultimately with larger, ineffable truths."

Over the years, Jones's own pragmatic style has evolved, grounded in the "organic" fundamentals articulated by Wright, but also informed by other architects and free of dogma. Something of Jones's own character has asserted itself. While even his earliest houses show signs of departure from Wright, Jones moved further and further away from any Wrightian "style."

It is difficult to guess how much of this is the result of a conscious weaning away, how much has been a natural creeping away, and how much stemmed from Wright's own encouragement. Jones says that when Wright looked at his house and chopped his hands up and down, the student didn't quite see what the master was getting at.

But Thorncrown Chapel, the little twenty-four-foot-wide-by sixty-foot-long sacred space Jones built in the woods outside Eureka Springs, makes the point quite clearly. Thorncrown recalls Wright only in its elegance and use of indigenous materials. It could not have been imagined by any Wright copyist.

Jones is widely recognized as an artist of the first rank. In 1991, Thorncrown Chapel was voted the best American building since 1980 by the American Institute of Architects. In 1990, Jones himself was awarded the AIA Gold Medal, the highest honor an architect can achieve.

Unlike some who studied under Wright in his rural compounds, Jones resisted becoming an architectural cultist or a Wright mimic. He instead absorbed the underlying principles of Wright's work, using them to create remarkably satisfying houses that are not clones of the master. While Jones's buildings generally adhere to the tenets of Wright's philosophy by weighing such factors as the character of the materials employed, the affinity of the building with its site, and the relationship of each part to the whole, they are not calibrated to Wrightian specifications. In Jones's work there is a hard geometry and some whimsical ornamentation that might not have passed muster with Wright. Jones occasionally employed deliberately contrarian ideas in an attempt to "move off dead center."

He used what he needed of Wright's principles but sometimes found it helpful to contravene them—so long as breaking the rules made sense and served the building.

"Sometimes I would rather use strong, high, delineating light rather than straight-in horizontal light," Jones says. "You're still working with the characteristics of light, you're still dealing with what is fundamental and elemental in the whole thing, but you're trying to express it in a somewhat different way."

So while some of Wright's houses can be absurdly dark, Jones's designs generally feature skylights or clerestory windows to bring plenty of light directly into the core of the home.

His approach to roofs—traditionally a problem in Wright's houses—is also markedly different. While Wright preferred flat, low roofs, Jones employs large overhanging structures that snap downward like folded wings. Jones's characteristic long, prominent sloping roof with a deep overhang evokes a reassuring sense of shelter and at the same time affords immense practicality: It keeps walls dry, deflects wind from the windows and doors, and prevents the interior from being overheated by the sun.

Jones's career is easily understood; he has committed himself to a series of enduring ideas instead of accommodating himself to the fashion of the day. Bauhausism and Deconstructivism and other fads never laid a glove on him.

His work speaks for itself—and for the human condition.

"Architecture is not just building," Jones says. "It's not just some theory. Architecture is space and light and form and balance and scale, and then it's people's response to the reality of architecture.... It is fundamental that something is built of good materials, that it is structurally sound and safe and all those things. But that's good building, that's not architecture.

"Architecture has got to transcend mere construction, it has got to be expressive of something more than just mere accommodation. It's not just caught up in stylistic fetters; in the finer sense it has got to get into the realm of the human spirit and to transcend technical correctness and functional achievement. That puts it in the realm of art."

1993

The Heretic's Song: Tom Wolfe's Latest South

Tom Wolfe is nothing if not ambitious; he wants to be nothing less than the American Tolstoy, though one suspects he'd settle for Dickens if the compensation package is better.

The dandy in the ice-cream suit with the seven-million-dollar advance has already secured a place in the history of American letters by his avocation and his practice of what came to be called New Journalism in the '60s and '70s. And having set journalism straight—or awry, as straight journalists usually would have it—Wolfe decided to inflict his vision of what the American novel should be on the world at large.

First, in 1987, there was *Bonfire of the Vanities,* a sprawling book about an arrogant Wall Street investment banker (one of the "Masters of the Universe") who was served his comeuppance in a roiling nightmare of racial politics and bad luck. It was a wild, well-observed ride, filled with teeming detail, that invited comparison to Trollope's busy nineteenth-century "ant colony" novels that purported to show every strata of society. If Wolfe wasn't exactly deep, at least he was sharp—he sliced up the sociocultural pretensions of the big bam boom '80s like a surgeon on methamphetamine.

And then he went further.

To back up his bestseller, to lend it the ballast of literary theory, he published a blithe and bubbly twenty-nine-thousand-word manifesto in *Harper's* called "The Billion-Footed Beast" in which he proposed the American novel should be wrought from "a highly detailed realism based on reporting"—just like *Bonfire of the Vanities.* Wolfe expressed impatience with novelists who seemed to be more concerned with the interior lives of characters than with "the metropolis or any other big, rich slices of contemporary life." Wolfe complained that American fiction had "abandoned realism" for "literary games" such as minimalism or the Raymond Carver–Gordon Lish school.

The antidote for this navel-gazing, Wolfe declared, was a robust interest in the way things work. Only by going out and utilizing the skills of the reporter could the novelist hope to reinvigorate American fiction. All those slim gray works, those nagging, neurotic excavations of the self, were sterile and limp, and they were killing the American novel.

To resuscitate the novel, Wolfe lectured, one would have to follow the example of Emile Zola, whose "documentation trips" took him into the coal mines of northern France. Wolfe invoked the muckraking spirit of Sinclair Lewis and argued it was reportorial detail more than psychological blathering that lent the novel its power to involve and engross readers—"the *petits faits vrais* (little true things) that create verisimilitude and make a novel gripping or absorbing."

More remarkably, Wolfe went on to declare that "no one was ever moved to tears by reading about the unhappy fates of heroes and heroines in Homer, Sophocles, Moliere, . . . or Shakespeare."

Really?

✧ ✧ ✧

But if Wolfe's literary ideas might seem a bit unconventional—or even heretical—he might be granted at least a few points. *Bonfire of the Vanities* was a rich and compelling book, a kind of joy ride for the mind. It was sleek and funny and it moved as fast as a John Grisham legal thriller and with the preciseness of one of Tom Clancy's late–Cold War era munitions manuals. It was fun. It was smart. And if you weren't paying close attention you might have even mistaken it for a great novel. Some people thought it was. Tom Wolfe, for instance.

There was nothing wrong with *Bonfire of the Vanities*—except it wasn't really realistic. It was more like a movie reduced to words than a novel of great insight. Had Wolfe not picked a fight with the American novelists, there would be no reason to criticize it. But he had, so a few things needed to be said.

The avant-garde minimalism Wolfe found so objectionable was already in recession by the time he published his manifesto. What was literary realism if it wasn't John Updike's Rabbit Angstrom books? What was Richard Ford's *The Sportswriter?* American fiction has had its dry patches, and to be sure there were a lot of fey little books in the '80s—all those shiny Vintage paperbacks—but for the most part those books had as little impact as they had blood.

Bonfire of the Vanities was a good book, but to insist on its importance is to oversell it. It was flashy and sensational, and the characters were all archetypes that the author—the real master of that richly imagined universe— moved about at will. Compare Sherman McCoy to Harry "Rabbit" Angstrom or to Frank Bascombe? McCoy is a emblem, he stands for the sucking greed and presumption of privilege that we associated with wheeler-dealer financial masters of the '80s. Rabbit and Frank are, well, guys—more or less average men with complex emotional entanglements and real strengths and weaknesses. They are, for better or worse, more real than Sherman McCoy. And their worlds—the books they inhabit—are, for better or worse, more realistic.

Tom Wolfe is magnificent, a wonderful writer, an entertaining novelist—but he is not a realistic one.

✧ ✧ ✧

What is interesting is that Wolfe—a sensational figure, the last living literary fop—seems to genuinely think that life is as spiked with vulgarity and gaudiness as his books. Perhaps this is the way the reporter looks at life from a fourteen-room Upper East Side apartment with a view of Central Park. Maybe life is like that for Tom Wolfe, but most of us live a less fevered existence. For us, reading *Bonfire of the Vanities* or Wolfe's latest, *A Man in Full,* is more like watching an episode of *Lifestyles of the Rich and Famous* than reviewing our own calendars. Wolfe's novels invite us to vicarious experiences, the same way good mysteries or detective fiction can.

None of this would be worth thinking about were Wolfe not so much the white-hot writer of the moment. His *A Man in Full* is another bestseller, 750 pages, a big, noisy blockbuster book. Unlike most bestsellers, it seems likely that most people who buy the book will actually end up reading it—it is compulsively readable, juicy and cinematic, and ultimately unchallenging. Like *Bonfire of the Vanities,* there is nothing very wrong with it as a ripping read.

But it's not as good as Wolfe and a lot of critics seem to think. It is pumped-up pulp—albeit pulp informed by a genuinely fine reportorial talent. That's great, or at least it would be if Wolfe weren't being seriously touted as Dickens's heir by the likes of *Time,* the *Washington Post,* and *Newsweek.*

"Right now, no writer—reporter or novelist—is getting [America] on paper better than Tom Wolfe," *Newsweek* gushed; *Time* weighed in with a review that concluded that "no summary of *A Man in Full* can do justice to the novel's ethical nuances." The *New York Times* offered the opinion that Wolf had, in *A Man in Full,* written "passages as powerful and as beautiful as anything written not merely by contemporary American novelists but by any American novelist."

But the sensibility that drives *A Man in Full* is not really a literary sensibility; that is to say Wolfe seems relatively unconcerned with the explication of the "little true things" that complicate the human situation and drive the human heart. He's interested in big, loud things, noisy situations, and he employs larger-than-life archetypes rather than characters. *A Man in Full* has more in common with a Middle English morality play than it does with *Anna Karenina* or *Bleak House*. *A Man in Full* is, above all, an unsubtle book. For all its snaking plotlines, it is not complex—it is essentially a simple story about simple people told in a style that suggests complexity without ever delivering it.

✧ ✧ ✧

A Man in Full is a 750-page novel that can be read in a couple of sittings; it has the same holding power as a well-made Hollywood film. Steven Spielberg would be the perfect director for this project, much better than the art-happy Brian De Palma, who directed the failed (but not genuinely bad) film version of *Bonfire of the Vanities.* But then Wolfe's book hardly needs a movie version, he's already stocked it with immediately tagable "characters": the arrogant and viral real-estate tycoon, the black lawyer who seems white, the ghetto athlete poised to make millions in the pros, the poor but honest young man in reaction to his hippie upbringing, the trophy wife, etc.

He's given a lot of these characters vaguely Dickensian names: Charlie Croker, Raymond Peepgass, Buck McNutter, Fareek Fanon, Wismer Stroock. Wolfe has made a study of the assonances of Dickens's nomenclature and adapted them to late-twentieth-century America. But these characters seem capable of signifying only one emotion at a time; their dynamic range is limited—even in the book we recognize them as sturdy but basically utilitarian types.

Wolfe's story revolves around sixty-year-old Charlie Croker, a former college football player whose appetites are as prodigious as his girth. Croker is the Atlanta real-estate tycoon whose empire is in danger of crashing down under the weight of his hubris—he has sunk too much of his own money into an immense and nearly vacant office complex called Croker Concourse. He owes the bank $500 million and the bankers are getting nervous.

As Croker struggles to hang onto his precious, twenty-nine-thousand-acre quail-shooting retreat (called "Turpmtine" in imitation of slave parlance) and his Gulfstream 5 jet, a local black football hero—Fanon, nicknamed "the Cannon"—is being accused of date rape by the daughter of an extraordinarily wealthy power broker. The mayor of Atlanta offers Croker a deal—if he'll speak up for Fanon and help avoid what the mayor sees as a possible racial conflagration, then perhaps the city can help Croker with his problems.

There are several subplots, and all of them are intriguing. Wolfe gets to show off a lot of what he knows about various topics, such as rap music (turns out he doesn't know too much about that), the conditions in food-service warehouses, corporate jets, and bank "work-out sessions." Much of it is impressive, but about three-quarters of the way through the need to bring the subplots together causes the novel to creak and sway a bit. Wolfe can't sustain the energy and—unlike Updike—apparently can't simply jack up his knowledge to Ph.D. level anytime he wills it. So the novel ends on a relatively unsatisfying note, afflicted by convenient coincidence and unconvincing shifts in worldview.

Like an early experimental aircraft, *A Man in Full* flies for a while before sputtering and quaking and finally—"crashes" is too violent a word—touching down and pitching forward, dead and failed. The pilot clambers out, waving his cap, cursing gravity.

1999

Encounters and Equivocations

Father's Day

There are things that I try to remember, things that elude me. They squirt through my mind like drops of mercury; they haunt the corners of my peripheral inner vision, nagging yet reticent. I can remember the old houses, the sharp smells of wet dog and wool, the crunch of snow, and the tender nap of flannel pajamas, but names and places and circumstances are much harder to recall.

Yet I persist. I close my eyes and try not to grab hold of the first easy, saving word. I try to dissolve the code, to reach back to the faint colors stirring deep in my muddy-bottomed brain. It's all in there, the doctors say, everything we've seen and felt, every sound, everything noticed and unnoticed, all the clues.

They say that we can retrieve the pertinent facts and feelings, that we can talk ourselves clear of the tangling rubble of the past and be free. They say that it is good to do this, to escape the gravitational pull of the past, to establish ourselves as beings independent of the hurt and damage our parents (however inadvertently) inflicted upon us. Remember Philip Larkin's lines?

> *They fuck you up, your mom and dad*
> *They may not mean to, but they do*
> *They fill you with the faults they had*
> *And add some extra, just for you*

I doubt I would know of Philip Larkin had it not been for my father, who read him and in whose books I first found those lines. In retrospect it seems strange that my father should have had such a book—the only poet I can remember him ever mentioning was Kipling, the only lines I ever heard him quote were from Tennyson's "Charge of the Light Brigade."

I close my eyes and I can hear him, softly reciting, "Half a league, half a league, half a league onward . . ."

He learned the poem at Belmont Abbey, the North Carolina prep school he attended on scholarship. He was a poor boy, more accurately a poor relation, but he could run and throw. He never knew his own father, or his brother's father. He played on the same American Legion baseball team as Jimmy Hall, who set a rookie record for home runs when he came up with

135

the Minnesota Twins in 1963. He was a shortstop most of his life—he was a soldier, an intelligence officer, an altar boy. I remember his rough hands and the way the stubble on his chin scratched me when he hugged me. I remember the way he could snap a baseball through bright air, how he could make the ball seem a humming, vibrating, living thing.

I remember the blue haze of his cigarette smoke. I can remember the wartime absences and the gray and yellow-striped queerness of an early morning tarmac, the earth-rattling roar of B-52s, and the emptied belly of a KC-135. I remember the old bathtub-white Thunderbird he had for a while and the blue suit I "borrowed" from him while I was in high school. Details swarm together and for an instant form a picture; just as quickly they float away like ashes.

There are tangibles—I have his baseball glove. In my mother's house there is a drawer full of military ribbons, old watches, Zippo lighters, all the paraphernalia of a certain kind of masculine existence. I am in possession of the facts; I could make the dates fit together; I can recall specific moments, days. There are photographs. There is evidence, documentation—no one goes through the world without leaving a mark.

❖ ❖ ❖

I am, for better or worse, my father's mark.

I am, I suppose, more of the part of him that read Larkin than the part that gripped wrenches and baseballs, but the older I grow the more I remind myself of him. I am now not much younger than he was when he died, and I think that men whose fathers die young acquire a certain fatalism. I look like his photos; I imagine that I feel some of the same things he must have felt.

It is difficult to know how much we can attribute to our fathers, how much to our mothers, how much to the crowd we happened to have fallen in with, how much to the blood, and how much to the secret small voices within each of us. We are tricky and complex and not easily reducible to component parts.

Here I am, near the end of this bloodiest century, and I am missing a man I have not seen for sixteen years. Even now I dream of my father and wake in quiet sorrow that he is not here. Sometimes I think I should not be surprised to pick up the phone and hear his voice. Sometimes I think I expect that.

Perhaps a personal past is nothing more than a myth, an assumptive narrative we create for ourselves to give our unruly lives a sense of order and purpose. Our stories are the way we justify ourselves to the world, the way we justify ourselves to ourselves.

When I say I remember my father I wonder if I am not ascribing to him qualities he would not claim for himself. Would he think of himself as a kind man, a quiet man, a strong man? I must admit that I am not sure—my father was not one to talk much about himself, much less about how he viewed himself. If he constructed a private biography for himself, he kept it private.

I do not remember my father talking much, though I hear his voice—his inflections, his hesitancy, a little vocal catch that signals his groping for the right word—in my own. I have made his mispronunciations my own; I have assimilated his gestures and, they tell me, his smile.

Near the end, my father told some stories, stories about growing up in Asheville, about his single professional boxing match, about a cobra and a Jeep in the jungles of Thailand. These stories were offered more as anecdotes than as answers, as scraps of information from which we might patch together a kind of comfort, a quilt in which to wrap us. They weren't meant to explain; at the time there seemed nothing to explain other than the large mystery of why people are born to die and why dying sometimes has to hurt so much.

I think in a way I was glad for him when he finally gave out, when the suffering was over. But maybe it wasn't like that, maybe I was more selfish than that, maybe I was tired of the hospital smell and the waiting. Maybe I was not as good a son as I might have been.

This is hard for me to think about, to think that I might have wished him dead for selfish reasons. I know that I could not help it, that awful thoughts breeze through the minds of saints. But I think about it and I wonder if I let him down.

It would not have been the first time, though we never had the break that some sons and fathers have. I loved him and he loved me and things were never so difficult that we couldn't talk.

I think we could be friends today, that he would like me and the life I've made. I think he would be OK with how things turned out. And, oh, I miss him sometimes, but I'm not sad when I remember him, and in the end I suppose that is all that we can hope.

1999

Homecomings

It was an accident of nativity that put "Savannah" on my passport. I can claim this city as my birthplace—the hospital I was born in is now a museum—and my mother's hometown, but it would be romantic to assert a deeper connection. I only lived here a few months before being swept away to upstate New York, and I haven't been back in nearly thirty years. Since then Georgia, for me, has been that long shadowless walk through the Atlanta airport.

There are reasons I have not been back, and most of those reasons are selfish. I have been busy and I seem to lack the familial instinct that drives one to reunions and the like.

It is more than that: Even as a child I never felt completely at ease with my mother's people, especially my mother's brothers. They seemed ever volatile, charged with a pregnant gloom that might at any moment darkly erupt. Some of that, no doubt, was the perhaps wistful workings of a childish imagination, a mingling of the observed and the conjured-up. I imagined my uncles were outlaw men. When I last saw them they were younger than I am now—whiskey-breathed sumbucks with sandpaper beards and scabbards attached to their thick country belts. To tell the truth, those farm boys scared me then.

It wasn't all confabulation. There were disappointments and minor legal scrapes and a few sad accidents. They grew up working tobacco fields and weren't going to do it when they'd grown; after my grandfather died they began selling off his land, allowing the woods to take back the fields. Businesses were attempted and abandoned, jobs secured and inevitably lost. I heard about these setbacks from my mother, who for thirty years served as my ambassador to Georgia, passing on my regards and channeling the necessary news. At her house in Louisiana, she received the occasional passing-through relative, and every year she went back for a couple of weeks.

Then, a year ago, my mother retired. Last summer she contracted to build a house near the airport in Savannah. She moved in November and I knew that a trip back was inevitable. We'd have to see the new house; we'd have to make an obligatory trip west to Bulloch County, through the smothering Georgia dark, to the old home place, to visit my grandmother and whoever else might be gathered at her place.

We left, after supper, fortified by a couple of glasses of wine, my mother at the wheel of her flash Cadillac; she was a first-class tour guide, pointing out points of interest in what otherwise might have seemed an eerily empty night. The woods were full of ghosts and cousins I had never met.

For a few miles we picked up the interstate, and when we exited a wave of longing and trepidation slapped me square. I was on familiar, uncomfortable ground: I knew where the vanished gas station–country store had stood. I knew where the creek sometimes flooded to make a swimming hole. To the right was a part in the pines wide enough to drive a car. This was the road to the old house, still unpaved after all these years, a landing strip of packed clay and sand.

A county sign announced the name I never knew it had: Seedtick Road. We drove down it a little ways and on the left was a little brick ranch house: Granny's place.

"Drive down a little further," I asked. "I want to see where the old house stood."

"The new owners rebuilt it," my mother said.

It was only about a quarter-mile down the road. It had been bricked and streamlined and seemed smaller than I remembered. The barn with the hogs was gone, as was the cornfield across the road. There had been a pasture and a smokehouse and a chicken coop and on the other side of the house the beginnings of the tobacco fields that ran almost the length of the road. Now, it looked like an abortive subdivision—there was a lonely looping drive and a single house off in the distance.

"There was a tobacco barn over there," I said. The fields went for a couple of miles down this road. At the end of the road is a cemetery.

✧ ✧ ✧

Granny's house was tight with cigarette smoke and the close smells of old ladies; everywhere was fragrance and reek. Food simmered in pots; untethered children scrambled underfoot. There were hugs and introductions, and walls covered with dark paneling and hung with what seemed like hundreds of mismatched photographs: my high school graduation photo, a family portrait when I was a sophomore in high school, photos of my mother, her sisters, her brothers—a Chasen's wall full of familiars and strangers. Some of the photographs were thirty years old, some were much older.

One of my mother's sisters told me that from time to time one of the family would go through the photos on Granny's wall, harvesting the ex's and the most preposterous hairstyles. Granny would never take a photo down; you had to fend for yourself.

After a while it felt like a spice hold in there, the warmth laced the air with flavors. Gingerly as astronauts we stepped out the back into a night that seemed as black and fathomless as deep space. We gulped thin, bracing air and slipped back inside for the finale.

Thirty years is a long time, long enough to round off hard faces, to loosen jowls and pad cheekbones. It is long enough to turn wild young men into watery-eyed old men. I saw my Uncle Buddy, kittenish and mild and nursing a plastic tumbler of sweet iced tea as he watched Jimmy Stewart on the big-screen TV. I understand he means no one any harm; I doubt he ever did.

My Uncle Mike—who's only a couple of years older than me—was there as well, with his new (to me, at least) wife and his old kids. He seemed genuinely glad to see me, and I found myself surprised to realize that I was genuinely glad to see him as well. We learned that Mandy was up in Macon—he's got a job there—and that though Roy's trailer was just a few yards away, he didn't much care for crowds so we weren't likely to see him this night. I nodded, because I understood that.

We only stayed about an hour; one of my aunts gave us a Christmas gift and another squared my shoulders and looked me dead in the face.

"You haven't changed," she said. "You haven't changed at all."

And all the time I was thinking, "No, ma'am, I have changed. I'm changing all the time. Sometimes I think it's all I really do."

2000

Vermeer and the Left-Handed Epistemologist

There is some evidence that Jan Vermeer painted with the aid of a camera obscura; that he sometimes used this device that allowed him to project an image on his canvas and then copy it in a paint-by-number fashion. Vermeer is believed by some to have turned a whole room into a camera obscura to paint his famous *View of Delft,* the only landscape he is known to have painted and, by acclamation, his greatest achievement.

Some art historians suspect Vermeer may have "cheated" in this manner because they detect in Vermeer's work telltale "disks of confusion," little circles of colored light that are the result of light bending through an unsophisticated lens.

Look at an object with the naked eye and you will see the object. Bend light through raw lenses and you will see sparkling highlights where the focus slips, and foreground aspects may appear exaggerated. (If you cheat with a camera obscura, Vermeer, we will catch you.)

Ironically, what the modern audience values most in Vermeer's work is the uncanny objectivity with which the artist was able to record the eye's experience. We look at how he rendered the soft play of daylight on his subjects, at a kind of photographic precision (achieved despite the sometimes rough layering of his paint), and wonder. How could the painter's mind contain such detail? How could he see so much?

Despite his alleged use of optical assistance, Vermeer's genius is real. It does not lie in his mechanically aided ability to reproduce the tangle of light that plays on the human retina, but in the ineffable quality with which he invests his subjects. The atoms of his paintings hum.

Vermeer creates a world just out of phase with our expectation—he almost imperceptibly skews his world toward beauty. Vermeer shows us a world that very nearly exists, the soft-focused world of the dazzled.

For all the miracles he painted, Vermeer's fabled objectivity is a lie—as are all things that pretend to know the way things really are.

Recently I read a provocative sentence, said to be the first sentence of a physics textbook. I approximate it: "All progress mankind has ever made can be attributed to the careful taking of measurements."

Science is not much more than belief in measurements, a faith in the actual that is no less brave for its dourness. Science assumes that some things—actually, quite a few things—are knowable. Science presumes there are forces we can rely on, certain immutable laws that govern the universe. Maybe you know some of them:

Matter can be neither created nor destroyed.
Bodies in motion tend to remain in motion; bodies at rest tend to remain at rest.
What goes up must come down.
The sun rises in the east and sets in the west.

These are things we can depend on, if we can depend on anything, if we have faith in science, if we believe in "facts."

You might think it is dangerous for a journalist to put the word "facts" in quotes; a journalist suspicious of facts is sort of like a carpenter who doubts his planks and hammers. Why even raise the question? What happens when we lose our faith in facts?

Maybe "facts" are something different from facts, which may very well be mythological creatures. Now truth is a different matter; truth is something worth believing in, but are facts that fail to serve the truth facts at all?

It is a fact that O. J. Simpson is legally not guilty. It is a fact that one of this country's most pressing issues is whether seven-year-old girls should be allowed to fly—and to crash—airplanes. It is a fact that, as the millennium approaches, more and more of us will find ourselves hunkering in bunkers in vast, indifferent places like Montana or Stone County, fear quickening in our veins.

✧ ✧ ✧

I have a friend who is an epistemologist as well as a left-handed pitcher. He is my teammate on an over-thirty baseball team. He is interested in both how the human animal drugs itself with certainty and how tightly he must spin a baseball so that it will break at just the right point to fool a batter. His spectrum of concern embraces both the esoteric and the practical; it is probably not too much to say that he is a typical lefty, a philosopher-technician looking for ways to corroborate the facts.

A few weeks ago he sent me an e-mail message—it started on his computer screen, then zipped through phone lines to a big computer somewhere

(I imagine) in the Northeast. Then I turned on my computer, dialed my service, and fetched down from that electronic harbor my new e-mail.

His question asked whether, as an opinion journalist, I was ever persuaded to take a position on an issue based simply on the quality of the sentences I could craft in support of that position (actually, he said it more gracefully, but I have allowed the original version to blow away in some cyber wind). In other words, which comes first, language or idea?

I honestly do not know. I know that sometimes it is tempting to adopt a position that allows full enjoyment of a joke, that there are times when contrarianism for contrarianism's sake seems a useful strategy. I think it is interesting of my friend to ask me this question when there seems so little of which I am sure—I know that it is sometimes hard to get at exactly what I want to say. Yet what I want to say is rarely blunt and hardly ever certain.

I use the words to find the meaning. I know that there are things I believe and things I can't know, that—as Whittaker Chambers said—man without mysticism is a monster, and that—as Stevie Wonder said—superstition ain't the way.

Another fact or two: Vermeer died poor and left eleven children. His widow declared bankruptcy. Vermeer's will named the artist's friend Antony van Leewenhoek, inventor of the microscope and discoverer of the paramecium, executor of his estate. Art historians speculate that an interest in optics brought the two men together.

I often think of Vermeer and his "objectivity"—the "facts" surrounding his *View of Delft*. And I can look at what he did and, even suspecting he had help from science, find something surpassingly enriching in his not-quite-factual accomplishment.

Beauty exists; it is real, as real as dreams.

1996

Curt Flood

I used to have a baseball card of Curt Flood, a 1970 Topps. The photo on the front of the card was a close-up of the player's head and shoulders, taken from a low angle so that the gray underside of the cap's bill was visible but not the embroidered team logo.

The people at Topps chose this shot because Flood had been photographed in the uniform of the St. Louis Cardinals, the team for which he'd played a dozen seasons, and had been traded to the Philadelphia Phillies during the off-season. While this might not pose a problem in the digital age, when any photograph can be manipulated to show anything (today they could put Curt Flood in an astronaut suit or give him a pair of Bruno Magli shoes), back then the baseball-card people could only instruct their photographers to take "safety photos" of players who might be traded, avoiding identifiable team logos. That way, if a player was traded during the off-season, it was possible to avoid the embarrassment of showing a new Philadelphia Phillie in the uniform of his old team. Such things seemed important then, at least to the eleven-year-old boys who were the primary consumers of baseball cards.

It was mildly surprising that Topps would have a safety shot of Flood; in 1969 he didn't seem particularly likely to be traded. He was a fixture in the Cardinal outfield, an elegant center fielder who batted over .300 seven times and led the league in hits in 1964. A three-time All-Star and a seven-time Gold Glove winner, he playedfor two world champions (and were it not for Jim Northrop's fly ball that Flood misplayed in the seventh inning of the seventh game of the 1968 World Series, he might have played for a third). Though he had played eight games for the Cincinnati Reds at the beginning of his career, there was no player more emblematic of those scrappy, scientific Cardinal teams of the '60s than Curt Flood.

But he was traded, along with catcher Tim McCarver, in a deal that brought troubled Phillie slugger Richie (later "Dick") Allen to the Cardinals. Topps scrambled to produce the card I used to own, showing an unbranded Flood in his neutralized uniform, a man between teams.

Flood refused to report to the Phillies. Maybe it was because the Phillies were a bad team, both on the field and in the front office, perennial losers who played before perpetually ill-tempered fans. Maybe he sensed injustice in a system that treated men like chattel. Baseball's reserve clause bound a player to the team that originally signed him for the duration of his career. While the team could trade the player to another team, once a player had signed his first professional contract there was no mechanism by which he could ever offer his services to the highest bidder or decide he would rather play for one team rather than another. Flood didn't want to go to Philadelphia, but the reserve clause kept him from pursuing his livelihood anywhere else.

Flood asked then-commissioner Bowie Kuhn—an employee of the baseball owners—to declare him a free agent and was summarily turned down. He then filed a lawsuit, claiming that baseball had violated antitrust laws.

He sat out the entire 1970 season, living the life of an expatriate painter in Denmark while his case wound through the courts. The Phillies and Cardinals worked out their trade, and after the 1970 season, the Phillies dealt Flood to the expansive Washington Senators. Though he agreed to come back, Flood no longer seemed to have the heart for the game. He played only thirteen games for the Senators before retiring. He was thirty-three.

In 1972, the U.S. Supreme Court ruled against Flood. Three years later, it didn't matter—an arbitrator threw out baseball's reserve clause and emancipated professional athletes. Now we all know about the ridiculous salaries athletes earn. Whether you like it or not, they do earn them. However much we bemoan spoiled professional athletes, the fact is they generate the revenue; fans wouldn't pay the inflated ticket prices if they couldn't afford or didn't want to pay them.

✧ ✧ ✧

I remember 1969. I remember people hated Curt Flood.

None of the obituaries that ran last week mentioned the general approbation that Flood's principled stand earned him. Not only were the lords of baseball and their lackeys aligned against him, but Joe Garagiola, the game's own Art Linkletter (and vicious spiker of Jackie Robinson during his playing days), testified that the elimination of the reserve clause would destroy baseball. There was a certain reactive temper that somehow construed Flood's stand as un-American, vaguely communistic. Much of Philip Roth's *Our Gang*—a very funny, extended cheap shot at the Nixon White House, disguised as a novel—concerns President Tricky Dick's attempts to blame the country's myriad troubles on "communist" Curt Flood.

I was probably more aware of the Flood situation than most eleven-year-old baseball fans because my father slightly knew Flood. They had played against each other in a couple of minor leagues in the '50s and once or twice had raced from home plate to the center-field wall as a pregame diversion for the fans. Flood always won.

My father remembered Flood as a man of ferocious dignity and reserve. He told me about a time, not many years after black players began showing up in baseball, when Flood became the first black man to play with white boys in a certain medium-sized Southern city. Though there was a half-hearted attempt to pass Flood off as Cuban, it didn't matter to some of the uglier bleacher denizens, who brought a bag of rotten vegetables with which they meant to express their displeasure at having to tolerate an opposing center fielder of color.

In the bottom of the first inning, Flood took up his position in center field and the biggest and bravest of the idiots stood up and tossed a tomato that landed at Flood's feet. Without saying a word, Flood simply turned and glared toward the stands. The tomato-flinger locked eyes with him for a moment, then melted silently into his seat.

I'm not a collector, but I wish I still had that Curt Flood baseball card.

I don't know what Flood gave up in order to fight, other than $100,000 a year in a time when that was big money. (McCarver, the player traded along with him, said it never occurred to him to challenge the status quo. It was the way things were.)

One can speculate: if he had continued to play, he might have played five or eight more years, and if he had played near the level he set in the '60s, he might have had an outside shot at three thousand hits. He probably wouldn't have got there; he probably wouldn't have had a chance at the Hall of Fame. Based on what he achieved as a player, Flood probably doesn't belong in the Hall of Fame. He was very good, but he was not great—not that way.

In his own way.

1997

Blues for Robert Palmer

Robert Palmer died November 20, 1997. He was fifty-two.

It is a shame if you don't know who he is, or if you've confused him with some other more famous Robert Palmer. It is a shame, but it is not your fault. Palmer wasn't a glamorous man, though he was often in the company of glamorous people. He was a rock critic, one of the best, a writer who understood that sometimes it is necessary to take the apparently trivial seriously. Palmer knew that any understanding of the American character was impossible without first understanding the music that common people listened to and claimed for their own; that rock 'n 'roll is not just transitory fashion but a democratic art form that could (and did) literally change the world.

After he died I fielded a couple of phone calls and e-mail messages from people who did know who he was and who wanted to know why news of his passing hadn't shown up in this newspaper the next day. I don't really know why. I'm not sure anyone does—the wire service apparently didn't move the story quickly enough for our deadlines. We got an obituary in as quickly as we could.

I knew Bob, a little. We'd talked a few times. I'd said nice things about his work in print; he'd thanked me for that. But we weren't friends—I don't have any stories to tell about him. I respected him. I envied him. He was generous with me.

Palmer was the first full-time pop music writer ever employed by the *New York Times* and one of the strongest voices to emerge from *Rolling Stone* magazine. He wrote *Deep Blues,* which is simply the best book ever about the music that crawled out of the Mississippi Delta; he put together a couple of documentary films and was the chief advisor on *Rock & Roll,* the ten-part PBS documentary that aired a couple of years ago.

He was from Little Rock, "raised and educated here," the biographical notes to *Deep Blues* read. But that education was not strictly, or even primarily, academic. In the introduction to his book, *Rock & Roll: An Unruly History,* the companion volume to the PBS series, he wrote about his days as a teenaged saxophonist in a mostly black combo playing the rough South Main Businessman's Club, just around the corner from the Ninth Street strip.

Palmer and Fred Tackett—who went on to be one of the most sought-after session guitarists in the industry—played together in another makeshift group, fronted, Palmer wrote, by two "frat men/hustlers at the local community college" who "played corny trumpet and trombone by ear."

"One thing we didn't talk about," Palmer wrote, "was what a contemporary music critic might call the astonishing eclecticism of our musical offering. There we were stirring Dixieland and surf music, rockabilly and r & b, pseudo and honky-tonk country and western into a big gumbo. We had no idea we were breaking down barriers and cross-fertilizing genres. In those days the definitions were not so firmly fixed."

Palmer was a writer who never gave in to the modern tendency to categorize and segregate musical styles—he recognized that the tendency to sort music into bins labeled "jazz," "rock," "country," etc., was driven by the need for nonmusicians to find some comfortable, nontechnical way to discuss music. And while they may have their uses, the categories are artificial boundaries usually ignored by musicians.

As a musician writing about music, Palmer sought to convey the passion and the coherency of forms that might have been unintelligible to the unreceptive ear. He was able to write about the interstices of the technical and the sublime, to communicate some of his own love of the music to a reader who hadn't heard (or hadn't really heard) the work in question. And he could illuminate—find a fresh channel of delight—in work that was imminently familiar.

He was the best at telling you what you were hearing, at explaining how and why the sounds affected you the way they did. Here's a passage from his essay "The Church of the Sonic Guitar," included in *Rock & Roll: An Unruly History*, that explains the benefits, beyond amplification, of electricification:

> *The electric guitar can merely make the instrument's single-note lines a little louder, so that the musician can solo like a saxophonist or a brass player. But once a certain volume threshold has been passed, the electric guitar becomes another instrument entirely. Its tuning flexibility can now be used to set up sympathetic resonances between the strings, so that techniques such as open tunings and barre chords can get the entire instrument humming sonorously, sustained by amplification until it becomes a representation in sound of the wonder of creation itself. . . .*
>
> *The electric guitar, once the volume has surpassed the sustain threshold, doesn't just "ring." It also produces overtones, sum and difference tones, interference patterns and other acoustical phenomena. Variant tunings bring particular aspects of these phenomena to the fore, as in the work of Sonic Youth and similar bands who have learned to write melodious, memo-*

rable pop tunes without recourse to conventional harmony. In rock of this sort, acoustical effects can become so pronounced that they seem to "eat," or cancel out, the original tones whose interactions produced them. But underlying all of these more or less unstable tonal relationships is an unchanging mathematics of resonance and vibration, a system of ratios or tonal proportions that not only exists independently in nature but may underlie reality itself. The idea that "nature is vibration" is the basis of ancient Indian and Chinese metaphysics, has been an underground tradition in Western thought since Pythagoras, and seems to be supported by some of the theoretical and experimental findings of postrelativity physics. . . . when we hear these mathematical proportions manifested in sound, we intuitively recognize that profound information on "fundamental vibrational structure" is being revealed. This is the intuition that we feel, as a kind of religious awe, when we worship in the Church of the Sonic Guitar.

That is a remarkable insight, and anyone who has ever been moved by a Jimi Hendrix record ought to recognize Palmer is right. Rock 'n' roll (including its cultural precursors) is rightly understood as a phenomenon, but it is also music, and no critic was ever as good as Palmer at writing about that music. Greil Marcus may be pop's greatest social historian, and the late Lester Bangs may have been its most fervent advocate, but Palmer was the best at describing how the stuff got into your guts.

He'll be missed—I don't know anyone who possesses a similar combination of technical expertise, writing chops, and genuine love for his subject. He was what a critic ought to be; he never succumbed to easy judgments or reflexive irony.

And I think the best way to remember him is to read his work. I'm sure it's all he'd ask.

1997

Edwin Cheney's Heart

There are times in most people's lives when they want to burn down hospitals, when they look across the table at someone they love and learn some hard truth, when the phone buzzes and a stranger says he's sorry.

The heart is a numb muscle, a knot of blood and gristle at the center of a man. How can it hurt so without bursting? How dare it? People die and we can accept that, though it is harder when they are young and so in love with living.

Yet we do move on, past cradles and caskets. We thread through cathedrals and courthouses and cancer wards, each of us reeking of mortality and destined to abandon the earth. I found a magazine in the gym and read a story about Ted Williams, seventy-eight years old and raging at God, praying to Jesus to die before his ten-year-old dog. Grief is like that; it can make our heroes beg. Who wants to be the last left standing?

Grief is hard and unshareable; there comes a time when the consoling hand on the shoulder becomes too much, when we look into the liquid eyes of caring folks and want to spit: This grief is mine!

We don't, of course. There is nothing so civil as a fresh widow. The well-intentioned are just that; the bereaved make them feel better by accepting their condolences, as they stand there bereft, with their soft gloves, with their refrigerators stuffed with silver-covered Pyrex, with their tiny smiles and soft voices telling the appropriate social lies. It isn't seemly to fall apart, and so they don't, though no one would blame them if they did.

✧ ✧ ✧

Edwin Cheney wanted to build a house for his wife in the Chicago suburb of Oak Park. He hired an architect named Frank Lloyd Wright to design it. While Wright was working on the house, he fell in love with Mrs. Cheney. She left her husband, Wright left his wife and six children, and together they fled abroad on what she called a "spiritual hegira."

When they returned, Wright built, in the Wisconsin countryside, a sprawling house for Mrs. Cheney. He called it Taliesin, after a second-rate masque that referred to "the prairies of a man's heart." Wright said Taliesin was Welsh for "shining brow," and he meant for the house to make the brow of the little hill on which it stood. "Not on the hill but of the hill," was how he often described it, and because Wright was a genius as well as a cad, his house is genuinely wondrous, one of the great houses on this continent.

Wright lived there with Mrs. Cheney for three years. During that time he struggled to rebuild his architecture practice, which had been all but ruined by the scandal. Because he was a genius he began to receive new commissions, for the Imperial Hotel in Tokyo, for an experimental entertainment complex in Chicago called Midway Gardens. The new work led him to commute between Taliesin and Chicago; he was in Chicago that day in August 1914.

Mrs. Cheney was at Taliesin. Her two children had joined her for a brief holiday. Wright's carpenter William Weston and his thirteen-year-old son were also there, so were two draftsmen and two handymen. Not long before, Wright had hired a couple from Barbados to serve as butler and cook at Taliesin.

Wright was in his office in Chicago, eating lunch with his grown son John when the call came—"Taliesin destroyed by fire." But it was worse than that; the new butler, Julian Carleton, had gone berserk with an ax and killed seven of those in the house. Only Weston had escaped, he had struggled with the madman and fled, returning to find the house in flames.

(Carleton was later found hiding in the ruins of the house. Shortly before he was captured he attempted suicide by drinking hydrochloric acid; the acid burned his throat so that he was unable to speak or eat. Seven weeks after the incident he died of starvation in the local jail; apparently he never tried to explain.)

In his memoir, *My Father Who Is on Earth*, John Lloyd Wright added a few details to the story. John wrote that he made arrangements for his father to travel back to Taliesin:

> Mr. Cheney was on the train too. I got a compartment and shoved Dad and Mr. Cheney into it to save them from being crushed by reporters who were already crowding in on us. Mr. Cheney was the father of the two little girls who were visiting their mother, his former wife. From the moment he clasped Dad's hand there was a closeness between them, a grief-stricken, mute understanding. From there on the only words I remember hearing uttered between them were when Mr. Cheney took his departure at noon the next day. The remains of his two little girls were in a box he held in one hand.
>
> "Good-bye, Frank, I'm going now." Dad clasped his hand.
> "Good-bye, Ed." They stood looking into each other's eyes.
> "Good-bye, Frank," Mr. Cheney repeated. There was no strife, no

trouble in their voices. In farewell they spoke as men with a deep grief—a despairing, heart-rending understanding.

An "understanding." The word also appears in the *Chicago Tribune* account of Edwin Cheney's leave-taking from Taliesin with the bodies of his children. Wright biographer Brendan Gill identifies the writer of the unbylined story as the famous Walter Noble Burns, thought to be one of the inspirations for the Charles MacArthur–Ben Hecht play *The Front Page*.

The story reads thus:

> There was no trouble in their voices at the farewell. . . . Cheney stepped into the automobile beside the small wooden box that held the bodies of his children and rolled away without a backward glance at the place where the woman who was once his wife lay dead.
>
> At the station . . . Mr. Cheney personally saw to the placing of the bodies on the train and read a pile of messages of condolences from Oak Park friends.
>
> "You are not remaining for the burial of Mrs. [Cheney]?" he was asked.
>
> "No," he answered slowly. "I am only here to take the bodies of my children home. . . . Concerning Mrs. [Cheney] you must talk to—to someone else."
>
> He deliberated and did not utter the name of Wright.

We only know of Edwin Cheney secondhand, through Wright's myriad biographers, who tell us he was a colorless, unexciting man, an electrical engineer ripe for cuckolding. He asked her many times before she consented to marry him; she left him for a pompous little ass. Cheney was unfortunate, a mere man—well-mannered and stoic—in the path of ruthless genius.

But lately I have been thinking of Edwin Cheney, of that long, slow train pulling through Wisconsin, of the air in that compartment unstirred by voices. I think I am a fan of his. It is possible to live, to look fate in the face and not fold up.

More and more often, it seems, the news is bad. There are friends who won't be here next year. Hug who you can.

1997

On Board the Porno Flight

On a flight from the West Coast to Dallas, a young man sits in an aisle seat in coach class. He looks standard issue, with pleasant, intelligent eyes and a rusty goatee. He wears khaki trousers and a dark long-sleeved pullover knit shirt with a soft collar. He is the kind of young man you wouldn't much notice if not for what he is about to do.

He reaches into his attaché and extracts a magazine—a pornographic magazine. Not a copy of *Playboy* or even *Hustler* or any other relatively demure "men's" magazine, but one of those garish stroke books that are usually bound in shrink wrap and kept behind counters. One of those publications that prosecuting attorneys occasionally decide are a menace to public health and safety—a really nasty, garish, hard-core porno smut publication.

No one says anything.

After a few minutes, the man in the next seat casually engages the reader (looker?) in a conversation about the fortunes of the Dallas Mavericks and Dennis Rodman. The reader adopts an attitude of reflection, allowing the magazine to flop open on his lap as he ponders the relative merits of adding a voracious rebounder head-case to the mix. Fields of flesh gape open in his lap.

No one seems alarmed—though it is impossible to imagine that no one notices. Perhaps an open porno magazine is like a glass eye; perhaps it would be rude to mention it. It is interesting that we feel constrained, that we feel that we must be particularly careful of the feelings of the young man with the porno mag flopped open on his thighs, but that is exactly how we feel.

Is it that we feel a kind of pity for the porno user? Maybe it is the same kind of commiseration we might feel for a movie rube who shows up for a job interview in a rented powder-blue tuxedo. What kind of sensibility allows a person to commit this kind of social faux pas? Poor thing, he doesn't know what he is doing.

No, there is nothing naive-seeming about this young man. It is more likely that he understands people will be shocked and affronted by his flagrant display; it is likely he also knows no one will challenge him. No doubt he sees himself as the kind of person who isn't politically correct, who doesn't kowtow to the conventional. He is daring us to speak to him, to say something about his choice of looking material. He is his own man, strong and secure, a steely Howard Roark amid the Milquetoasts.

That's the kind of man who opens a porno mag on an airplane, the kind of man who's bought into an image of himself as a rebel. He does what he wants—and in the ever-coarsening society, he is perpetually seeking new ways to stimulate his fellow creatures to outrage. Their mild protests, which melt before his cold gaze, amuse him. It is likely that it disappoints him that no one—not even the flight attendants—have said anything to him about his magazine. He settles back, reclines his seat into the lap of the person behind him.

There are bullies of all kinds. Some people admire them. Some people admire their "strength," their indifference to general opprobrium. It is probably not too much to say that shamelessness is, if not yet regarded as a full-fledged virtue, at least a useful mechanism for coping with modern times.

❖ ❖ ❖

Someone—I—should have said something. The only defense I can offer is that I was a few seats away and that it would have required making a few steps (and possibly a scene) to approach the porno bully. And I don't know quite what I should have said to him, other than he ought to put his toys away until later. I don't know what I could have said or done without making the situation worse, without drawing attention to the fact that I was confronting this young man. You never know what a man who opens up a porno mag on a plane might do—he might have been inspired to slug me.

(And I haven't been slugged in years. I mightn't have responded well. I might have felt compelled to slug him back. I might have blown my job, my marriage, and possibly even my freedom trying to point out an obvious affront to public decency. These things go through your head when you contemplate confronting a bully. You run a kind of calculus of risk versus reward.)

Like a lot of people, I struggle with my temper. I carry little grudges; I can hold harsh opinions. But I try not to be rude, not even to people I know need to hear something stronger than gentle remonstrations. While most people would be horrified to have their rudeness pointed out to them—most of us don't strive to offend—there is a significant contingent who think good manners are an indication of either phoniness or weakness.

It has become something of a truism to say we have become a nation of victims, whining about our imagined powerlessness as we look for targets on which we can unload our generalized, free-floating discontent. Invariably, those targets are among the weakest among us: fresh immigrants, the poor, the young. In good times, like those they say we are enjoying now, the drumbeat softens somewhat—the more comfortable we are, the less likely we are to be mean—but never really abates. And there is the possibility we are becoming meaner.

As Christopher Lasch wrote in *The Culture of Narcissism,* "we are a much more solipsistic people now. We have turned from the community to ourselves, from the common good to our own good, becoming fixated with our personal development, our material well-being, our emotional satisfaction."

We are different than we used to be. The human attention span has been attenuated. We can no longer call on a collective mental library of classical imagery. And we are less concerned with how our words and actions might impinge on the sensibilities of others. We are meaner.

We are meaner, despite the fact that times are good. This is the most difficult thing to understand. In tougher times—or when we perceive times are tougher—we dispense with unessential qualities such as love and sympathy. We lock down our higher faculties and revert to the lizard brain. OK, but that's when times are tough.

Maybe corporate Darwinism has created the perception that America can't support everyone and the strong must push the more vulnerable out of the way in order to flourish.

I wonder if "hard times" don't simply provide us an excuse to exercise our darkest reflexes; perhaps we enjoy being mean so much that almost any excuse will do. One of the reasons it is wrong for politicians to scare people unduly—to engage in demagoguery—is because it is so easy to incite people to cruelty. This is evident when people who live in neighborhoods where crime is virtually nonexistent howl about street crime, when silly rap stars make millions with nihilistic lyrics that debase women and taunt rivals, when alert young men who should know better display pornography in airplanes.

2000

Travels with Yanko

Yanko says he used to be shy. But that was long ago. He enlisted in the army seven months before Pearl Harbor. He went through the war and came out a changed man. Having survived it, he allows that it was good for him.

For one thing, he lost his shyness overseas. He came back from the war a talker and a negotiator. He learned to wrangle with salesmen, to work them for deals. These days he talks to waitresses and millionaires, to policemen and party guests and people in the street. He is genuinely interested in them, in their lives and aspirations. It is a good quality to have.

Yanko comes down to visit every couple of years. He lives in Cleveland, where the Indians play and where every other lawn supports a caricature of an Indian brave—"Chief Wahoo," his name is. Yanko follows the Indians, identifies with the team. When he talks about them he uses the pronoun "we." He says, "Boy, the Red Sox sure beat us good last night" and "We've got a good one in that Ramirez kid." He knows who's up next in the rotation, what the manager Hargrove has set as his goals for the year.

(Actually Yanko lives in Parma, where the frequency of Chief Wahoo signs is somewhat higher than in Cleveland proper. But people know—or at least think they know—where Cleveland is, so it's easier to say Cleveland. Yanko says Cleveland, but he means Parma.)

Yank looks twenty years younger than he actually is—not because he is vain about his appearance but because he comes from hardy Croatian stock. His genes are good. He is strong, with big hands and arms. He looks prosperous. He is a man of modest appetites. He doesn't eat more than he ought to; he doesn't spend much money on himself. He'll have a highball in the evening when he's on vacation, but he's not a drinker. He gave up smoking years ago. But while Yanko may be careful, he's not timid—he smiles big in the world's face.

✧ ✧ ✧

Yanko does not quite know what to make of the South, of Arkansas. It sure is hot here. He long ago learned not to expect to see barefoot hillbillies on the streets; he knows they stay up in the hollers. His daughter came down here more than twenty years ago, and that's OK. She likes it, good enough.

She married this Southern boy. He's OK too. He plays golf and maybe he ought to try out for the Senior Tour when he's old enough. Those guys, they make some kind of dough. Maybe he should just go on TV; TV people, they make good money, don't they? Better than writers, right?

Ah, well, what are you going to do. They're happy.

✧ ✧ ✧

It is good to have him down here, to hear his stories. Last time we went to Cleveland, Yanko's daughter brought a microcassette recorder and got him telling stories about the old days. She filled up two hours of tape and there's plenty more to tell.

About the Philippines, during the war: Yanko was a medical corpsman there, digging trenches to drain off malaria. He heard bullets whistle, but the most danger he was ever in was when he was chased by a wild boar. He and the other corpsmen had left their rifles in the jeep and had to run for it.

"It was the first time the army ever issued weapons to medics," Yanko explains, noting that the Japanese seemed not to respect the Red Cross armbands they wore.

Somebody shot the boar and they had it for dinner.

Yanko never did master the art of cracking coconuts apart with a machete, though he watched the Filipinos do it expertly.

"Some of those rich guys on the island, before the Japanese got there, buried their Mercedes—they put them down in a hole and covered them up with leaves," Yanko remembers. Then, when the Americans liberated the island, they raked back the palm fronds and drove the cars out. It was the damnedest thing.

Yanko remembers that the *Cleveland Plain Dealer* ran a story about his family—they had five brothers who served in the war. Against the odds, all of them came back.

George was always an island ahead of Yanko in the Pacific, Ely was in Europe until Berlin fell. Then he was shipped over to help finish off Tojo. After MacArthur forced the peace, three of the brothers were reunited on Okinawa and came home on the same ship.

Ely is gone now. He was the dude of the family—a sharp dresser and a bit of a con man. He wore tailored uniforms; he looked like a colonel even though he was a buck sergeant. He played the angles and used to borrow Yanko's car for hot dates on Saturday nights. Sunday mornings the gas tank was always empty.

But everyone loved the rascal Ely, with his oil-smooth ways.

Yanko's dad must have been something else again. He outlived four wives. Every time one of his wives would die—usually in childbirth—he would take the boat back to the old country, back to Yugoslavia. He would find another girl and bring her over to the States. It was like that in the early part of the century; Yanko's father felt an obligation to bring over another girl if he could.

America was that kind of place then. No Croatian girl could resist a man with an American passport and a steady job. Even after Yanko's dad lost his eye in an accident—the railroad paid him off, so there was no need to sue—he could pretty much have his pick of women in the old country.

Now there's just George and Pete and Goldie left. George is too thin, Yanko thinks. Pete plays the market. He's loaded. Goldie—well, Goldie is something else: a bit of a politician, certainly the family matriarch, a big deal in the Croatian-American societies. She goes to Yugoslavia every year or so. Yanko has never felt any desire to go.

Yanko gets along real well. His house is paid for, and though he hasn't worked—for money—since 1982, he has everything he wants and a little extra. He can travel a little; a couple of years ago he went to Ellis Island to see where the American experience had started for his family.

Now that U.S. Air is flying regional jets into Little Rock National, it might not be so long before he comes back here.

Yanko is more than a talker; he is a conversationalist. He is engaged with the world—he watches the news and every morning walks down to the corner store and buys a newspaper. He thinks that Milosevic is in some respects a Serbian retaliation for the abuses they suffered under Tito.

"Tito treated the Serbs really bad," Yanko says. "I guess the guy Milosevic is nuts, but he's getting back for all that."

Yanko remembers when it was no big deal if one was a Serb or a Croat, he knows of marriages between the groups that have worked out fine. Those marriages, however, were consecrated in America.

Yanko is American, as American as anyone, more American than most. He doesn't presume to think this, much less say it, but I do.

1999

Bharati's Crocodile

For Bharati Mukherjee

Cancun, Mexico: we left Bharati waiting for the crocodile. Or not exactly—she was just promising to come back to see the crocodile later that day. In the meantime, she had to go and work on the piece on Mother Theresa she was writing for *Time.*

She said the crocodile was supposed to show up precisely at 7:30 P.M. and she didn't want to miss it. We didn't know anything about the crocodile, other than there was a sign posted that said we weren't supposed to feed it. That seemed fair enough; once you start feeding crocodiles it becomes difficult to get rid of them.

To tell the truth, I didn't believe in the crocodile. It didn't seem credible. After all, we were at one of those all-inclusive resorts, the kind that feature beach volleyball and snorkeling and windsurfing and tennis and promise guests there's no need to tip. There were hundreds of sun-blocked vacationers about, some of whom made more noise than others. Club Med just didn't seem a convivial spot for crocodiles. If there was a crocodile, it seemed likely that he would be drawn across the lagoon on a track. I imagined a Disney crocodile, with blue eyes and bow tie.

So we walked on, toward the evening's seminar, to hear the writers talk about the people for whom they write. It wasn't a bad panel, but we were at the end of the week, the final night of the conference, and everyone was leaving in the morning. People were beginning to weary of the blasting sun, sandy shoes, and irritatingly warm winds. The inherent inauthenticity of the tropics was beginning to grate on everyone—paradise is never real.

Especially not in Cancun. Acapulco and Puerto Vallarta were quaint fishing villages before they were discovered by developers and sun worshippers, but Cancun was created as a resort city; before 1970 or so there wasn't much here but a few Mayan ruins and scrub jungle—maybe some crocodiles. One creation myth holds that in 1968 the Mexican government, looking for a spot to locate the ideal resort, fed a computer vital statistics—including climate, beach conditions, and proximity to the United States. After the lights stopped flashing and the gears quit whirring, the card that was spit out read "Cancun."

But it wasn't the artificiality of the place that the writers wanted to escape; it was the candy colors and the tequila drinks, the mild wines of the dining halls, the boring cheerfulness of the young guests and staff. Most of the writers weren't particularly beachy. They wanted to get back to their little rooms, their gray cities, their keyboards, and their work.

Mexico has always struck me as an odd choice for a vacation; when I think of Mexico I think of border towns and maquiladoras—those export assembly factories set up just over the U.S. border to take advantage of NAFTA. I've never become inured to the juxtaposition of relatively wealthy American and European tourists and bitterly poor campesinos.

One of the attractions of this place where we're staying is that one doesn't have to come in contact with the free-range poor; there are the young women cleaning the breezeway by spilling out carbolic acid and scraping at the stone with spatulas, and the young man stooping on the walk near the tennis courts, whacking away for hours with a hatchet (for what purpose?), but they did not speak or even make eye contact unless they were spoken to—and even then they limited their conversation to a soft "buenos dias."

To get to Mexico from Club Med, you have to walk a mile or so to the road where the buses run. (It is quicker, though technically against the rules, to go a hundred yards down the beach and through the lobby of the adjacent Westin.) Then for fifty cents—or 4.5 pesos—you can ride the twenty-two kilometers through the New Jerusalem of the hotel zone, past the Plaza Kukulcan mall, past the Hard Rock and the Planet Hollywood and the All-Star Cafe, past Mango Tango and Senor Frog's, onto the mainland and into town.

If you're not careful you can miss the tourist market—El Centro—along Avenue Tulum and wind up past the Wal-Mart and the baseball stadium, in the working class neighborhood around Calle 113.

It is a quiet and respectable poor community; however threadbare and run down it seems, it does not look dangerous. The schoolkids all wear uniforms; the children are all beautiful. There's none of the reflexive sullenness that seems to infect cities north of the border. People may be curious as to why and how you've found your way down here, but they are helpful and polite. There is nothing desperate about el barrio—it is free of the carny barking and begging of the border towns. There is a backstage feel to el barrio—it is a district in which real people really live.

And as such it is utterly uninteresting, except perhaps to anthropologists. So we rode the bus back to campus.

✧ ✧ ✧

We left again to eat in a restaurant. Club Med provides meals (and the food is good), but we are less buffet people than we are beach people. We are restaurant people, and we found—more or less by mistake—a good one. We had seafood and drank margaritas and four men dressed in *guayaberas* and carrying guitars came to our table and played tunes called "Mariachi Loco" and "Besame Mucho."

I gave them all the change I had in my pocket—which, much later, we decided must have been about four U.S. dollars—and left in a good mood that wasn't ruined even when the bus driver declined to take us all the way back to Club Med, instead depositing us at the Westin. Had our heads been clearer, we might have walked through the lobby of the Westin, out onto the beach, and then back to our room. But we didn't think of that.

When we finally got back, we wandered down toward the bar to try to use up all the drink coupons we had left. And on the way we stopped and looked down into the lagoon, not expecting anything but checking just the same.

At first we didn't see him, but the crocodile was there, his chocolate eyes shining above the mud. I thought that he looked more like an alligator, that crocodiles had pointed snouts, but I was corrected. He was green, not brown, the crowd that was starting to gather allowed. So alligators are brown?

He didn't move but we could tell he was alive; and despite the sign I wished I had half a chicken to chuck down to him, to see how quick he could move if he wanted. But none of us fed the crocodile; we let him be.

We turned and headed for the bar and then we saw Bharati—she was smiling, luminous as a book jacket. She wanted to know if we had seen the crocodile. I had to admit that I had.

1999

My Dinner with Barry

I once had dinner with Barry Goldwater.

It wasn't, as you might suppose, in the line of duty. It was a purely coincidental meeting. When I was living in Arizona I took a woman to dinner at an Italian restaurant in Scottsdale called Un Bacio Ristoranti. There weren't many people there that night, but the hostess just happened to seat us next to Goldwater and his then-new wife, Susan Wechsler. He was within reach; had I wanted to I could have reached over and clapped him on the shoulder.

I didn't want to. I knew who he was, but I wasn't quite sure how I felt about Goldwater. He was the sort of person one forms ideas about—I don't think I would have voted for him, but I admired him. I had heard that he was not always a gentleman, that he could be crude and even cruel. He certainly was not a saint—no businessman can afford to be.

My father had liked Goldwater—to a point. He thought he made good sense; he thought there was something to the "In your heart, you know he's right" business. But he thought that Goldwater might turn Vietnam into a full-fledged war, and he worried about that. (And when Lyndon Johnson escalated the war, my dad wanted his vote back.)

I later found out some things about Goldwater myself.

Goldwater was born to privilege and he believed in privilege and wouldn't return phone calls from people who worked for the newspaper that employed me then. His marriage to Susan had raised a mild local scandal; she had been his nurse, and some people fretted that she had connived to win the affection of a weakened old warrior. People said that she was a gold digger and that Goldwater had gone feeble, but when I read the quotes he gave the *Arizona Republic,* I thought he made a lot of sense.

So I didn't introduce myself to Goldwater. I didn't do anything other than nod politely in his direction. I noticed that he had two martinis; I noticed that he didn't touch his soup. We might have sat side-by-side for a couple of hours without saying anything to each other had not the boys from Tempe showed up.

That is how I think of them—the "boys from Tempe." They might not have been that at all. They might have been from Mesa or from Phoenix. They might not have even been from Arizona. They might not have been the frat boys that I took them for, but conventioneers or junior executives. I choose to believe that they were students at Arizona State, but I do not remember exactly why I believe that.

Anyway, there were three of them, with loosened ties and pushed-up sleeves, and they were drunk.

Not bad drunk, not unpleasantly drunk, just a little less inhibited than perhaps they should have been. They laughed a little too loud; they were a little too solicitous of the waitress; they seemed like decent guys, but they were on the brink of behaving badly.

They got their drinks and took a table by the window. And one of them noticed Goldwater.

He was a hero to them all, or so they believed. They were the type of bright young boys who imagined themselves princes of the entrepreneurial class, they had no use for "liberals"—a word one of them spat out like a piece of rotten fruit.

They advanced on Goldwater, crowding the old man's table.

"Man, we really missed the vote when we didn't elect you president in '72."

"You're a great American, Barry. A great conservative."

"Let us buy you a drink, Mr. Goldwater?"

✧ ✧ ✧

Goldwater smiled and turned to them. He declined the drink, but he thanked them politely.

The guys looked at me, and because of my proximity to Goldwater they must have assumed that I was with him, that we might have had business to discuss. They realized they might be intruding—they weren't so drunk that they didn't realize they were making a scene. I nodded at them; they went back to their own table.

And Goldwater turned to me.

"That doesn't happen often anymore," he said quietly.

"It doesn't? I would imagine you're as famous as any man in Arizona, Mr. Goldwater," I said.

"Not with young people. They don't generally know me. That was kind of interesting."

"But he did get the year wrong. It was 1964."

"That's right, 1964. LBJ dropped the bomb on me."

"I suppose he did. But it looks like you won the battle of ideas. There are no New Dealers left; everybody is some kind of a conservative."

"There are a few conservatives. There are a lot of jerks."

And Goldwater and I talked. When he asked, I told him I was a writer and relatively new to Arizona and he let it go at that. I told him I had admired his impatience with partisan convention and his willingness to speak out even when his views were impolitic. I told him that I was impressed when he called Pat Robertson a kook and when he endorsed a Democrat for Congress and that I hoped the Maricopa County Republicans didn't retaliate by removing Goldwater's name from the building that housed their headquarters.

He said he didn't give a damn whether they removed his name or not; he said he was "too old and mean" to worry about the machinations of petty bureaucrats.

I told Goldwater that I had read his book, *The Conscience of a Conservative,* and that it had been an important book in my life. I added that I thought he might have served his country better as a senator from Arizona, as an uncompromised spokesman for the principles of Edmund Burke and common sense, better than he would have been able to as president.

"Didn't vote for me, huh?" he laughed.

"No, Senator. I was too young to vote in 1964." And, I almost added, "I wouldn't have voted for you anyway. Sorry."

Goldwater didn't mind.

"It was the wrong time. I was right, but people couldn't see it. People were filled with spirit, and when John Kennedy got killed I knew I wasn't going to be able to overcome that. Lee Harvey Oswald was the worst thing that could have happened to us as a country. I still think about that."

After a while, our conversation ran its course and we turned back to our plates of pasta. Goldwater and Susan got up to leave and as he stood up he put his hand on my shoulder and said he was glad to have met me.

I'm glad I met you too, Barry. Take care.

1998

Central High: Forty Years On

Forty years since Central High, and things are better now.

Things are better because everyone—aside from the professionally discontent local distributor of windshield fliers—says that things are better. We can regard each other with unforced warmth, sit down at lunch counters together and understand that we want the same things for our children. We can work in the same offices, shower in the same gymnasiums, talk politics together, and grumble about our tax burdens and the pressures of keeping decent in a world that increasingly seems to reward indecency.

We avoid the same bad neighborhoods; we laugh at the same bright young black comedian—you know, the one who says he "loves black people but hates niggers."

It should go without saying that black people in America have more in common with white people in America than they have with black people in Africa, though there may in fact be something to W.E.B. Dubois's idea that there is, in the words of his time, an innate Negro identity—consisting of "Negro soul" and "Negro blood." In genetic terms, "race" means next to nothing; the people whom we identify—who identify themselves—as "black" physically have no more or less in common with other black folk than they have with white folk. Some people have more melanin; usually "black" people have darker skin than "white" people.

Of course, it cannot be as simple as that. There is a psychological component as well; it means something to be black, just as it means something to be a Jew or the great-grandson of one of Lee's lieutenants. It is flip and disrespectful to suggest that it makes no difference, to suggest that the souls of black folk record the world the same as the eyes of Pharaoh.

Still, things are better between black and white people than they were forty years ago. Only the unsophisticated persist under the old codes; these days even bigots can make common cause with different-colored bigots. There aren't so many lynchings; people are generally outraged by the outrageous.

There are moments when we almost find it possible to forget the fact of the Other's color and the separate yet equal histories that have brought each of us to the point where we stand searching the Other's eyes for what is familiar and recognizable, straining to connect across a great yawning gulf of false grievance and genuine misery. It is important that we continue to strain toward the Other, toward each other, important that we not give in to moral exhaustion, that we not leave unfinished the work begun so long ago by people like those who integrated Little Rock's Central High.

✧ ✧ ✧

Things are better now, but "better" is a relative term and it's clear to anyone of conscience that race—however shaky it may be as a scientific concept—is still the intractable American problem. The color line is as real for you and me as it was for DuBois or Martin Luther King Jr. American apartheid is no less real for being extralegal—our kids still do not go to school together and there are still influential bigots (white and black) about.

It is fashionable to think civil rights legislation is either diversionary or antibusiness. It is fashionable to use the old ugly words to show that we are "not politically correct." It is fashionable to be selfish and to believe that what is good for you personally must be good for the country, for the future of mankind.

It is fashionable to disbelieve in all kinds of Darwinism except the economic kind and to hold the poor and the powerless accountable for their own sorry condition. It is fashionable to say that there are absolutes in the world, that relativism is for the weak of will and spirit, that things are more black and white than gray.

And, yes, some things are absolute. There are things we will not, can not, argue about: There is such a thing as moral truth, and there is evil in the world.

One of the things that is true and inarguable and absolute is that the repression of black folk was this country's great crime—the original sin that stained this nation's soul. Our transgressions are compounded because we—our ancestors—knew the extent of this evil; make whatever excuses you will about the vagaries of the old ways, but Thomas Jefferson and Robert E. Lee and the ancient Greeks knew it was wrong to treat human beings as chattel, just as the Theodore Bilbos and the Bull Connors and the George Wallaces and the Orval Faubuses knew that their various acts of obstruction were evil.

Just as the mean hearts and the petty sneaks, the cheats and the advantage-takers comprehend the full measure of their transgressions, the slave masters and the lynch mobbers and the White Citizens' Council members knew exactly what they were doing. They knew it was worse than wrong, but the person who will let qualms of conscience interfere with physical comfort is rare indeed. We humans are the only lucky creatures who can apprehend the rightness or wrongness of the things we do; to be human is to know sin, to taste it—and sometimes to relish it.

All of us Americans are haunted by race, and we shall not be released from this curse until the worst nightmares of the White Citizens' Council come to fruition. It is possible that someday the old shame may be dissolved by miscegenation, that the mongrelization of these disparate races may produce a new kind of American, unhyphenated yet alert to history, an alloy of two (or three or six) cultures, unimpeded by ancient wounds and unafraid of people who look or talk differently. Maybe. That is optimistic.

Forty years after Central High and things are better, but there is no assurance things will be better forty years from now. We have established a permanent urban underclass in this country; we breed monsters—young, post-literate, and heavily armed—in the shadows of our abandoned warehouses. We have put gates on our communities and bars on our windows and we look at old newspapers and hold dinners and congratulate ourselves on how much things have changed in forty years.

And ignore the evil tingling in our bones.

1997

Gone with the Wind, 1998

From the distance of nearly sixty years, it might be difficult to see exactly why *Gone with the Wind*—back in theaters this June—is still considered by many to be the quintessential American epic and a great movie. Perhaps it is, as it was once fashionable to suggest, an overrated film.

There are certainly problems to which the unconvinced can point, not the least of which is that it is a reasonably faithful adaptation of Margaret Mitchell's thousand-page novel and as such is nearly four hours long. And for all the fuss over a few extraordinary scenes—the thousands of wounded soldiers, laid out forever; the horse-drawn carriage silhouetted by consuming flames; the bloody, expressionistic skies—most of the camera work is fairly pedestrian. Some scenes are ridiculously overlit—no doubt because Technicolor was still a glorious new gimmick in 1939.

Vivian Leigh's performance as Scarlett O'Hara may be iconic, but it is hardly supple. She comes across as melodramatic, and she displays an extraordinarily narrow range. She pouts well enough, but she seems as equally distressed over Daddy dying and Rhett Butler leaving her as she does about her waistline. Clark Gable seems embarrassed by his appearance in the film—at times he looks like a man smiling bravely through his lumbago. Hattie McDaniel probably deserved her Best Supporting Actress Oscar (Olivia De Havilland was also nominated for her role as Melanie), and, as Prissy, Butterfly McQueen managed to invest a comic performance with genuine dignity, but in general the level of acting is not first-rate.

While Victor Fleming is credited as the movie's director and won an Academy Award for his contribution, in retrospect it hardly seems a tour de force. A certain stylistic inconsistency might be attributed to the fact that George Cukor, Sam Wood, and William Cameron Menzies also directed several scenes without credit.

Similarly, though Sidney Howard was the only writer aside from Mitchell to receive a writing credit, there were at least ten other writers involved in scripting the movie, including producer David O. Selznick, Ben Hecht, and Charles MacArthur. If *Gone with the Wind* is a masterpiece, then it is a masterpiece by committee.

＊ ＊ ＊

But there is something beyond the technical that makes *Gone with the Wind* what it is—ineffable and sublime. It is soap opera, but it is soap opera of such magnitude that it shames all objections. It is the biggest movie from back in the day when movies were big; it is gaudy and silly and sad, overblown and overwrought and overhyped—to resist it is to admit your cynicism, your proclivity to spoilsport.

Like all myths, it is a simple story, rich in the old verities of honor, passion, courage, and perseverance. Compare willful, petulant, spoiled Scarlett O'Hara (did any heroine ever have a better name? Thank goodness Mitchell did not settle on "Pansy" or "Storm," two names she tried out in early draft) to Kate Winslet's character in *Titanic,* the recent movie that is most reminiscent of *Gone with the Wind.*

While Scarlett is petty and greedy and sometimes downright mean, over the course of the film she becomes an adult, fighting for her land, running a business, and acquiescing to three loveless marriages in order to provide for her family. On the other hand, Winslet's Rose is practically the anti-Scarlett; she rejects the arranged marriage that would ensure her family's financial health in order to have a three-night fling with a wild-eyed artist who looks like a twelve-year-old.

(It is interesting to note that while the female leads of the movies are approximately the same age, Clark Gable was thirty-eight years old when *Gone with the Wind* had its premiere, a full generation older than Leonardo Di Caprio, who was twenty-two when *Titanic* was filmed.)

Whatever modern audiences may think of the two heroines' choices— modern audiences indoctrinated with the idea that self-fulfillment is the ultimate mission of the individual may be more likely than Depression-era audiences to sympathize with Rose's choices—it's clear that despite the superficial similarities between these blockbusters, they don't make movies like *Gone with the Wind* anymore.

While both the novel and the book have been criticized as romantic, nostalgic paeans to the Lost Cause of the Confederacy and the original sin of slavery, there is nothing romantic in its depictions of the horror of war as seen through the eyes of women. Mitchell was a creature of her times, and her stereotypical depictions of black folk can seem jarring to modern readers, but her critique of the Southern aristocracy was acute. There is social realism in the book, and moral ambiguity too.

Rhett Butler is no more standard-issue hero material than Scarlett is your average heroine; the greatest virtue of *Gone with the Wind,* the alleged romance, is that it doesn't gloss over the lovers' flaws or offer the kind of happily-ever-after remedy that Hollywood has come to insist upon. Rhett and Scarlett are in love, but they are also who they are—they are doomed by their own character.

One doesn't have to accept Mitchell's novel as great literature to recognize that it aspires to great literature; Mitchell was trying to be an American Dostoyevsky—and some people think she came awfully close to being just that.

Others think she had to settle for writing the best-selling (and no doubt best-read) American novel of all time.

◇ ◇ ◇

Gone with the Wind has persisted in the American consciousness not because it is a good film of a great book (or vice versa) but because it was the right film at the right time. Perhaps there is a reason that 1939—the year of *The Wizard of Oz, Mr. Smith Goes to Washington, Wuthering Heights, Stagecoach,* and *Ninotchka* as well as *Gone with the Wind*—was such a good year for movies. Europe was reigniting; the Great Depression was receding; maybe people needed to retreat into the dark of the theater.

For whatever reason, *Gone with the Wind* was installed as an essential American myth, a cultural artifact that can hardly be avoided. While it might seem old-fashioned or quaint to modern audiences, it is a force with which we all must deal—even if we deal with it by avoiding it or by adopting an attitude of smug condescension toward Grandma's favorite movie.

Sixty years on, it is difficult to judge the film. It eludes us—the choices seem to narrow. Either we accept it, plunge headlong into its rich, bittersweet pageantry, or we hold it at arm's length like a curious purple bug.

So perhaps it is best to turn back to the ancient judgments. When the book was first published—to considerable ballyhoo, it sold fifty thousand copies the first day—the anonymous reviewer in the *New York Times Book Review* offered the following appraisal: "This is beyond doubt one of the most remarkable first novels produced by an American writer. It is also one of the best . . . a bounteous feast of excellent storytelling . . . Mitchell's real triumph is Scarlett O'Hara, a heroine lacking in many virtues—in nearly all, one might say, but courage."

To counterbalance that, we might remember the story told about MGM executive Irving Thalberg, who, when he heard Louis B. Mayer was planning on turning Mitchell's book into a movie, told the studio chief, "Forget it, Louis. No Civil War picture ever made a nickel."

1998

Bill Clinton Time

The President Next Door

*He had come a long way to this blue lawn, and his dream must
have seemed so close that he could hardly fail to grasp it. He did
not know it was already behind him, somewhere back in that
vast obscurity beyond the city, where the dark fields of the republic rolled on under the night.*
—*F. Scott Fitzgerald*, The Great Gatsby

Ten years ago I was Bill Clinton's neighbor; I rented the bottom floor of
a small house directly behind the Arkansas governor's mansion. I am told
that in a few months, we will be neighbors again. Clinton plans to spend a lot
of time in Little Rock after he leaves the White House; he means to be present while his presidential library is being constructed. I'm told the library
plans include an apartment for the president and his family, but until it's finished he'll live with his mother-in-law in a townhouse in the Hillcrest area of
Little Rock. That townhouse is less than forty yards from my front door.

When we moved in two years ago, the previous owner alerted us to the
proximity of the presidential mother-in-law; she told us two or three times a
year Bill and Hillary came to visit. During those visits, our neighborhood
would be swarmed over with Secret Service, military personnel, and police.
Not without some pride she told us that during those visits the president's
personal physician had been quartered in what was now our third bedroom.

During the obligatory inspection occasioned by the house's sale, a
tangle of wire was found in our crawl space. The inspector could make no
sense of it and noted it on his report. It turned out that the president's pro-
tectors had installed a sub-rosa telephone line beneath our house to use in
case of some emergency. We ripped it out.

For some reason, the Secret Service has never asked us to put anyone
up, or even to change our routine to accommodate the president's occasional
visits. They have taken pains to see that we are not put out in the least by
these visits; they are consistently courteous and far more flexible than I would
ever have imagined possible. It's likely I would have quartered the president's
doctor had they asked—even if they had sworn me to secrecy and forbidden
me to ever mention my service to the republic.

After we took possession of the house it took us a few months to remodel it to our liking; we knocked down and put up walls and remodeled a kitchen and bathroom. We planned a housewarming party.

A week after we sent out invitations, a Secret Service agent knocked on our door and told us the president was planning a visit to Little Rock and would be staying at his mother-in-law's. He would arrive on a Saturday afternoon, a few hours before our scheduled party, and spend the night. They expected that he would leave Sunday morning to attend church, but that he might return to the townhouse Sunday afternoon before flying back to Washington.

In preparation for this visit, the agent needed to get just a little information from us—he needed the license plate numbers of our vehicles and confirmation that my wife and I were the only residents of the house. Oh, and were we expecting any guests this weekend?

I told him what we had planned. I told him we'd cancel.

"Oh, no," he insisted. "Maybe we can park him [I believe he actually said 'Potus,' federal semaphore for 'President of the United States'] somewhere else for the evening. But if we can't, go ahead with your party. We don't want to upset anyone's plans. But could you supply us with a guest list?"

We didn't actually have a guest list. It was easy enough to remember the friends to whom we'd sent invitations, but we'd issued a more or less blanket invitation to all the folks who worked at our newspaper, and I imagine I had told dozens or more acquaintances about the party. We'd even left a few invitations on the doors of our new neighbors—some of whom we hadn't even met yet.

I went to my office and pulled out our address book and after a couple of hours came up with my best guess of names. I noted at the bottom of the list that there might be people who'd show up whose names weren't on the list. If they needed verification, they could call us.

I told the agent that if the president got bored, he could come on up, have a glass of wine. We'd have the Razorback basketball game on for him.

✧ ✧ ✧

The president arrived that afternoon, along with thirty or forty ancillary vehicles—sedans, limousines, and vans with blacked-out windows. They filled up our little cul-de-sac. And not long after the president had settled in, our guests began to trickle in, open-mouthed.

The Secret Service and the police had set up a roadblock at the end of our street, at the bottom of the hill on which our house rests. As our guests showed up, they were asked to step out of their cars while they were searched

174

and a dog trained to sniff out bombs scrambled over their seats. A light rain had begun to fall.

Most of our guests were amused by the experience—only a couple claimed to be put out. A particularly libertarian-minded friend refused to submit to the search and missed the party. But mostly it seemed like a lagniappe for our guests. Some of them ended up congregating in our bedroom, which afforded the best view of the presidential limousine and the milling of the president's men.

I should point out that most of these people were journalists, most of them had met and talked with Bill Clinton before. Still, the idea of having the president next door caused them to clump together like groupies outside a rock star's hotel window, waiting for some stir to betray the presence of greatness within.

✧ ✧ ✧

At one point in the party, a friend I'll call Bob Smith asked me about the preparations, and I told him I had provided the Secret Service with a guest list.

"I assumed that," he said. "But how did you know my full name?"

I was puzzled by this—I told him that I only knew him by the name I knew him by, Bob Smith.

But he said the Secret Service had his full name on their list—Algernon Robert Smith.

✧ ✧ ✧

A few weeks later I asked a golfing buddy, a retired Secret Service agent who'd been part of Jimmy Carter's detail, about that. He told me that the Secret Service had probably completed criminal background checks on all my guests. He said that it wasn't a big deal, but that ever since John Wayne Gacy had gotten close enough to have his picture taken with Rosalyn Carter at a fund-raiser, such background checks were routine.

He said maybe the president had actually considered walking over to our housewarming party. Maybe the agents thought it was a possibility. They just wanted to be ready for any contingencies.

✧ ✧ ✧

Since that first visit, the president has been back several times. He waves at us, though he's never dropped by for a chat or a beer. These most recent visits, late in his presidency, have been more relaxed. Often we haven't even been contacted by the Secret Service before he shows up; they know we know

175

the drill and don't object to the petty inconveniences the president's presence occasions. We understand their security concerns.

During his most recent visit, my wife, Karen, encountered a Secret Service agent in our backyard as she was about to take the dogs out for a run. He asked her if we could see the president when he walked from his limo to his mother-in-law's front door.

"Oh sure," she said. "From our bedroom window we've got a clear—"

"Please, don't say 'shot,'" he pleaded.

❖ ❖ ❖

I don't mean to imply that I am close to Bill Clinton in anything other than a physical sense. I know him, I've written about him, we have friends in common, but we are not friends. I feel kindly toward him, but I've written tough things about him and I imagine that he keeps score on those kinds of things. He's never sent me any Christmas cards. I doubt he ever thinks of me at all.

On the other hand, it seems I cannot escape Clinton. In this I am not unlike most other Arkansans—whenever I am out of state I can expect a few questions about him. People will ask if I know him, as though Arkansas were just a big small town (which in many ways it is). If they realize that I write for a newspaper, there are more questions.

I know Bill Clinton. I don't know him. He seems to be following me around. Just the other day I flipped open a fresh review copy of Joe Esterhaz's *American Rhapsody* to a random page. I saw my own name there—misspelled "Phillip" but unmistakably me—next to a quote that I reported a long, long time ago. Clinton has been great for my career—I think. At least I get to go on television sometimes and people I don't expect to know my work seem to know it.

❖ ❖ ❖

People figure I'll have some insight into Bill Clinton's psyche. I don't know that I do. I know some things about him, but I can't pretend this knowledge adds up to any kind of coherent, unified field theory of the man. I think a lot of things about him; I think he is a serial disappointer and—almost in spite of himself—a great man. I think he married up. I think he's smarter than I am but not as smart as he thinks. And I think to get close to understanding who he is and what he means and what his legacy might be you have to try to understand a little about the place from whence he came and to which he occasionally returns.

Until Bill Clinton came along, most people probably thought of Arkansas as a land of ignorant hillbillies, the realm of Lil' Abner and Daisy Mae and Snuffy Smith and Jed Clampett. True, ours is still a frontier state, raw and remote and sometimes less than civilized. True, if any state deserves to be called anti-intellectual, then Arkansas is it. Too many of us think that dogs and guns and commerce are the only proper pursuits for men, that ideas and art are the province of the anemic and the weak.

Philip Roth has compared Arkansas to Israel, a country unto itself, surrounded by the Other. Of course in our case, the Other is the United States of America, the richest and most powerful nation on earth. While we may not be so backward as we fear, even as we enter a new millennium there is a whiff of the Third World about our state.

Arkansas was what was left over after Missouri and Louisiana were chiseled out of the Louisiana Purchase and after Oklahoma was designated Indian Territory. Poor farmers with large families, little cash, and very few slaves settled this unwanted region, the—as H. L. Mencken put it—"miasmatic jungles of Arkansas."

Yet, there is much of Arkansas that is worthy of being called beautiful, and more that is surprising. Our countryside is as pretty as any; up in the hills rivers boil through spectacular, bluff-lined passes. The changing fall foliage rivals New England's.

Little Rock, Clinton's first capital, sits on the southern bank of the Arkansas River, where the flatlands of the Mississippi Delta meet the hills, very near the geographical center of the state. Our state's only real city, Little Rock, is more cultured and cosmopolitan than one might expect. There are a number of fine restaurants, some good book stores, and a ready supply of alert professionals who work for Jack Stephens's downtown bond house, the University of Arkansas for Medical Sciences, various media outlets, state government, and the courts. For a town of its size—roughly 175,000 people live in the city or its suburbs—the theater is good and so is the local arts center.

Other towns hold diverse and often painfully subtle charms. The mountain resort of Eureka Springs is a looney version of an artists' colony, lately infiltrated by country music Christians. Hot Springs, where Bill Clinton grew up, is a high-camp cross between Las Vegas and Disneyland, smack in the middle of the Bible Belt; in its glory days it was a favorite retreat of the likes of Babe Ruth and Al Capone. Fayetteville is a remote and hilly college town, home of the beloved Arkansas Razorbacks. Pine Bluff, the state's second-largest population center, once enjoyed the distinction of being named by

Rand-McNally as the worst place to live in the nation. Texarkana, a border-straddling oddity in the extreme southwest corner of the state, was the boyhood home of H. Ross Perot.

There is an amiable resourcefulness about most Arkansans, they are good-humored people who can live well with the most modest of resources. They have had to make do with what they can scrape together.

We have our billionaires—the late Sam Walton's children, the Stephens brothers, J. B. Hunt, and a Rockefeller—but the disparity between our very few rich and powerful and the mostly rural masses is uncomfortable. For four decades, starting with World War II, Arkansas's economy grew faster than the national average; still, we have yet to catch up with the rest of the country in per capita income. The average Arkansan makes about 25 percent less than the average American. We lead the country in the production of chicken and rice, but we have fewer natural resources than our neighbors and no major, growing industry. The aluminum fields of the central part of the state are depleted, as are the timber lands of the east.

In terms of area, Arkansas is the smallest state between the Mississippi and the Pacific. In terms of population, it is the smallest Southern state. Despite the undeniable progress that was accomplished during—and before—Bill Clinton's years as governor, Arkansas remains near the bottom of the states in terms of literacy rate and teacher salaries. We have fewer museums and libraries, and fewer books in the libraries we do have. Conversely, we lead the states in the incidence of venereal disease and unwed mothers; the infant mortality rate is inexcusable. For years the unofficial state motto has been "Thank God for Mississippi."

Though Arkansas was part of the Confederacy, it is really not of the South—in the South, certainly, but not of the South. At the time of the War between the States, only the cotton plantation country near the Mississippi River was completely settled. Even in the faded towns along the Mississippi, where today great slouching homes overlook public housing tracts, there is little of the sense of cloying ruin that permeates the real South.

There is no real aristocracy here, no founding families. There were no great robber barons, no great plantation owners. There are none of William Faulkner's Compsons, only striving or bitter Snopeses, each scrambling for a place at the table. To be from Arkansas is to be turned away from the big house, to be designated redneck or trash.

This is not all bad; until a few years ago the license plates on our cars announced we were living in the "Land of Opportunity." With no tight traditions, Arkansas has long honored the bright young person with creative ideas. Upward mobility is no myth here. It is said that anyone who can write

178

a thousand dollar check to a charity can become part of Little Rock society, invited to all manner of balls, soirees, and fêtes.

In this regard, Arkansas has more a Western than Southern sensibility—family counts for less than ability. Even our billionaires have modest roots: Sam Walton began his career running small-town dime stores; Jack Stephens and his late brother, Witt, built their fortunes from scratch.

Yet for all the admirable attributes of the Arkansas character, it sometimes seems the most Southern thing about the state is its people's habit of self-deprecation and instinct for shame, a pathology of melancholia and self-loathing that manifests itself as a kind of palpable inferiority complex. Arkansans reflexively assume anything of local origin to be second-rate; we mistrust the most innovative and original among us. Likewise, we often suspect the worst of ourselves; like all hell-fearing beings we continually question our motives and hold fast to guilt.

Because of this insecurity, this inappropriate defensiveness, we fear the harsh judgments of outlanders. Because we are from Arkansas, we have none of the advantages. We are quickly and deeply hurt, even when censure is offered constructively. We see offense where none is intended. To be from Arkansas is to simultaneously seek and scorn the approval of the Other.

❖ ❖ ❖

Hope, Arkansas, in the southwestern corner of the state, is a fairly conventional American small town, perhaps poorer than most. While today an outsider might have considerable difficulty distinguishing the working-class white neighborhoods from their black counterparts or discovering a qualitative difference between the squalid trailers favored by "white trash" and the silver-wood shotgun shacks of poor blacks, there are clear caste boundaries in this little town. The locals know which streets are which and generally keep to their own. Those still-extant boundaries were more pronounced and enforced in August 1946, when the boy who was to become Bill Clinton entered the milieu.

He was born William Jefferson Blythe IV, some eleven months after the end of World War II and some three months after his father, a salesman for a heavy equipment firm, was killed in a freakish one-car accident. (The elder Blythe, we now know, was a bit of a rounder and possibly a bigamist—after Clinton's inauguration, a man appeared claiming, apparently truthfully, to be the president's half brother.) Relatives say they can even now discern in the president the familiar tics of the father he never knew; they see it in the puppyish way he cocks his head, in his slender fingers and easy smile.

Five months after his birth, Billy Blythe's mother, Virginia, turned the child over to her parents and returned to nursing school in Louisiana to gain certification as an nurse anesthetist. These early vacancies might account for at least a portion of young Blythe's precocity—he was, by all accounts, an exceptionally serious child. His grandparents, Elridge and Edith Cassidy, were uncommonly decent people. They ran a general store, in an rural area near Hope, that had a reputation as one of a very few places where black people could freely mingle with whites. The Cassidys would even extend credit to blacks and are remembered by some in Hope as rather self-righteous social liberals. The uglier phrase, which still has surprising currency in south Arkansas today, is "nigger lover." Billy Blythe heard the words frequently.

When Billy was four years old, his mother returned. Three years later, she married Roger Clinton. The family moved to Hot Springs, where Roger took a job in his brother's Buick dealership. The union was not a completely happy one; Roger Clinton was an alcoholic who sometimes beat his wife and once fired off a handgun in the living room. Perhaps as a reaction to the turmoil at home, Billy Blythe threw himself into his schoolwork, becoming a model student. He remembers engaging his mother—a voluble and opinionated woman—in sprightly conversations about the issues of the day.

Some have suggested that Virginia was—consciously or not—pushing her son to develop his already apparent intellectual gifts, preparing him for a public life that would take him far beyond Hot Springs. In any event, Virginia and her clever eldest son spent many hours in the kitchen in earnest discussions that likely provided both of them with an escape from the domestic terror that would start with Roger's first glass of bourbon.

A familiar chapter in the Bill Clinton hagiography has the preteen Billy Blythe lecturing his mother on the inherent evil of American apartheid, and Bill Clinton has claimed that the Central High School crisis of 1957, which occurred when he was eleven years old, was a significant event in the development of his intellectual character.

✧ ✧ ✧

Two anecdotes from Billy Blythe's early teens mark him as a child of unusual sensitivity and courage. After Virginia divorced and then quickly reconciled with Roger Clinton, fifteen-year-old Bill adopted his stepfather's surname in an effort to heal the fractured family. Then—following the incident in which Roger fired his pistol in the house—Bill took his mother and younger half brother by the hand as he confronted his stepfather.

"You will never hit either of them again," he said. "If you want them, you'll have to go through me." While Roger Clinton continued to drink, apparently the young man's warning had the desired effect—the violence at home ceased.

Years later, the half brother who had held Bill Clinton's hand that fateful evening, Roger Clinton Jr., would tell reporters that Bill was virtually a father to him while he was growing up. "He was always there," Roger said. "After my father died, he practically raised me—and I adored him."

Meanwhile, Bill Clinton was becoming the perfect student, the sort of driven overachiever whom teachers love and classmates usually detest. Although Clinton was not the most popular kid in school, neither was he a nerdy pariah. He seems to have existed comfortably among the upper reaches of high school society, an exceptionally able and gifted kid determined to rise above his decidedly white trash roots. As a high schooler, he was selected as a senator to Boys Nation, an annual exercise in mock government sponsored by the American Legion. He traveled to Washington, where he famously met John F. Kennedy in a ceremony in the Rose Garden.

That image of the thin, bushy-headed boy in a white polo shirt with an oversized Legion crest, encumbered by the inevitable, unfortunate name tag, leaning into a handshake with the impossibly young, doomed president, surfaced during Clinton's 1992 presidential campaign, in both still photo and grainy film formats. It is a remarkable record—young Clinton seems to have pushed himself to the front of the crowd, there to be noticed, selected by the most glamorous American politician ever. There is something earnest in the face of that young man, something that was not lost on all his former high school and college classmates who now say they were certain Bill Clinton would one day become president.

Clinton himself marks that moment as the instant his political ambitions jelled. While he says he had earlier considered a career in music—his saxophone was good enough for the statewide scholastic honor band—or medicine, after experiencing the electric shock of brushing against JFK, he never thought of any career but public service.

He enrolled at Georgetown University largely to be in Washington, near the seat of power he hoped someday to occupy. While he was at Georgetown, the elder Roger Clinton was dying of cancer at Duke University Hospital. For months, twenty-year-old Clinton would make the drive from Washington to Durham, North Carolina, every weekend to visit his dying stepfather, the man who had created the domestic misery young Bill wanted so desperately to escape.

The rapprochement came on Easter weekend in 1966 as the two men attended services at Duke Chapel. Clinton later described the moment to

Peter Applebome of the *New York Times:* "It was, God, beautiful. I think he knew I was coming down there just because I loved him. There was nothing else to fight over, nothing else to run from. It was a wonderful time in my life, and I think, his."

Then came Oxford, Clinton's Rhodes Scholarship (an old joke has us Arkies misunderstanding it as a "Roads Scholarship" and considering it a very fine practical diploma), and the subsequent deepening of his activism and putative vision of governance. It was here the machinations surrounding Clinton's avoidance of the draft took place, culminating in the remarkable, impassioned letter he sent to his ROTC colonel, Eugene Holmes, thanking him for "saving [him] from the draft." While Clinton critics have used the letter as evidence that Clinton took extraordinary measures to escape military service in Vietnam—the letter was dated December 3, 1969, three months after Clinton received a very high lottery number—it is difficult to read the text of the letter without being moved and impressed by its thoughtful young author. In it, Clinton describes himself and his peers as "still loving their country but loathing the military, to which you and other good men have devoted years, lifetimes of the best service you could give."

It is at best simplistic, and more likely disingenuous, to read into those words a distaste for American servicemen. "Loathing the military" seems, in context, to refer to the ongoing actions in Vietnam, not to the "good men" who did serve. On the other hand, it is apparent that Bill Clinton—like many of the ablest young men of his generation—chose to use whatever sneaky means he could to avoid military service. In the practical, if not strictly legal sense, he did in fact dodge the draft. And it is equally clear that, when confronted with the evidence years later, he chose to dissemble and spin the facts rather than own up to doing what he did.

Bill Clinton did not return home and enroll in the ROTC program at the University of Arkansas as he promised Colonel Holmes he would. Instead he entered Yale Law School, where he met and wooed and eventually moved in with Hillary Rodham, another middle-class striver from a comfortable Chicago suburb. Hillary Rodham was and is every bit Clinton's intellectual equal, and in her career as an activist attorney she has consistently seemed less willing to compromise her principles for political reasons than the ever-pragmatic Clinton.

In 1972, Hillary and Bill worked together as he ran George McGovern's ill-fated presidential campaign in Texas. She then moved on to Washington, where she worked for the special impeachment investigation staff of the House Judiciary Committee. When that job abruptly ended with the resignation of Richard Nixon, Hillary joined Clinton back home in Arkansas. For a time, they both taught law in Fayetteville. They married in 1975, after Clinton had run an unsuccessful, but ultimately encouraging race for Congress against an entrenched Republican. But he was elected state attorney general in 1976, and in 1979 he became, at thirty-two, the youngest governor in the country since thirty-one-year-old Harold Stassen was elected in Minnesota in 1938.

✧ ✧ ✧

Clinton's first term as governor resembles, in a way, his presidency. He came in furious, with a program for every problem, and surrounded himself with a coterie of young, smart, and bearded reformers from out of state. It at times seemed like a calculated attempt at a Southern Camelot, though it had its less-than-graceful episodes. For instance, to celebrate his inauguration, Clinton threw a huge rock 'n' roll dance party—unfortunately themed, like a high school prom, "Denim and Diamonds." For good measure, near the end of the night, he joined the band on stage for a saxophone solo.

With his longish hair and uncommonly liberal—for Arkansas, at least—ideas, Clinton was a dashing figure, unafraid to pick fights with some of the state's most powerful interests. He argued with the state's timber companies and trucking interests and anonymously co-authored a newspaper article that denounced Arkansas Power and Light Company's involvement in a nuclear power plant in Mississippi. Immediately he set about fulfilling his campaign promise to upgrade the state's highway system by raising gasoline taxes and automobile licensing fees to finance road improvements. He also expressed misgivings about the state's death penalty—though he was careful to add that he thought capital punishment could be an effective deterrent to crime.

Democratic party insiders quickly recognized him as a potential star, and Clinton addressed the party convention in 1980, where he claimed to represent "a new generation of party leaders." His speech did not, however, foreshadow his "New Democrat" rhetoric of 1992 so much as look backward to the liberal idealism of Hubert Humphrey.

"We have proved that our party is more sensitive than the Republicans to equality and justice, to the poor and the dispossessed," he said. "But now we must prove that we offer more in the way of creative and realistic solutions to our economic and energy and environmental problems, and that we can have a vision that can withstand the erosion of special interest politics that is gripping our land."

But however high Bill Clinton's national stock had risen, at home many Arkansans took exception to his Ivy League kitchen cabinet, many of whom seemed to regard Arkansas's hoi polloi as backward hicks. Clinton's national ambitions seemed a little too obvious. Popular mythology has it that many Arkansans felt their governor and his wife—who at that time still called herself Hillary Rodham—had grown arrogant, and that they voted for his Republican opponent, a gregarious savings-and-loan executive named Frank White, in 1980 merely in order to send Clinton a message. In reality, other factors played at least as large a role as Clinton's imperiousness.

After becoming the youngest ex-governor in American history, Clinton retreated to the relative safety of his friend Bruce Lindsey's Little Rock law firm. A year after his defeat, he was running again; he went on television, apologized to the voters, and asked for another chance.

There is no question that Clinton's setback radically altered his political style, that Frank White ripped the fearlessness from Bill Clinton. His defeat could very easily have been the end of a political career that Clinton had trained like an athlete for since his youth. Those who believe themselves close to Bill Clinton say that during much of 1981 he was depressed, fretting that his chosen trajectory might not, after all, be available. He returned to the public eye contrite, with his longish hair shorn and without his carpetbagger advisers. He was suddenly a more incremental, moderate politician. Gone were any lagging doubts about the usefulness of lethal injection; gone were his vocal broadsides against the timber companies and other powerful interests. Hillary Rodham became Hillary Clinton. And, in 1982, Bill Clinton once more became governor of Arkansas.

He would remain governor until after he was elected president.

✧ ✧ ✧

"There is the world of ideas and the world of practice," Matthew Arnold wrote. Government, the science of determining how a country's citizens will live, is ideally (though rarely) suspended in the juncture of these two spheres. Policy is best enacted by specialists but driven by visionaries. Even so, it is considered naive to argue for a vision of a good society unpolluted by partisan politics. Democratic government works only so long as an intellectual superego—a leader—is in place to harness the collective id of the masses. Demagogues, such as Wisconsin's Joe McCarthy, Mississippi's Theodore Bilbo, Louisiana's Huey Long, North Carolina's Jesse Helms, and Arkansas's Orval Faubus, arise when charismatic and cunning leaders neglect their moral duty and bend the mass whim to their own political ends.

After regaining the statehouse in 1982, Bill Clinton seemed determined never to repeat the mistakes of 1980. His new issues were, appropriately enough for a state in Arkansas's miserable economic condition, education and the development of new jobs. During the next eight years, Clinton would return to these issues again and again, while occasionally emphasizing utility reform, ethics in government, highway issues, and even the environment. But he was much more measured than he was in his first term, as his teenage predilection for peacemaking seemed to reemerge—Clinton developed a passion for consensus-building, developing what my friend and former colleague Stephen Buel has called the "politics of agreement."

With his perennially boyish looks and easy smile, Clinton maintained Richard Corey's common touch while, for the most part, fighting the good fight against a know-nothing legislature. While education reform is surely the safest issue a progressive Southerner can champion, Clinton staked out the high ground. He also advocated an ambitious restructuring of the state's tax system. His education reform package passed in 1983, and his job-training program in 1985. In 1988 he took a code of ethics for legislators to voters in a referendum, even though this last victory angered lawmakers and injured his ability to work with the legislature.

He even had a moment of startling moral clarity and courage. In 1984, when the state police came to Clinton and told him they had evidence Roger Clinton was selling cocaine, Clinton approved the sting that resulted in his younger brother's arrest and imprisonment.

Yet such instances were becoming increasingly rare. There were, in the post-1980 Clinton, some troubling tendencies. He controlled his risks. As he was preparing to run for reelection in 1990, he made some murky pronouncements, on issues such as capital punishment and flag-burning, that seemed desperately cynical, designed not to cost him the yahoo vote. During a Democratic Leadership Conference, Clinton said that in order to compete with Republicans for the White House Democrats had to "get on the right side of" emotional issues such as flag-burning—advice that seemed uncomfortably near endorsing situational demagoguery. Throughout the 1980s, Clinton ran his gubernatorial races not as a man determined to impress his vision upon a land he loves, but as a politician attempting to cling to a power base. Damaged by his 1980 defeat, Clinton turned skittish—it often seemed he was willing to hedge his notion of virtue rather than risk rejection by the voters.

(By the time the 1990 gubernatorial election rolled around, many Arkansans who in other years would have supported Clinton had begun to wonder if his very longevity in office had not adversely affected the state's welfare. Clinton's hold on power, they suggested, had calcified the power structure, creating a kind of imperial executive and stifling the development of young leaders. There was widespread speculation that Clinton would not make the race in 1990, in order to concentrate on running for the presidency in 1992.)

During 1986 and 1987, Clinton was chairman of the National Governors Association, a position that gave him rein to travel the country and gauge his support. Clinton made thirty-four trips to twenty-one states during his tenure, and he said later that his trips convinced him he could run well. Most Arkansans expected their governor to announce he would run for president. Then, on July 14, 1987, Clinton stunned his supporters—and many journalists—by announcing in a press release that he would not run.

A hall had been rented for the next day, and the governor had scheduled a press conference. Ray Strother, a well-known Democratic consultant, was already in town planning media strategy. There seems little question that Clinton was planning to make the race in 1988, and then, at the last possible moment, backed out. There has always been speculation that the problems encountered by Gary Hart of Colorado—forced out of the race following revelations of womanizing—had much to do with the decision. Suddenly, the rules were changed and any candidate could expect to have his private life scrutinized by an emboldened press.

At the time, Clinton denied his decision was based on anything other than family considerations. He recalled the uncertainty of his own childhood and said he feared the effect the distractions and pressure of a national campaign would have on his then-eight-year-old daughter, Chelsea.

A year later, Clinton's national political fortunes seemed to plummet further when he delivered a stupefying thirty-three-minute keynote speech at the 1988 Democratic National Convention in Atlanta. After becoming a national joke, Clinton showed two conflicting yet very genuine sides of his personality. First he whined, blaming his speech on the guidelines set forth by nominee Michael Dukakis's camp. Then he redeemed himself by going on *The Tonight Show with Johnny Carson* and blowing a credible rendition of George Gershwin's "Summertime" on his saxophone.

I remember watching Clinton's *Tonight Show* appearance with two friends of Bill, both of whom were nervous and doubted the wisdom of Clinton's appearing on a show where he had become a running joke. But as I watched the easy-grinning governor on television, I experienced something of a recognition—I suddenly realized that Bill Clinton was indeed a person of destiny.

Among those who thought Clinton was vulnerable was the late Lee Atwater, the genius GOP campaign strategist and the architect of George Bush's rather nasty—and undeniably successful—1988 presidential campaign. Driven to some extent by his personal dislike for Clinton, Atwater recruited the then-Democratic congressman from Little Rock, a wild-eyed loose cannon named Tommy Robinson, to run as a Republican against Clinton. Robinson, a former sheriff and Clinton appointee, was best known for his reckless willingness to say anything about anyone. Atwater and other GOP strategists thought that even if Clinton could survive what would surely be a vicious, mud-slinging attack by Robinson, his reputation would be so sullied that any national ambitions would have to be, once again, postponed.

Here in Arkansas we anticipated a bloodbath—that Robinson would accuse Clinton not only of womanizing, but possibly of miscegenation, fathering bastards, or drug abuse, or even worse. Robinson was the most colorful kind of Southern demagogue; whenever convenient, he could conflate rumor and innuendo into charges that, however unsubstantiated, could not be ignored.

In fact, when Clinton reluctantly announced he was, in fact, going to run for governor in 1990, he said his chief reason for making the campaign was to save the state from the "black shadow" of Tommy Robinson. Clinton averred that no other Democrat could defeat the popular former sheriff, and he may have been right. But when the smoke cleared in the GOP primary, it was Sheffield Nelson, another former Clinton ally gone over to the Republicans, who had vanquished Robinson. Clinton—after promising to serve his full four-year term as governor, a promise that seemed to preclude his running for president in 1992—easily handled Nelson in the general election.

✧ ✧ ✧

Much has been written about the kind of response Clinton evokes in people, especially journalists, even as he looks over your shoulder for the next hand to shake. His personal skills are extraordinary and are trivialized by television. Bill Clinton can make you think you are the smartest, most insightful person in the world—just as he can dazzle you with his own command of facts and figures. He can deliver just the right dose of simulated intimacy; he told me once that, despite all outward appearances, he was very nervous when he appeared on the *Tonight Show*—"I remember Joe Cocker was on there with me," Clinton confided. "I wanted to play with him, but I was too scared to ask—he had a wild-ass band."

As difficult as it may be to imagine Bill Clinton intimidated by a rock star's bass player, when the anecdote is relayed by the current president, it charms and flatters. Never think Bill Clinton untalented.

But Bill Clinton can also infuriate. Let us return to that central issue of American life, the one thing that Bill Clinton claims motivates him before all else—the idea of social justice and Arkansas's regrettable history with race and rights.

I said that to understand Bill Clinton, one must understand Arkansas. And to understand Arkansas, one must understand Central High and its residual guilt. For some of us in Arkansas, Bill Clinton still stands as our best hope for redemption. Others of us think his anguish and spirit have shrunken, that he is as hollow as he is gifted.

Beneath the sepulchral, marble-spread stillness of the state capitol there resides an ugly monument. In 1990, with some stealth and—fairness requires this be noted—without the benefit of public money, supporters and friends of Orval E. Faubus installed a brown bronze bust of the obstructionist architect of the 1957 Central High crisis in a hallway off the second-floor rotunda.

An enigmatic, sphinx-like smile cracks the erstwhile six-term governor's frozen aspect. The effect is further confused by the nearly touching, sad cast of its eyes. This is a statue that seems not to know whether to laugh or weep. Though even the model himself does not thoroughly approve of the knurled and creased likeness, complaining that Winthrop Rockefeller's bust is "much better," it is one of only three busts as yet placed in the capitol and, as such, it must be regarded as high tribute.

To the out-of-state visitor, as well as to many lifelong residents, the bust might suggest an ugliness more insidious than unhandsomeness. It must seem a strange recognition to bestow on the most infamous Arkansan, a man best known for his defiance of federal law.

Faubus is the governor who ordered the Arkansas National Guard to seize Little Rock's Central High School in an effort to prevent nine black students from enrolling there. It was Faubus who, in August 1958, shepherded through the state legislature a bill that established a "legal basis to close schools forced to integrate and transfer public funds to private schools."

On September 27, 1958, Little Rock voters elected to do just that, and the public schools remained closed for the entire 1958–59 school year. Only after the U.S. Circuit Court of Appeals for the Eighth Circuit ruled the closing law unconstitutional and the business elite of the city mobilized, leading to the election of three desegregation candidates to the school board in May 1959, did the high schools reopen—with limited integration.

While there is evidence to suggest Faubus became a segregationist hero more from political opportunism than pathology, his actions helped throw the schools of Little Rock into a still-extant cycle of turmoil and bad faith, with economic and social ramifications that cost the state at least as much as the estimated $123 million settlement. Faubus converted one of the most ignorant strains of the American character into political capital; he exploited racial mistrust and dread in order to secure a political base.

While the maneuvers of politicians such as Faubus and Alabama's George Wallace might seem silly and perverse to the great majority of Americans today, one might wonder whether things have really changed so much in the intervening years. Racism is one of the most persistent and potent undercurrents of civilization; only since the end of World War II has America found it necessary to officially expunge the remnants of Jim Crow from its legal and political systems.

The social crisis facing blacks is certainly no secret; so long as a class of people remains economically and politically dispossessed, no real assimilative progress is possible. Race is the problem—W.E.B. DuBois noted that the color line was the emphatic fact of American society. That color line, however camouflaged, remains today, infecting every facet of American life.

For a Southern state, Arkansas's black population is relatively small (about 16 percent) and concentrated in the state's southern and eastern regions. The racial dynamic is different than in other Southern states, largely because the legacy of slavery has had only a relatively minor effect on Arkansas. Since only 3 percent of Arkansas landowners kept slaves at the onset of the Civil War—and only a small minority of these held more than a few slaves—more recent tensions between the races stem more from economic competition between blacks and whites than from a continuation of the plantation system.

While white attitudes towards blacks in places like Mississippi, Georgia, and Alabama are informed by a certain noblesse oblige, Arkansas stands apart. The racism practiced in Arkansas rarely manifests itself in the "gentle" patronizing of black folkways associated with the stereotypical Southern aristocrat. In Arkansas, racism is more fearful than condescending, more like the variety practiced in Northern cities like Chicago and Boston than in, say, Oxford, Mississippi.

Take the example of Nolan Richardson, the flamboyant basketball coach at the University of Arkansas in Fayetteville. In 1987, Richardson was going through a tragic time. His daughter had died of cancer. More distressing to some was the fact that his teams were losing almost as often as they won. After a move to fire Richardson in the wake of his daughter's funeral failed, it was alleged that a heavyweight alumni association called the Razorback Club had "instructed" the university's then-president Ray Thornton and athletic director Frank Broyles never to hire another black head coach.

Similarly, in 1989, a white teacher in the small town of England, Arkansas, defended the segregationist policies of the town's public swimming pool by explaining that she personally felt "uncomfortable around blacks." Bill Powell, a Little Rock radio talk-show host, took to the air to defend the teacher, not on a First Amendment basis, but because it was "natural" to feel uncomfortable around people of a different color. In 1990, Ralph Forbes, a white supremacist and former associate of hate-monger Tom Metzger, ran a credible campaign for lieutenant governor.

Racism of the most virulent sort is invariably a form of self-loathing, a fear fed by weakness. It is unfortunate there are still many in Arkansas who loathe Bill Clinton largely because, as governor, black people loved and supported him in extraordinary numbers. While Clinton's record on civil rights issues is not infallible and certainly not as good as advertised, he did at least appoint unprecedented numbers of black folk to state boards and commissions as well as to high-profile policy-making positions, manufacturing role models while at the same time encouraging black political fealty. Dr. Joycelyn Elders, who served as director of the state Health Department and also went on to become Surgeon General of the United States, is but one example of Clinton's able black appointees.

Stephen Buel, who for several years published an alternative newspaper in Little Rock and covered Clinton's 1992 presidential campaign for United Press International, calls Clinton's record on civil rights "fearless."

"Race is the one subject on which Bill Clinton is unreproachable," Buel said in an interview conducted shortly after the Los Angeles riots. "It is the one issue on which he's consistently enlightened and where he's followed his own heart."

But political appointments—jobs delivered by a beneficent authority figure—may not carry much political currency. Selecting leaders, as opposed to electing them, is problematic. Black people who attain the necessary level of success to attract the attention of those who would select them to sit on boards or commissions have probably physically divorced themselves from the neighborhoods where most black people live. As they move into areas that are more affluent, they move away from the problems endemic to the black community—the fractured families, the crime, the psychological upheaval of ghettoization. Pulling oneself up by one's own bootstraps is fine, but it is a scenario that provides only individual escape, not the general uplifting of a ethnic group.

Gordon Morgan, a professor of sociology at the University of Arkansas who was, not incidentally, that school's first black faculty member, said that while Clinton's appointments have, for the most part, been highly qualified and effective, people generally remain "suspicious of appointed leadership."

Paul Greenberg, the Pulitzer prize–winning editorial-page editor of the *Arkansas Democrat-Gazette,* is perhaps Bill Clinton's fiercest critic. Greenberg, who was likely the first to use the phrase "Slick Willie" to describe Clinton, contends Clinton's black appointments were not made at the risk of the governor's popularity.

"He has substituted patronage for progress," Greenberg said during the 1992 presidential campaign. "We do not have a state civil rights law . . . we don't have a fair-housing law in this state—that would also have cost him some popularity. He dodges and weaves whenever it might cost him something to support civil rights. I don't think appointing black folks to boards and commissions has hurt him. I don't think there's any great groundswell of opposition to black members on these boards and commissions. A state civil rights bill, a fair-housing law, that would mean that he'd be risking something politically."

Sadly, Bill Clinton, stung a dozen years ago, does not make a habit of taking political risks. He abandoned his promise to make the U.S. military treat gay soldiers the same as straight, and he allowed Lani Gunier, his most creative appointment, to slide indecorously into the muck of history.

❖ ❖ ❖

I am not much concerned with whether Bill Clinton has met the textbook definition of a good husband. As a mutual friend once told me, any man over forty who has not done something stupid with his clothes off probably has not had the opportunity to do so. The Clintons are attractive and powerful people and they grew up in a time when American puritanism had—however briefly—ebbed. Their marriage is their business, and I suspect Hillary can take care of herself.

Still, the sexual indiscretions of the president are not something I can ignore. My new neighbor has a reputation, and though I don't exactly hold it against him, I know things about him that I would rather not know. And it is not completely the fault of inquisitor Ken Starr and a genuine confederation of Clinton's enemies. He behaved recklessly and selfishly. Monica Lewinsky may have been a predator, but she was also a little girl, no matter what she thought of herself. He should have known better.

But I have friends who have behaved badly at various times in their life, friends who never felt the pressures of the presidency. I can't excuse Bill

Clinton's behavior, but I can understand it and even imagine myself in his place. Like Goethe, I can't imagine a crime which I could not, under the right circumstances, commit. I do not expect that my neighbor will keep odd hours or disrupt my sleep with loud driveway arguments. Marriages are strange things, and the Clintons' marriage is not my business.

Human beings are frail creatures; as I write this, the most talked about story in Arkansas is about some prominent citizens who apparently imported young women from China for the purposes of their own sexual gratification. Our newspaper has so far refrained from blaring "Chinese Sex Slaves!" in seventy-two-point type, but the temptation is there.

Things are always entertaining here in Arkansas.

A couple of years ago, I stopped in Hope to buy gas in the middle of the night. There are many landmarks in the town now. One gentleman has taken to giving tours of these streets, pointing out both of the houses little Billy Blythe lived in as a child. Even this fluorescent-lit service station had a rack of souvenirs and T-shirts strung along its walls. Right by the register there was a four-inch stack of crude bumper stickers. For a dollar, you could signify that you "didn't vote for the dope from Hope." A prophet is without honor, I guess.

Though Bill Clinton is elsewhere, he still haunts the streets of my town. Every day I drive past that too-famous McDonalds; sometimes I lunch at Doe's Eat Place or at Your Mama's Good Food, where James Carville hung out. I used to work out in the same YMCA as Bill Clinton, back when we were neighbors the first time around. I saw him in the neighborhood; I waved and the governor waved back. It is hard to say how it is here, hard to make people in Phoenix or Chicago or San Francisco understand. There is a kind of intimacy, available here in Little Rock, that is at once comforting and stifling. We know our big goofy former governor; in a way we feel comfortable with him. It is odd to see him paid such deference, to see him so examined.

I am no friend of Bill Clinton, at least not in the way I understand friendship. He is—was—a person one saw, one ran into, one thought and wrote about. I do know a lot of people who do claim to know him, some who like him and some who don't.

But I wonder if any of us ever knew Bill Clinton, if we ever got past his bluff innocence and flashy intellect. Almost by accident I discovered there were gaps in his knowledge of pop culture, that despite his prodigious reading there were things Bill Clinton did not know. I have seen him look positively gooberish, like he wants to mouth "Hi, Mom!" and wave into the camera. He often seems out of place, with his triathlete's watch and his blooming ripe body. He should not wear those running shorts. His ties used

192

to be atrocious. He still seems like the big country kid with the wild eyes and the talent no one seems to be able to account for—a happy freak of nature, Bill Clinton was born to run. He never seemed to notice the rather inappropriate message of his first campaign's theme song, Fleetwood Mac's "Don't Stop Thinkin' about Tomorrow." (I'm thinking of these lines: "Though you don't believe that it's true / I never meant any harm to you.")

Though Bill Clinton disappoints me, I'm still fond of him. After all, it is not for lack of effort that he is not Thomas Jefferson or Jack Kennedy.

It is difficult to take seriously an adult who says, in all apparent seriousness, "I feel your pain," but there is something of the healer in this president. He has had his moments and I suspect he will have more.

✧ ✧ ✧

During the 1992 presidential campaign, Clinton suggested to David Shribman of the *Wall Street Journal* that character was less an intrinsic trait than an ongoing "quest," a process rather than a condition that might be secured. In describing it thusly, Clinton made clear that while he had no present claim to stainlessness, he reserved the right to aspire to virtue.

That is an interesting and apt way to think about the issue, which matters perhaps less in politics than in most varieties of human endeavor. If character—by which I suppose we mean something like moral courage tempered with the appropriate humility—is something that may be gained, rather than something immutable, then there is hope for the wretched. Everybody needs a shot at redemption, and the American compact has always included a second chance or two. Take, for example, Richard Nixon, the undisputed champion.

So there is still hope for us and our young president. Sweet forgiveness awaits the earnest striver for character.

This is a relativist argument, the sort of idea advanced by those suspicious of absolutes. It is also the truth, insofar as there is plenty of empirical evidence that people can grow into better people and that as some people mature they become both wiser and less certain of their superstitions.

So Philip Johnson once thought Hitler had an interesting turn of mind? Now he recognizes his own stupidity. So Louis Farrakhan has said intemperate, racist things? Now he saws through Mendelssohn not so badly and talks about undoing with music what his regrettable words have done. If the spirits of architects and violinists can enlarge and improve, then why not presidents?

Maybe the unguarded Bill Clinton—the Clinton who seems to acknowledge he is capable of self-deception and prone to hubris—was doing more than expressing the proper modesty when he made that statement to the *Journal*. Maybe his pride was exhausted; maybe he was groping toward something genuine. Maybe Clinton walked right up to the brink of self-awareness and found himself staring into the abyss. Who can fail to empathize with the terror of a man contemplating his own vacancies?

If that is what happened, it was not the act of a coward.

Other things being equal, I would prefer not to be cynical, for cynicism, the inner rot that attacks our capacity to trust, is the most debilitating factor in the ongoing conversation about how Americans ought to live. To be cynical is to take yourself out of the game, to concede that lying has become a necessary skill, not only for those seeking office but for all those seeking to avoid blame. I know Bill Clinton dissembles, but I don't believe that he has to or even that he wants to.

Bill Clinton is a human being, not so innocent as he would have us believe but no demon either. He is a capable man, diminished more by the inoculating effects of constant exposure and scrutiny. He is, as someone once said of Voltaire, a "chaos of clear ideas." He is the most powerful man on the face of the earth and he is still that boy in the kitchen of his strong-willed mother's hospital-clean ranch house, listening to her mutter about the world's idiocy and injustice. He is the slightly sheepish character who seems amazed at how far he's come, who delights in room service and sneaking away from the Secret Service to make small talk with his friends.

Bill Clinton is not trash, but he is a Snopes—because he is from Arkansas and here we are all Snopeses, no matter how hard we want to become Kennedys or Compsons. I am looking forward to his coming home. I am interested in what my new neighbor will do with the rest of his life.

2000

Riding with the Sun King

This is the oldest piece in the book, a straight bit of reportage about a day spent with Bill Clinton back when he was running for governor of Arkansas the last time. With the exception of a few minor cuts, this is how the story appeared in *Spectrum Weekly*, a Little Rock alternative newspaper, on October 31, 1990.

He is the Sun King and if you look too long at him you will be blind, your senses flooded with his gold-spined brilliance. As e. e. cummings might have said of him, Jesus, he is a handsome man—despite his too big head and hands and feet and his roomy, rheumy, allergy-ridden nose. There must some elemental undercurrent here that generates envy in other men, not just the musk of power but something pheromonic. Since it is not polite to compare your governor to Mussolini, or even Huey Long, then let's say he is like one of those Kennedy boys, or that rare thing, a soulful politician.

Bill Clinton has a common touch, a dangerous charisma, and a sense of his own mortality. At forty-four, he is running for governor for the sixth time, though men like Clinton and Joe DiMaggio seem to glide more than run. He has debated his gubernatorial opponent Sheffield Nelson twice in recent weeks, and spoken after him at perhaps a dozen rallies and meetings around the state. While Nelson generally acquits himself well, adopting a measured, informal speaking style that seems tailored to fit his hoped-for image as a tough-minded businessman with a heart, he concedes that Clinton usually wins the style points.

"Bill is an excellent campaigner," Nelson says. "He can excite a crowd. I just hope there's enough people who can see through that, so I can win on substantive issues."

The other candidates in the governor's race don't say Clinton is dishonest, only that he has lashed Arkansas to ambitious, expensive dreams that will never come true. They make him out to be a pusher of hope, a goofy-eyed liberal crazy for power, a guest who has overstayed his welcome. They say Bill Clinton has one eye on Washington, that he behaves like the Western-educated potentate of a backward Third World country. They say he doesn't follow through, isn't suited to detail work, has an attention span of about . . .

But nobody says Bill Clinton isn't a good candidate. He is a fearsome counter-puncher and a stirring speaker. On the stump, he can blister or warm, sweeping a crowd through its full range of emotions. He's even better one-on-one, eye-to-eye. He flashes his keen intelligence like a rapier and he whips it out for even the most mundane tasks—as when he gently reminds a school superintendent concerned about declining enrollment and stagnant teacher salaries that dollars *ought* to be linked to children, *not* teachers. While his opponent Nelson will occasionally admit he's unfamiliar with a problem, Clinton can explain practically anything. He has a seemingly informed, thoughtful answer to virtually every question he is posed. He remembers names and faces. He tosses off facts, numbers, anecdotes, and rude, rustic stories.

He can be ruthless when aroused, and though he started this campaign in low gear, he hit his stride about a month ago and seems determined to keep the pressure on right up until election day. He is not campaigning like an arrogant incumbent. He is up early and out at 'em, making those 7 A.M. breakfast meetings and those 9 P.M. barbecues, getting back to the governor's mansion at midnight and working—there is still a state to be run—sometimes until 2:30 or 3 A.M.

As friends and foes quickly discover, it is impossible to stay objective about Bill Clinton—there is too much to envy.

❖ ❖ ❖

Two weeks before the voters do their November duty, on a day with a sky as clear as vodka and his heart unclogged with any residual doubt about his candidacy, Bill Clinton arranges himself in the shotgun seat of a Ford Aerostar van, kicking one snakeskin boot up and shifting his weight around so he can talk over his left shoulder to the reporter behind him.

Yes, Bill Clinton has flushed the hesitation from his booming heart and is glad in the campaign. He's glad to be busting down this blue-gray streak of interstate toward Malvern with his Arkansas State Police driver Carl Kirkland and campaign aide Hal Honeycutt, who has sacked out on the bench seat in the way back. We are running late, the obligatory fifteen or twenty minutes that puts us on what the beat reporters call "Bill Clinton time."

This *is* Bill Clinton time, the early fall of an election year. This is not the same Bill Clinton who nine months ago stood in the cool rotunda of the state capitol and announced that though he lacked the requisite "fire in the belly" for the coming campaign, he was going to suck it up and run again to save the state from the "dark shadow" of Tommy Robinson. Also, he felt he was the only one who could shepherd his prize education programs to fruition in the '90s. That winter Clinton was resigned, grim and determined, not a man who could admit he was "having a lot of fun campaigning."

This race has finally got his juices flowing. He is flat-out rocking now.

Clinton may have hit peak form on October 11, at an outdoor rally sponsored by Blue Cross and Blue Shield of Arkansas. Taking the stage after a typical measured speech by GOP challenger Sheffield Nelson—who disposed of dark shadow Robinson in the primary—Clinton snorted and growled through an apparently extemporaneous attack on both his opponent and the fiscal policies of the Reagan-Bush administrations that placed larger burdens on state governments while raising taxpayer expectations with sunny rhetoric.

"They have given us deficits all over the South," he said, his arms flung wide. "And they come back and sanctimoniously attack us for raising taxes. How dare they! Shame on them! Shame on them!"

As Clinton blazed on, slinging and pounding and rattling his true and terrible sword, some of Nelson's supporters taunted and tried to dispute his claims. The governor swung round on them, enjoying the exchange, notching up the bluster as he challenged the malcontents, whose catcalls were soon drowned out by cheers and applause.

"I got my adrenaline going," Clinton said later. "I felt real good up there."

Now, weeks later in the van, he still feels good.

"If we don't make any mistakes, if we don't let up and keep our folks working just as hard as we have up to now, I think we'll win," Clinton says. "It's easy to lose a lead—you have to maintain an energy and a spirit in a campaign. You have to keep the level of feeling and emotion high to get flesh-and-blood people to want to work for you."

❖ ❖ ❖

Clinton knows what it is like to lose. Various polls show him with a comfortable lead over Nelson, but Clinton remembers the 1980 "Cubans and Car Tags" election when the polls showed him sixteen points ahead of amiable savings-and-loan president and political novice Frank White.

When the smoke cleared, Bill Clinton was the youngest ex-governor in United States history.

It is important to understand the election of 1980 and its residual effects on Bill Clinton. That was the year that witnessed the ascendancy of Ronald Reagan and country-western Republicanism in the South. Jimmy Carter faltered, and so did Bill Clinton. The consensus is that a lot of people felt their boy governor had forgotten his roots, that he was too obvious in his aspirations for national office. But it isn't quite that simple—Clinton himself insists it was more than his own arrogance that beat him.

When he won the office in 1978, Clinton became the youngest governor since Harold Stassen was elected in Minnesota forty years before. Immediately he set about fulfilling his campaign promise to upgrade the state's highway system by raising gasoline taxes and automobile licensing fees to finance road improvements. It was an unpopular move, and Clinton later admitted he had tried to do too much too fast.

"I made a young man's mistake," he said on the eve of his comeback Democratic primary in 1982. "I had an agenda a mile long that you couldn't achieve [even in] a four-year term. I was so busy doing what I wanted to do I didn't have time to correct mistakes."

Yet if Clinton misread the public temper on the car tags issue, he says there was nothing he could do about the "Cubans" part of the equation. The Carter administration had, over the protests of the state of Arkansas, placed some eighteen thousand Cuban refugees at Fort Chaffee. In May and June of 1980, hundreds of these Cubans escaped, some making their way as far as the town of Barling on the outskirts of Fort Smith before being recaptured. Then, on June 1, about two hundred of the detainees burned down the barracks they were being housed in. Forty people were injured in the riot and Clinton was forced to call in the National Guard and ask the federal government to tighten security at the base.

"There wasn't anything I could do about that," Clinton says. "I asked Jimmy Carter not to put them here. I was as mad about the Cuban deal as anyone else."

A few moments later the governor of Arkansas excuses himself, turns back in his seat to face the road and slumps in his seat. We are fifteen minutes away from Malvern, and he'd like to get ten minutes of sleep. His eyes close and the sun bastes his ruddy face.

✧ ✧ ✧

The Malvern Senior Citizens Center, its linoleum floors gleaming, is a familiar stop for the campaigning Clinton, and he strides into its big open hall with the self-assurance of an old quarterback—he's still young but chocked with memories. Though he has a paunch and his hair is beginning to go gray, there is yet glory in his body. He bids the four or five ladies arranged about the piano to keep singing as he meanders through the rows of tables that hold perhaps two hundred elderly men and women. These people—especially the women—dote on their young governor. He takes them by the hand and greets some of them by name.

They reach toward him as though he were a faith healer, their confidence absolute, their eyes dancing.

Finally, after every name has lit for a second on the governor's lips, he takes the microphone and the Walker Evans faces go rapt. It is a simple talk. Clinton notices the improvements made in the building, how they've decorated. He notes the absence of an "old friend"—Paw Paw Jones—with whom he would speak every time he visited the center. He runs a hand through his hair and reminds them he is "no longer the boy politician of Arkansas."

He tells them that the fastest growing demographic group in America is "people over eighty" and that a few days before he met a 101-year-old woman in Van Buren who was "bright as a penny."

"Everywhere I go in this campaign, I'm running into people over a hundred years old," he says. "It used to be that I would run into one or two a year, now it seems like I meet three or four a month."

Clinton has—as a shushing lady in the back notes—their "undivided." The kitchen help creep out to stand in front of their door and listen. The governor loads up and winds down.

"I met an old gentleman in Mena the other day," he says, "who came up to me and said, 'Son, I'm a Democrat, a conservative, and an Arkansawyer—you suit me just fine.'"

Applause, laughter, bells, and sirens. Now Clinton gives them the good news: He is about to announce a program, called Elder Choices, that will free up Medicare money that would normally be dedicated to providing nursing-home care to be used for alternatives for elderly folks who choose to stay out of nursing homes.

"The most important thing to Americans is that they be given a choice in the lives they lead," Clinton says. "This program will give some people the opportunity to stay out of the nursing home if that's what they want to do—it will give people more control over their own lives."

Let there be no mistake about it. Bill Clinton believes in government. He believes in the ability of state programs to improve the lives of Arkansans. He believes that moral people have an obligation to make the future better and that the nineties might see a "kind of fusion of our strongest conservative and liberal impulses"—"the rise of a progressive liberal agenda that is married to the emphasis of the past few years on market solutions to problems and the importance of individual responsibility."

Clinton's talk at the senior center is like so many others of his campaign appearances in that, before he finishes talking, he has explained how a specific state program of his will benefit the specific constituency he is addressing. Whether he's talking to senior citizens, the Association of Arkansas

Entrepreneurs, or the Arkansas Hospitality Association, for every group he addresses, Clinton comes loaded with an anecdote and a program or two.

After the senior center talk, Clinton meanders a bit more, has some cake and a brisk talk with the mayor of Malvern, who will drive the governor to his next appointment, a milling-about affair at the Hot Spring County Democratic Party Headquarters. Some of the senior citizens approach the governor with Instamatics in hand and he poses for a few photos. The crowd drains out, back to cars and vans that will take them home.

As he leaves the center, Clinton turns to a state senator and pointedly asks, "Where are all the black folks? When we used to come here it seemed that one in four or five was black. Today they were just a handful."

"I would think that's a function of better transportation," the senator answers. "They're able to get out into the county now, bring more people in from the surrounding area."

Clinton replies, "And there aren't as many black folks in the county as live right around here?"

"No."

The governor nods, satisfied for now.

◇ ◇ ◇

Arkansas is rural and poor, and some people say it is backward. Clinton is frustrated by the state's genetically inscribed inferiority complex and its stubborn mistrust of intellectuals. Clinton, after all, is an intellectual—at least by the standards Arkansans hold for politicians. He is a graduate of Yale's law school and a Rhodes scholar who, along with the White House's Roger Porter, drew up George Bush's education goals. For Clinton there are many questions and the answer is education. Education is what will eventually bring the jobs that Arkansas needs; education is what will make us strong and prosperous. To him, it seems simple.

"We've got to do four things to bring our per capita income up in line with other states," he says. "Number one, we've got to recognize that education is not just for kids, and we need to provide access to education throughout a lifetime. If we could get everybody with a job reading at a high school level, we'd see a real increase in income.

"Number two, we need to put every Arkansas citizen within driving range of a vo-tech/community college."

Clinton envisions a system of hybrid schools that would offer both job training skills and academic classes—though he chafes a bit at the distinction between practical and academic, tossing off examples of how "academic courses" like "statistical process control" can have a real impact in the very palpable world of, say, chain-saw manufacture.

"Number three, we need to get help for our non-college-bound students in the form of apprenticeship programs, and, number four, we need to make it easier for the children of working-class people to go to college."

In addition to a college bond program on the November ballot, Clinton would like to see a program where every child from a household with an income of less than twenty thousand dollars who maintains a B average in high school is given a full-tuition scholarship to a state university.

"Now that's a real thing that would really affect people's lives," Clinton says. "Don't you know that would give some of these kids some incentive to stay out of the streets and in the libraries? If all they had to do was maintain a B average?"

Though his opponent Nelson dismisses Clinton's record of school reform as a sham and says that all Clinton's various programs have done is alienate teachers, in the public mind Clinton is inexorably linked to the education issue. Maybe that is why a woman stopped Clinton on the streets of Malvern to show him examples of her daughter's homework. The mother thinks her daughter should be moved up a grade.

"This is what she's doing now."

She hands the governor a scrawly mess.

"She gets in there and sees the other kids scribbling, and she's bored, so she starts doing what they're doing. I'm afraid, she's, uh—"

"Regressing?" Clinton's aide Honeycutt offers.

"Yeah, that's it." The woman is crying.

Clinton seems genuinely touched by her concern. He turns to the mayor of Malvern, who promises to go with the woman if she will set up an appointment with the school superintendent. Honeycutt writes her name and number down on a yellow legal pad and promises to follow up in a few weeks.

Clinton looks long into her eyes, takes her hand.

"Thank you for caring," he says.

Later, while Clinton is closeted away in the back office of the Chamber of Commerce, granting an interview to the editor of the *Malvern Daily Record,* the mayor and the school superintendent talk about the woman's problem. They'll do the necessary screening, and if the child needs to be placed in first grade, well, they'll see that she is placed in the first grade.

"And you can write her a letter, give the governor credit for this," the superintendent tells Honeycutt, who smiles and nods.

All is calm, the last campaign speech of the day has been delivered, and the governor's plane has lifted off. Now the governor of Arkansas reaches up and switches off the overhead light to cast the cabin in a dim gloom. There is one more story he wants to tell.

"When I was in junior high school, I had a friend who had a brother, maybe a year or two older than us. . . . He was a perfect kid, handsome as a damn movie star, a great athlete, smart, popular with the girls, one of those guys who everybody loved—just an amazing guy.

"He went to sleep one night and the next morning they found him dead.

"They never found out what killed him. It must have been a stroke, or a heart attack, but no one really knew. No sign of anything. He just died."

The governor sleeps.

✧ ✧ ✧

Clinton says he knew by the time he was sixteen years old that he wanted to be governor or senator or president someday. He almost ran for president in 1988.

During 1986 and 1987, he had been the chairman of the National Governor's Association, a position that gave him the freedom to travel the country, to gauge his support among the Democratic faithful. After Gary Hart was disgraced and after Arkansas senator Dale Bumpers announced he would not seek the office, a lot of people expected Clinton to enter the race. Tension built, press conferences were called, and then—on July 14, 1987—Clinton said he would not run.

"Mentally I was 100 percent committed to the race, but emotionally I wasn't," Clinton said at the time. He maintains his decision was based solely on family considerations. He said he remembered the uncertainty of his own childhood and feared the effect the pressures and distractions of a national campaign might have on his own daughter.

Bill Clinton still wants to be president. It hangs there in the back of his mind, a faded campaign banner strung so high that no one has ever had the will to fetch it down. It stays up; it's an eyesore to some; it has become part of the landscape. Some people think it's lost all meaning; some don't even see it anymore.

But Bill Clinton still wants to be president. You can tell. His eyes glint.

On that day nine months ago when he reluctantly announced he was running for governor, again, he said if he won he intended to stay in the mansion his full term—four years.

"I don't know what could make me change my mind," he said. That would seem to preclude a national bid in 1992, but when Clinton said that, George Bush's approval rating was above 60 percent. Now it's down—and could go lower. In the waning days of what surely will be his last gubernatorial campaign, Clinton is willing to talk about the presidential race, sort of. At least he's willing to talk about the mistakes the Democrats made in 1988.

"I don't know that I understand primary politics well enough to get the nomination," he says. "And I think I may be too conservative to carry the national ticket. But I wrote an answer, to the Willie Horton ads, that would have had the people screaming for Michael Dukakis. The Dukakis candidacy was the best argument in the world for a strong national defense. Mike showed what happened when there is unilateral disarmament—you get rolled over."

Though he began the campaign tentatively—some believe he did not decide to run for reelection until he stepped up on the podium in the capitol rotunda and looked around at all the anxious faces in the crowd—Bill Clinton is not tentative now. Mindful of the lessons taught by Frank White and Mike Dukakis, the Sun King knows what he wants and he will do what he has to do to get it. But first he must be governor, again.

1990

Afterword: What I Know about the South

One of the occupational hazards of being a newspaper columnist is being constantly pressed to produce. It is necessary to feed the beast so many words per week, so many column inches. I understand my position is one of privilege, that I serve at the pleasure of my editors, of my publisher. I understand there are plenty of hot young talents out there eager to take my job. I cannot complain—for, as my friend Paul Bowen likes to remind me, the writing life beats running a tree saw all day.

Still, in order to be a columnist, one must develop certain strategies for putting word after word day after day. One of the things I sometimes do is simply list some things "I know."

These "what-I-know" columns are among the most popular I write, because, I think, most of my audience gets the inherent joke. In most of my columns, I shy from certitude. I tend to creep up on the issue at hand, roll it over and rub its belly. I don't generally try to persuade my readers; I just try to hold up my end of an imaginary conversation. The what-I-know columns are a break from my usual equivocal, discursive, and—I pray—thoughtful meanderings.

They are also a gentle rejoinder to my critics—like everyone who writes for a newspaper, I have critics—who, I take it, would rather I get to the point. They'd rather I'd say what I have to say and get on with it. Am I fer it or agin it?

I was thinking of ending this book with a kind of what-I-know column. I know Jimmy Carter curses. (He told me so.) I know my habitual measuredness is symptomatic of my Southernness. I know my Southernness is—as C. Vann Woodward said—a kind of cloak I can drape over myself when it suits me.

But I find I can't end this book on such a flippant note—because I think maybe I have something else to say about the Southern character.

◇ ◇ ◇

There is a theory that holds human beings, like other animals, are nothing more than twitching meat, bone, blood, and suet. And so our thoughts and dreams are but accidents, electrical by-products of our essential drives to reproduce and to survive until we die. There are serious people who insist our understanding of the natural world is limited only by the inability of our minds to gather and process pertinent data. There are no ghosts, no magic—our understanding is incomplete, but there is nothing inexplicable if we look hard and long enough, if we apply the right set of equations.

I don't agree with these folks, but I understand their argument. Perhaps there is something sentimental and superstitious in me, something that might otherwise be described as a lack of intellectual rigor or discipline. But I prefer to believe in the inexplicable, in the ineffable. I prefer to think there are things beyond our knowing, things that can't be discovered in our chromosomes. And I think this tendency could be the greater part of what we could describe as the Southern character—a willingness to give oneself over to mystery.

◇ ◇ ◇

There I go again, I guess, worrying a question that mightn't even deserve asking. We're rapidly sliding into a post-American, post-nationalist world without meaningful cultural borders and I'm talking about a moot idea. After all, if the South ever existed, it was a nasty place, where the price of apparent consensus was dear. The South was a coercive community, a class-centered community where everyone knew their place, even if they couldn't keep it.

There is a cruelty to the concept, and those of us who rather proudly proclaim our Southernness (and even those of us who take it for granted) run the risk of denying the reality around us. For all the myth-building and the glorification of the South, there is a historical record with which to deal. Less than 150 years ago, people owned other people here and treated them more or less like beasts of burden. There are people who still hate other people based on the color of their skin. There have been thousands of murders committed by people who—by some evil quirk of the brain—were convinced their victims weren't quite human.

I know these arguments, and I know how to rebut them, and sometimes I find the energy but most often I just let them hang in the air. I have a kind of faith about the South, about my own assumed Southernness. I don't believe people are better or worse for where they are born and live. But sometimes I think they are different, and these differences are worth talking about.

So while a Marxist can characterize Will Percy's rhetoric of failure as symptomatic of a kind of exhaustion brought on by repressing sharecroppers, I prefer to believe in Uncle Will's inherent decency. When I read

Lanterns on the Levee, I read the wonderful memoir of an extraordinarily sensitive man, not the self-serving apology of a white master. Will Percy mightn't have been the progressive we wish he'd been—neither was Thomas Jefferson—but his language coaxes faith.

We don't have to overlook Will Percy's flaws to feel an affinity for him. His cousin and adopted son, Walker, satirized "Uncle Will" and his noblesse oblige in *The Moviegoer* through the Aunt Emily character. I don't think it means he didn't love him.

✧ ✧ ✧

I believe in Will and Walker Percy. I believe in Aunt Emily. And I know it's not fated; I know it's a choice I've made. I've chosen to have a kind of faith, to believe in mystery. Perhaps it's not the most rigorous path, perhaps it's not the most disciplined way to think, but I prefer it. I prefer to believe in demons and saints and the possibility of grace.

Genius erupts in unlikely places, they say, but there is something magic about this place we call the South. Something has washed up and settled here, and the culture that has evolved is strangely rich in unutterable, evanescent, human qualities.

How can we account for the incredible crop of creative talent that seems to emanate from the old wound of the Mississippi itself? It's often been observed that the Delta is a kind of primal swamp, the Tigris-Euphrates valley from which springs American popular music. But it's not just the music; there's a tradition of communication, of storytelling, and—most of all—of belief.

The proximity between William Faulkner and Elvis Presley is neither accidental nor merely geographic. Ike Turner invented rock 'n' roll not too far away from where W. C. Handy first heard "a lean, loose-jointed negro" playing "the weirdest music."

What links Eudora Welty and Robert Johnson, Jimmy Carter and James Brown, Walker Percy and Bessie Smith, Hank and Miller Williams is a sense of their own delimited humanity, which has as its expression a confidence in things unseen, in haints and angels and the Devil who walks the crossroads. While the South might not be haunted, it's for sure the Southerners—even the artificial Southerners—among us are.